MODERNIST FUTURES

In *Modernist Futures*, David James examines the implications of modernism's continuity in late-twentieth- and twenty-first-century writing by tracing its political and ethical valences in emerging novelistic practices. Focusing on the work of J. M. Coetzee, Milan Kundera, Ian McEwan, Toni Morrison, Michael Ondaatje and Phillip Roth, James reconsiders the purpose of literary innovation as it relates to the artistic and cultural interventions such writers perform. By rethinking critical and disciplinary parameters, James brings scholarship on contemporary fiction into dialogue with modernist studies, offering a nuanced account of narrative strategies that sheds new light on the form of the novel today. An ambitious and incisive contribution to the field, this book will appeal especially to scholars of modernism and contemporary literary culture as well as those in American and postcolonial studies.

DAVID JAMES is Lecturer in Modern and Contemporary Literature at Queen Mary, University of London. Author of *Contemporary British Fiction and the Artistry of Space: Style, Landscape, Perception* (2008), his articles have appeared in such venues as *Modernism/ Modernity*, *Journal of Modern Literature* and *Textual Practice*. He is editor of *The Legacies of Modernism: Historicising Postwar and Contemporary Fiction* (2011).

MODERNIST FUTURES

Innovation and Inheritance in the Contemporary Novel

DAVID JAMES

Queen Mary, University of London

CAMBRIDGE
UNIVERSITY PRESS

32 Avenue of the Americas, New York NY 10013-2473, USA

Cambridge University Press is part of the University of Cambridge.

It furthers the University's mission by disseminating knowledge in the pursuit of education, learning and research at the highest international levels of excellence.

www.cambridge.org
Information on this title: www.cambridge.org/9781107022478

© David James 2012

This publication is in copyright. Subject to statutory exception and to the provisions of relevant collective licensing agreements, no reproduction of any part may take place without the written permission of Cambridge University Press.

First published 2012

A catalogue record for this publication is available from the British Library

Library of Congress Cataloguing in Publication data
James, David, 1979–
Modernist futures : innovation and inheritance in the contemporary novel / David James.
p. cm.
Includes bibliographical references and index.
ISBN 978-1-107-02247-8 (hardback : alk. paper)
1. Modernism (Literature)   2. Fiction – 20th century – History and criticism.   3. Fiction – 21st century – History and criticism.   4. Postcolonialism in literature.   I. Title.
PN56.M54J36   2012
809'.9112–dc23
2012009119

ISBN 978-1-107-02247-8 Hardback

Cambridge University Press has no responsibility for the persistence or accuracy of URLs for external or third-party internet websites referred to in this publication, and does not guarantee that any content on such websites is, or will remain, accurate or appropriate.

For María

Contents

Acknowledgements		*page* ix
	Introduction: Contemporary fiction and the promise of modernism	1
1	'Advancing along the inherited path': Making it traditionally new in Milan Kundera and Philip Roth	43
2	'The perfect state for a novel': Michael Ondaatje's Cubist imagination	65
3	'Spare prose and a spare, thrifty world': J. M. Coetzee's politics of minimalism	96
4	'The dead hand of modernism': Ian McEwan, reluctant impressionist	135
5	'License to strut': Toni Morrison and the ethics of virtuosity	161
Notes		189
Index		221

Acknowledgements

To take stock of the numerous ways in which this book has become indebted to others over the years is to feel at once humbled and fortunate. At the University of Nottingham, my professional life has been enriched by immensely supportive colleagues. I thank Julie Sanders for being an exemplary mentor, before becoming an equally exemplary Head of School. No one matches her way of maintaining a calm sense of efficiency when you are in the office that safeguards your productivity when you are away from it. I continue to be indebted to her for showing me how to build a makeshift shelter in which to think and write amid the maelstrom of mid-semester administration. I'm similarly grateful to Dominic Head who, when he himself was leading the School, tolerated my tendency to drop by at the busiest times in search of impromptu conversations about the state of contemporary fiction studies. My propensity to exploit his truly encyclopaedic knowledge of the postwar novel is also something he has endured with unflagging enthusiasm and encouragement. Neal Alexander, Ron Carter, Matt Green, Josephine Guy, Andrew Harrison, Gillian Roberts, Mark Robson, Matthew Welton and Daniel Weston also have a penchant for impromptu discussions: thanks to their intellectual generosity, I have been able, simply by talking in a corridor, to clarify issues that could have otherwise gone unanswered in a library. It sounds like a platitude to say that teaching terms fly past with a speed that often allows little time to converse with colleagues about anything other than the next task ahead. For bucking precisely this trend towards conversational functionality, however, I would like to thank all those who have supported and contributed to the Contemporary Fiction Group at Nottingham – a forum for topflight debates about new writing that I have found very rewarding to chair. That group didn't start with me, however: the helm was graciously handed over by Sean Matthews, whose weekly hospitality elsewhere allowed me to keep envisioning this project in its most preliminary stages and through my earliest years in the job. Finally,

I would not have been able to complete the manuscript with patience, focus and composure without the generous period of research leave provided by the School of English.

It proved immensely helpful to have the opportunity to present several parts of this book to highly responsive audiences in both the United Kingdom and North America. I would particularly like to thank Jesse Matz for inviting me to speak on a MSA roundtable in 2008 about the relationship between modernism and the contemporary, reassuring me as that event did – and Jesse himself continues to do – that modernist continuities require further attention. By the same stroke, Matthew Hart reminded me to administer regular doses of self-scrutiny when plotting that story of continuance, and I thank him for his solidarity with respect to the way contemporary writing is more than ever demanding a fresh critical language. Whether they have known it or not, Susan Andrade, Richard Begam, Peter Boxall, Jay Clayton, Mark Currie, Amy Elias, Steve Ellis, Jim Hansen, Andrew Hoberek, Amy Hungerford, Roger Luckhurst, Peter Nicholls, Max Saunders, Tom Schaub and Rebecca Walkowitz have provided direction, indirectly or otherwise, at crucial points in this project's development, and I feel honoured to have had opportunities to converse (and in some cases to collaborate!) with such brilliant scholars. Closer to home, Peter Howarth and Finn Fordham never let me get away with much whenever I start mentioning the word modernism, let alone its future; Joe Brooker never lets me get away with anything to do with matters of style. I thank all three of them for their ability to play devil's advocate: the result of them doing so has sharpened the case this book makes about engaging historically as well as aesthetically with questions of form, and all remaining infelicities are wholly mine. Even the most sustained periods of scholarly effort benefit from healthy distractions – such as those provided so unselfishly by Julia Jordan, Eric Langley and David McAllister, who, when together, allow no one to take themselves too seriously. It was flattering to be invited to present some of the arguments in this book alongside my erstwhile supervisor, Laura Marcus, at the London Modernisms Seminar; and I continue to owe a debt of gratitude to Laura for the candid advice she has offered at many important stages. A fledgling version of the entire manuscript came under the exacting eye of Andrzej Gasiorek. As a friend with the knack for combing rigour and inspiration, his insights were not only scholarly but also pragmatic, and they gave me the momentum and confidence to say what I meant.

In addition to sharing ideas from this book before such audiences, I have had the opportunity to work with excellent editors and journals to bring burgeoning research into print. Some of the arguments informing the Introduction were articulated within a different framework in 'The New Purism', *Textual Practice*, 21:4 (2007): 687–714. Material that has subsequently been reshaped for Chapter 3 draws from 'By Thrifty Design: Ford's Bequest and Coetzee's Homage', in *International Ford Madox Ford Studies 7: Literary Networks and Cultural Transformations*, ed. Andrzej Gasiorek and Daniel Moore (Amsterdam and New York: Rodopi, 2008) and from '*Dusklands*', in *A Companion to the Work of J. M. Coetzee*, ed. Tim Mehigan (Rochester, NY: Camden House, 2011). An earlier version of Chapter 1 is included in my edited collection *The Legacies of Modernism: Historicising Postwar and Contemporary Fiction* (Cambridge University Press, 2011). To the editors and presses concerned, I am grateful for their permission to incorporate some of that work in revised form here.

At Cambridge University Press, I would like to thank Ray Ryan for his perceptive editorial guidance. With sharp foresight early on, he understood entirely what this book was trying to achieve, and he saw reason to invest in the project when it was still an embryo. I am genuinely grateful to the anonymous readers of this manuscript for offering judicious comments that helped me to augment the scope, heft and precision of my interventions. The Press's production team has represented the pinnacle of support and efficiency from start to finish, and it has been a pleasure to work with them again.

In putting together a book that is partly about literary heritage, I've become conscious of those traits I seem to have benefitted from inheriting. As a stonemason, my late father knew a good deal about what it means to pay attention to craft, and I hope the following pages bear some trace of his lessons in looking closer at how things are made. I have thanked my two older brothers before in print for not being academics and for being fabulous satirists instead: the gratitude is worth reiterating, because your relentless mockery of your little brother continues to do wonders in helping him keep his feet firmly on the ground. I marvel to think back at how my mum maintained her unflagging support for my commitment to an academic career, especially at times when such a pursuit seemed pretty reckless. She remains a paragon of reassurance, and without her support it is unlikely that I could have stayed on track through the uncertain years one spends gearing up for this profession. Uncertainties of other kinds have been rapidly dissolved with the love and encouragement of my family on the other side of the Atlantic: thanks to Tita and Jorge Sr., Lula and Andrés, and Jorge and Julie, for believing in me from the start and for offering the kindest welcome imaginable.

Learning from a comparatist can make you a more capacious reader; living with one is quite a different matter, especially when volumes in multiple languages vie for shelf space in an apartment that could hardly be described as capacious. This book bears the stamp of some of that learning and living; but more indelibly still, it bears witness to the love of a comparatist who became my companion. For her critical wisdom, her infinite patience, her sixth sense for what makes an argument ring true, and for the humour with which she reminded me to keep in mind our immediate futures whenever I was too absorbed in modernist ones, my final thanks are reserved for María del Pilar Blanco to whom this book is dedicated.

Introduction: Contemporary fiction and the promise of modernism

Any artistic project can be made to seem incomplete. Unrealised aspirations and unresolved arguments could describe why movements are remembered just as well as the finished masterworks for which they're renowned. But if stories of incompletion are there ready to be told, how do we go about telling them without ignoring anachronism and without relying on critical contrivance to prove claims for continuity? What does it really mean to consider that a given movement may also have a replenished moment, a phase of re-emergence – in another time, for another culture – through which its promise obtains renewed pertinence? Inevitably it's hard to view a period retrospectively and not review it at the same time, when enticed to see just how temporally elastic its parameters might be. Tempting as they are to fuel, though, debates about reperiodisation have a tendency to run their course through arguments of fleeting consequence; in modernism's case, that tale of continuance more compellingly unfolds when our work on revising paradigms is enriched by a closer look at creative practices. Providing such enrichment, Toni Morrison suggests that the 'ideal situation is to take from the past and apply it to the future'.[1] We would be hard pressed to think of a more audacious writer, one who, we might assume, has no truck with tradition. For surely Morrison's singularity sums up her freedom from inheritance, epitomising her irreverence toward any model that's not of her own making. Yet more than three decades later, Morrison's claim speaks to writers who variously partake in that 'ideal situation', and who find in it forms of imaginative praxis – forms that 'take from' modernism the potential for extending what fiction can do.

Precisely how and why modernist commitments, principles and aesthetics continue to inform the contemporary novel is the concern of this book. It brings together writers from a particular generation, whose careers have developed beyond the trends and traits of postmodernism, and who have drawn instead on modernism's legacy in the very process of fulfilling new formal, ethical and political objectives. Yet what does it mean to speak of modernism's continuance in the first place? Is it not the case that to argue for the persistence of recognisably modernist goals is surely something of a contradiction in itself, because to associate modernism with this talk of recuperation sounds quite opposed to the language of rupture on which so many vanguards of the early twentieth century staked their reputations? Surely the basic premise of any *modern*ism is, effectively, a demand: writers should forego all things vestigial or inherited in order to propel their methods forward and to produce art that reaches for alternative horizons. If this is the case, and if that demand is satisfied, how will we know what millennial modernisms look like when and if they arise? Will they be found in fiction that expresses 'a cultural shift' away from the high-modernist 'worship of form', as Urmila Seshagiri calls it, or instead in writers who make new interventions that at once extend aesthetic aims pioneered by early-twentieth-century fiction while challenging our critical expectations of what newness involves? Many of the answers to these questions will depend on whether we think the act of paying homage to modernism necessarily boils down to 'a literary moment as significant for what it departs from as for what it moves toward'.[2] Justified though these queries and caveats are, they forget modernism's own dialectical relation to tradition: fiction today partakes of an interaction between innovation and inheritance that is entirely consonant with what modernists themselves were doing more than a century ago, an interaction that enables writers to work *with* their lineage in the process of attempting new experiments with form.

So far, so convivial; at least that is how it seems in light of the more predictably antagonistic accounts of literary influence that have shaped our understanding of how writers pick up from and overtake their precursors. In this book, I draw attention to the way contemporary novelists forge less hostile or anxious lines of communication with the modernist tradition. The cultivation of this conviviality is something that Morrison herself encourages in the previously mentioned assertion, as she indicates the utility of the literary past for future ambitions. It is also a prospect that Raymond Williams entertained in *The Politics of Modernism*; although here, as we would expect from Williams, those interactions of past and present are couched in sociocultural rather than in stylistic or compositional terms:

If we are to break out of the non-historical fixity of *post*-modernism, then we must search out and counterpose an alternative tradition taken from the neglected works left in the wide margin of the century, a tradition which may address itself not to this by now exploitable because quite inhuman rewriting of the past but, for all our sakes, to a modern *future* in which community may be imagined again.[3]

In light of his argument that modernism has 'achieved comfortable integration into the new international capitalism', we could read Williams as confirming the idea that modernism has passed – what seemed so artistically radical is now culturally reified. Not only does he imply that it is a phase in literary history that can only be viewed in retrospect, its legacies addressed only via the prefix *post*; Williams is also keen to 'remind us that the innovations of what is called Modernism have become the new but fixed forms of our present moment'.[4] What role, then, does modernism play in a 'modern *future*'? The answer is more implicit, or inadvertent, in Williams's perorating comments. It is here that we need to read against the grain of his reconstruction of the fate of modernism's revolutionary protocols, painting as he does a picture of the project's exhaustion and its subsequent absorption into a 'comfortable' order of consumption. In other words, Williams would undoubtedly be wary of recuperating modernism as a contemporary concept, for it represents – in its early-twentieth-century manifestation – such a 'highly selective field';[5] his very terms, however, point beyond the rather fossilised version of institutional modernism that he frames. The implication is that we should 'counterpose' the assumptions that have 'fixed the moment of Modernism', because it is a fixity that is produced by the canonising 'machinery of selective tradition', whose categories may be inadequate for specifying how a new generation of writers are conversing with that tradition on more open-ended terms and, in so doing, exemplifying modernism's indispensability.[6] What might remain most pertinent about Williams's argument, therefore, could be precisely what runs athwart the twinned impulses of his critique: firstly, to uncover modernism's complicity in emergent forms of capitalist production; and, secondly, to call for a scholarly reinvestment in the neglected work of (regional) writers who have hitherto been excluded by the (metropolitan) sensibilities of high modernism.[7] Read counter-intuitively, Williams's intervention contains within itself an invitation, as it gestures to the viability of thinking about modernism's continued vitality, to the possibility of realising how it might be 'imagined again' after the vapidity of postmodernism.[8] We can accept such an invitation, providing we make the very distinction that Williams himself elides, one that would allow us to distinguish modernism as a 'selective' institutional construction, from modernism as the scene of an unfinished argument about the novel's critical and formal potentiality. Why some of the most audacious novelists have stepped into that scene in recent years is one of the questions motivating this book, as I consider how the relation between craft and critique in late-twentieth-century fiction corresponds with how 'the *social form* of modernism' in its earlier twentieth-century contexts, as Mark McGurl notes, was 'at once activated by and made manifest in the innovative *aesthetic forms* of the art-novel itself'.[9] If I take seriously Williams's notion about the way 'tradition' can 'address itself' to 'a modern *future*', I also take it to the next analytical level – and into a new historical epoch – by turning to novelists who have furthered modernist resources in order to meet fresh expectations about the purposes of literary experiment.

This study thus pursues the consequences of modernism's regeneration in contemporary fiction along two interrelated trajectories: the compositional and the political. The former indicates an attention to technique that shares Liam McIlvanney and Ray Ryan's contention that 'we are emerging from a period of heavily theoretical criticism and that, as a result, what might be called the novelness of novels is coming back into focus'.[10] This should not suggest that theoretical positions don't contribute to or facilitate the insights of this book. It implies instead that a closer scrutiny of the compositional elements of contemporary writing is required if we are to differentiate with any precision the strategies of writers whose affinities with modernism can be as complex and contradictory as they are explicit and self-conscious. Only then can we begin to explore at the levels of technique and context alike the reasons *why* modernist impulses remain so politically enabling for writers who have responded – as my six central writers do – to the material conditions that shape racial, sexual and social identification or injustice. This approach assumes that the particularities of form are therefore central, rather than incidental, to our estimation of contemporary fiction's involvement in ethical and political realms. In turn, that assumption helps us to counter the sense in which 'cultural critique', as Janice Radway has warned, 'typically attempts to make sense of the situation at the time of writing by relating it to past canons and rarely seeks to trace emergent, gradually building effects over time',[11] precisely because it also counters the idea that 'past canons' should remain our primary reference-point when we speak about artistic inheritance. As we shall see, a less programmatic account becomes available for the relation between literary innovation and cultural critique when we look more closely at contemporary writers' dynamic, if sometimes rebellious, conversations with the past in their process of developing 'emergent' narrative practices.

Any 'modernism after modernism', as Derek Attridge has put it, 'necessarily involves a reworking of modernism's methods, since nothing could be less modernist than a repetition of previous modes, however disruptive they were in their time'.[12] Running centrally throughout this book is my ambition to chart the creative motivations, thematic consequences and formal possibilities yielded by that process of reworking, but also to show why each of the very different novelists I consider should want to rework modernism in the first place. To explore why it matters that writers today re-evaluate modernist impulses and deploy them as their own, we need to join critics who, as Amy Hungerford wittily puts it, 'are not confined to those hefty postmodern slabs that formerly sat on syllabi as proof of the difficulty, and thus the worth, of contemporary writing in the academy'.[13] The goal of *Modernist Futures* is thus twofold: to propose alternative ways of thinking diachronically about the purpose of experimentation in contemporary fiction, and also, by doing so, to combine late-twentieth-century literary history with the commitments of close reading. Methodologically speaking, I try to be sensitive to the genealogical back-stories of the novel today – without recourse to that more familiar tale of postwar narrative as hedged in by 'hefty postmodern slabs' – even as I concentrate on the more local formal and affective properties that make particular novelists unique.

This is hardly an unprecedented move, nor is it the sole preserve of those who study the novel. Voices from art history, philosophy and aesthetics are joining the chorus that proclaims 'the premise that modernism is over is false'.[14] To substantiate this assertion – or to point out the disciplinary and hermeneutical consequences of refuting that 'premise' – J. M. Bernstein makes two further claims on behalf of modernism's continuity, claims that complement the notion I will be working with in this book: the *promise* of modernism has yet to be fully realised. The first of Bernstein's claims takes the form of an instruction to criticism itself, as he insists that we need to find modes of identifying how artists and writers have perpetuated that 'restless insistence on the transgression of past judgments in the new'.[15] His second and related claim is on behalf of modernism's currency, such that we need to find new ways of speaking about modernist practices *in* the present, rather than from the retrospective vantage point enabled *by* the present. Not simply an argument for extending modernism beyond its received period boundaries, it also addresses modernism as a set of persisting resources, rather than as a collection of historical artefacts. If the 'task of aesthetics', writes Bernstein, 'is to vindicate modernist art's *own* claim to mattering', then this is because modernism itself should be seen as a 'form of art that survives through a reiterated presentation of itself' and that also becomes the very 'stakes' of artistic practice and 'aesthetics in general'.[16] What Bernstein is implying, as I see it, is that we have been asking the wrong questions. The key issue is not whether modernist continuities exist, but how far, and at what price, modernism's extension into the procedures of contemporary literary or visual art has been obscured by critics who take the bygone vivacity of modernism for granted.

Bernstein raises an important series of metacritical issues, some of which will be explored in this Introduction. If the following chapters linger to some extent on the particularities of how novelists transcribe modernist innovations, I will take the opportunity here to step back somewhat from the writers in question, in order to clarify strands that connect their work and to point out some of the ways we are invited to approach them. In so doing, I not only intend to highlight unexpected correspondences between their creative aims, but also to reflect on how the very subject of contemporary literature's modernist 'heritage' relates to the disciplinary aims of the New Modernist Studies. Such implications for craft and criticism alike are highlighted throughout this study, and they enable me to account for interrelations within and between chapters more substantively than national or stylistic distinctions might imply. In turn, although this book expends much of its energy on exploring *how* modernist aesthetics resurface in contemporary fiction, of no less importance is the issue of *why* writers today extend such approaches to form in the first place – and what that might entail for our evolving critical practices.

MODERNIST FORM NOW

However they evolve, though, such practices are often freighted with suppositions. One might be led to suppose, for example, that a consideration of modernism's salience for contemporary fiction inevitably reinstates critical formalism over ideologically driven interpretations, as though turning from social effects to stylistic expressions were the only means of getting back in touch with the 'novelness of novels' today. Granted, 'the conjuring of "form" and "aesthetics" ', as Samuel Otter has remarked, 'discloses a variety of intellectual and emotional responses, spurred by a perceived indifference to verbal complexity, literary agency, textual explication (rather than critique), artistic wholes (rather than symptomatic parts), and readerly pleasures'.[17] The role of formally inspired readings in an approach to the political efficacy of the novel is only as vexed as the disciplinary tales we choose to retell about the pitfalls of close reading and its clashes with cultural analysis. Instead of re-inscribing such incompatibilities, one ought to be able to imagine 'less determined relationships between the formal and the historical and perspectives that might avoid the intoxicating cycle of antagonism or backlash', as Otter describes it, 'in which "form" and "history" are pitted against one another' – a story of methodological conflict that 'may no longer be (and may never have been) tenable'.[18] Sharing this scepticism about the perceived irreconcilability of craft and context in critical practice, throughout this book I adopt the premise that questions of form are indissolubly linked to questions concerning how fiction confronts the material world through its imaginative simulation of how that world is sensed and known. It is a premise that also concurs with Attridge's contention that '[w]hatever else the "modernist" text may be doing (and all literary texts function as a number of things besides literature), it is, through its form, which is to say through its staging of human meanings and intentions, a challenge that goes to the heart of the ethical and political'.[19] As these two pathways – the compositional and the politico-ethical – intersect in *Modernist Futures*, they address the issue of how we negotiate alternative directions for approaching modernism's persistence and recrudescence in contemporary fiction. We should observe such continuities from a writerly standpoint (in terms of the way they affect and reform the creative agendas of late-twentieth- and twenty-first-century novelists); yet I also trace their repercussions from an interpretive and literary-historical standpoint, so as to show why modernist aesthetics are not only compatible with, but are also actively opening up, new avenues for the novel's cultural interventions. As Rebecca Walkowitz has acknowledged, 'modernist strategies can be adapted for various political enterprises, as can critical attitudes',[20] and the six novelists considered in this book give a flavour of just how variously those adaptations occur. Certain shared commitments, however, can be discerned in ways that justify my selection of these writers; but in order to discern them, we first need to bring together a sufficiently agile definition of what *modernism* actually means before we consider what it does for novelists today.

In her study of the relevance of modernist methods for contemporary cosmopolitan fiction, Walkowitz defines modernism as 'involv[ing] strategies that respond to and engage with the experience of modernity',[21] drawing on Foucault's account of modernism as a 'consciousness' of modern life, 'a type of philosophical interrogation – one that simultaneously problematizes man's relation to the present, man's historical mode of being, and the constitution of the self as an autonomous subject'.[22] While this kind of interrogation is certainly one that concerns the writers I consider in this book, it doesn't provide a full range of answers to the question of why writers today are recalibrating modernist strategies to deal with the lived experience of *post*modernity, compelling us as they do to explore whether it's more preferable to characterise modernism with the logic of continuity instead of rupture. To say that modernism should be seen, as

Susan Stanford Friedman does, primarily 'as the structural principle of radical rupture – wherever, whenever, and in whatever forms it might occur',[23] is to reinstate a conflation of innovation with dissent that would simply not be recognised by writers who build on modernism's formal and critical potential. Models of rupture are familiar enough in accounts of early-twentieth-century literary experimentalism; they are models I want to complicate, though, not least because the rupturing of generic or linguistic conventions has not always guaranteed or aspired to politically progressive ends.[24] Chapter 1 thus establishes the conceptual and historical parameters within which we can utilise a more dialectical sense of the connection in fiction between inventiveness and literary heritage, a dialectic that informs the readings I then go on to perform in subsequent chapters. By gauging the political valences of this interaction of inheritance and innovation, I question, as Timothy Brennan has done, 'the idea that *rupture* rather than continuity is the sign of historical change'. Brennan remarks that '[t]his radical incantation of rupture – borrowed from the literary avant-gardes and a particular kind of modernism (Pound and Woolf rather than Eliot and Yeats) – is, in fact, conservative. For, if nothing else, the apparent calm of insisting on the flow and repeatability of tradition, as opposed to the Copernican shifts of the supposed year zero of the new, provides a mental landscape in which social transformation can actually be imagined'.[25] While the novelists considered in this study are scarcely unquestioning in their approach to 'the flow and repeatability of tradition', neither do they see that departing from what Milan Kundera calls 'the inherited path' along which writers move inventively in conversation with artistic precedents is inherently radical; instead, such writers combine acts of homage *with* fresh 'developments in modernist literary style' that, as Walkowitz has eloquently shown, may 'coincide with new ways of thinking about political critique'.[26] Modernist methods thus enable contemporary novelists to remap that 'mental landscape' where transformative contexts of social interaction, political assessment and ethical accountability can be envisioned.

Exploring *how* writers perform that process of imaginative remapping may not yield a startlingly new account of fiction's well-documented capacity for empathic projection and involvement, a capacity aptly summarised by Jonathan Franzen. Though he is, broadly speaking, a realist writer who would probably be reticent about being aligned with the modernist inheritance, Franzen pinpoints, nonetheless, precisely what is significant about certain modes of narration in contemporary fiction that couldn't be identified as anything other than modernist. For he insists that 'the novel is the greatest art form when it comes to forging a connection between the intensely interior and personal and the larger social reality'.[27] Pursuing this connection in fiction now prompts us to rethink the way we describe what is important (still) about some of the most familiar and exhaustively analysed innovations in twentieth-century writing. For example, if the novelists I examine in this book continue one of the hallmark aims of modernist fiction – to evoke interior subjectivity by simulating the effect of impressions, whether sustained or incoherent, to which subjects emotionally and intellectually respond – they also invite us to reconsider the supposedly inward orientation of that aim. In responding to modernism's experimental models of mentation, contemporary writers reveal the potential for modernist fiction to be more than simply a laboratory for examining consciousness as a hermetic domain. Instead, they incorporate techniques for showing how mental experiences are shaped by material circumstances, how protagonists' psychological states adapt to and are mutually pervaded by the social realms they navigate – revealing their working definition of the modernist novel as a medium for connecting interiority and accountability, braiding the description of characters' innermost reflections into the fabric of worldly situations.

This much may be familiar to readers of J. M. Coetzee, Milan Kundera, Ian McEwan, Toni Morrison, Michael Ondaatje and Philip Roth. Their fictions have often thematised whether in traumatic or enabling ways the relation between mind and world, perception and action, while testing the compatibility between the cultivation of personal agency and the demands of ethical responsibility. What remains to be answered, however, is the question of *why* these writers have chosen – creatively yet purposively – to extend modernist resources in representing their characters' phenomenal encounters with sociocultural environments and conflicts. This question matters to *Modernist Futures* not only because it lays the foundation for many of my interpretive aims and claims, but also because it justifies my corpus, a corpus drawn from a specific generation of novelists who began writing in the heyday of postmodernism and whose careers developed in its wake. After living through an age when self-referentiality as a creative compulsion reigned supreme, these figures are particularly concerned with exploring how the immediacy of inward experience relates to the interpersonal facets of social accountability. As they respond to an era typified by the fiction's parodic self-inspection, such writers reintegrate the novel's alternative capacities for interior and exterior forms of engagement – relating the potency of its simulation of emotive perceptions to the pertinence of its treatment of material realities.

It is thanks to the postmodern, then, that modernism has any future at all. Part of the purpose of this Introduction is to explain in literary-historical terms why that might be so, showing how those writers selected for the following five chapters reinvigorate modernist aesthetics in response to politically abortive metafiction. How we define that response, together with how we grasp what it is about modernist narrative that remains important for contemporary writers, will therefore depend on the kind of story we choose to tell about the development of postwar fiction — if indeed we choose to describe it in developmental terms in the first place. Some thirty years ago, Leslie Fiedler intimated the need for alternative accounts of modernism's reception at a time when fiction seemed more concerned with rescinding than with accepting whatever gifts were bestowed by earlier twentieth-century innovators. He noted, for instance, that '[t]hough a novelist like John Barth is clearly indebted to the example of James Joyce, he uses Joycean techniques not developmentally but terminally'.[28] This dissolution of modernism also announced the dismemberment of postmodernism's very enterprise, as metafiction turned in ever-tighter circles of self-interrogation. 'In light of this', reflects Fiedler,

> I was convinced for a long time that what was really dead in our culture was not the conventional novel at all, but *only* the kind of anticonventional long fiction which asked of the reader a constant awareness of its own artifice — and a concomitant admiration of the virtuosity of its artificer *as* artificer, as well as his ingenuity in making the death of the genre he purports to write its central subject. Clearly, it seems to me, such terminal fiction could not be written over and over without becoming an intolerable bore to its writers as well as its readers. But, alas, under the aegis of 'post-modernism', it has continued to be practiced to the very verge of the twenty-first century — and is still read by a tiny audience of a very special kind, whose nature can only be understood in terms of a radical change in the way long fictions have come to be consumed since the 1950s.[29]

The problem with this rather gloomy picture of postmodernism's destruction of the novel, and its critical absorption by an academy home to its own receptive but 'tiny audience of a very special kind', is that it forestalls the prospect of ever getting modernism *back into* that picture on the 'verge of the twenty-first century'. One of my contentions in this book is that contemporary writers are not only challenging any neat progression from modernist writing to the 'terminal fiction' of recent decades; they are also compelling us to wonder whether our understandings of how novelists now regard the politics of modernist forms have been built upon literary-historical charts that no longer seem accurate. To put it another way, in order to explore what writers now expect to achieve by reincorporating modernist techniques, we need to ask whether our conception of the novel's future – and modernism's role in it – has inherited, or at least been inflected by, a critical language centred on postmodernism's potential that is not entirely our own nor relevant to our present moment. The short answer would be: yes, inevitably it has. The long answer is played out across the pages of this book, as it shows why it is so important that we continue to develop critical vocabularies for recognising the import of modernism's reanimation in contemporary writing.

'The contemporary' itself, though, is no longer what it was. Likewise, the umbrella term 'postwar' now names a field for a discipline whose analytical priorities have at once proliferated and diverged. Fiction's journey from the postwar era into the contemporary scene has become too multifarious to be addressed as a single period, because of 'the simple fact', as Amy Hungerford rightly observes, 'that new forms of reading and writing are emerging on a vast scale'.[30] The risks of critical homogenisation, or at least inelegance, when thinking about what counts as contemporary become even more apparent once we bring that new generation of voices into the frame, including Monica Ali, Nicola Barker, Junot Díaz, Jonathan Safran Foer, Hari Kunzru, Andrea Levy, Tom McCarthy and David Mitchell, who only emerged through the 1990s, publishing their major works after the millennium. As already indicated, I will be concerned with a somewhat earlier group of innovators, in an effort to obtain a more historically nuanced sense of how modernism has operated in fiction written through and after the postmodern period, and to understand why that generation continues to play such a key role in reimagining what modernist conceptions of form might still become. One aspect of this analysis needs to account for the way writers have reassessed the idea of formal integrity after decades when postmodern fiction discredited such notions of cohesion. Pertinent here is the work of a British novelist who has shifted across generic boundaries, moving throughout her *oeuvre* from politically engaged fictions of socio-economic and racial inequality to dystopian visions of environmental peril.[31] Aptly enough, for this reason Maggie Gee thinks of herself as 'evidently a bit of a hybrid'. Yet the hybridity of which she speaks is formal as well as thematic, as she combines tradition with present aims. Committed to this synthesis of heritage and invention, she sees herself as the kind of writer who refuses to work *in the wake of* modernism because she doesn't see that modernism is over:

I have also consciously, in my career as a writer, become more aware of, and suspicious of, 'difficulty': i.e. I began as an 'experimental' writer, aka 'difficult', but came to believe the highbrow-commercial divide was a tragic one for contemporary literature, and that if one could, with a great deal of work, conceal complexity under a surface ease, this was a better way forward.[32]

Gee represents a refinement of high modernism's consciously pronounced sophistication, in terms of her awareness instead of what is the equally sophisticated task of articulating underlying 'complexity' with economy and control. Without resorting to so-called *lisible* transparency or comfortable traits of domestic realism, Gee suggests that creating an illusion of 'ease' in fact demands 'a great deal of work'. Aspiring to be no less experimental, even though her end result might appear more accessible, she goes on to assert that 'I still consider myself essentially a modernist, because I still believe in whole meanings for works of art: that the form of the whole should embody the meaning'.[33]

It is this belief in formal integrity, and the accompanying reticence towards postmodernism's self-reflexive dismemberment of subject matter and style, that recurs for each of the novelists addressed in the ensuing chapters. As an object of critical attention, this dimension of form may strike some readers as a rather blunt refusal of the consensus view of modernism's privileging of fragmentation. In part, it is; because I set about tracing modernism's continuance along less predictable lines, without seeing its contemporary persistence simply as a reflection, in David Tracy's phrase, of the 'fragmented character of our times'.[34] In turn, I regard literary innovation less as the product of cultural instabilities than as the very medium that brings the reader, through their intimate engagement with form, into a more ethically involved relation with *how* specific contexts of social crisis, racial injustice or political destabilisation are represented by novelists today.

Far from reverent, the six writers discussed in this book have certainly responded combatively to those modernist notions of individual genius that pertain to the novel's supremacy, artistic dignity, or supposed detachment from the public sphere of commodification. However, neither do they perpetuate the received view of modernism's search for aesthetic unification and mastery, a view that has been thoroughly complicated by recent work in modernist studies which has shown, as Andrzej Gasiorek and Patrick Parrinder remark, that while we can make 'all due allowance for the technical innovations of the great modernist writers', there was in reality 'no shared view of the nature, purposes and responsibilities of novel-writing in the period', and '[n]or was there a uniform response to the challenge of modernity'.[35] To say that contemporary writers are paying homage to the early-twentieth-century art novel as a vessel for now-lost principles of integrity would be to forget that modernist writing itself compelled its own readers to reflect on the discordances between manner and matter, technique and social critique. We should remember in turn that modernist novelists themselves 'engaged with contemporary life in a variety of fictional modes, reinventing the genre by means of radical experimentation with form' but also with 'less obvious transformations of established literary conventions'.[36] Nor are the six authors I centralise in this book remobilising that iconic effort of reparation in the face of modernity, an effort made most iconic by Eliot's *The Waste Land*, 'to create meaning from the flux and fragments of an atomized contemporary world', as Leonard Wilcox puts it, 'to pierce the veil, to reveal underlying truth'.[37] What sets my selected novelists apart from their contemporaries – and what motivates my engagement with *them* over other possible heirs to the modernist project – is their capacity to articulate modes of ethical and political commentary precisely through a sincere rather than self-parodic dedication to rendering perceptual experience. As Walkowitz points out, '[t]he analysis of perception and its provocations has been important to formal accounts of modernist experimentation as well as to cultural, political, and geographic accounts of urban experience and empire'.[38] The following chapters reveal that perception inspires 'a method' with a back-history, one that began with the early impressionism of Henry James and Ford Madox Ford, elaborated subsequently by the perspectival innovations of William Faulkner and Virginia Woolf, and is now extended today by such writers who appear in this book, who dramatise the 'provocations' of perception in narratives that embark upon different hemispheric and historical contexts.

It may seem unsurprising to regard the representation of perception as a lasting preoccupation, It provides a valuable point of focus, however, for considering how writers *are* dealing imaginatively with modernism's iconic concern with evoking the sensation of social worlds through the device of interior focalisation. This is most evident in contemporary novelists' concerns with dramatizing the relation of sensation to intellection, capturing in narrative form the flux of intimate thoughts. At first sight, such interactions point to a quintessentially impressionist set of goals, spurring Ford, Conrad and Woolf to undertake that task of correlating language and perspective, structure and sensory experience. Chapter 4 explores this lineage as it informs Ian McEwan's work, revealing impressionism's own extensive legacy beyond mid-century. Yet the attraction to the unity of perception and description that impressionism implies also continues in the work of novelists today who wouldn't associate their aims with the kind of free indirect discourse practiced perhaps most audaciously by James and Woolf. It is an attraction to the integration of form and content, structure and sensation, that marks Michael Ondaatje's affinity, as we will see in Chapter 2, with the logic of synthetic Cubism, just as it characterises the correlation of linguistic minimalism with depictions of agrarian thrift in J. M. Coetzee's fictions of provincial life. In each case, modernist aesthetics reoccur not as the mark of the writer's retrogressive reach for a pre-postmodern era of wholeness, but as a solution to specific representational concerns, a way of doing justice to the subject in hand – in short, as the realisation of a certain promise that remains in modernist conceptions of form.

But what exactly *is* modernist form in this context, and what kind of politico-ethical work might we expect it now to carry out in contemporary writing? Such deceptively simple questions of definition are key to our understanding of the stakes and implications of writers today fulfilling modernism's unrealised promises. For Angela Leighton, form is precisely what escapes definition, eluding our stock assumptions and exceeding prosodic or narratological categorisations. 'Form', she writes, 'is what remains when all the various somethings – matter, content, message – have been got out of the way'.[39] Nothingness necessarily accompanies, as this argument goes, our phenomenological grasp of a work's form: however much we want to name and typologise the properties we apprehend, the work 'takes on a curious, transgressive momentum of its own, evading capture as that neutral "form" which changeably reappears in various human guises', such that the very label *form* denotes 'both the object and the outline, the thing and its formal impression in the mind'.[40] If form is ultimately a word (rather than a prescribed or analysable set of properties) that 'already toys with its own content, enjoying the hologram effect of being a thing and an absence, a sound and an emptiness, there and not there',[41] then how might we approach a literary field, like modernism, across which the novel form became for writers the subject of conscious and careful reformulation? Dissolving the idea of form as technique may well liberate criticism from the tendency to draw on neologisms from narrative theory or to resort to the systematicity of descriptive stylistics. That belief in form's intangibility and indeterminacy, however, doesn't get us any closer to achieving a more precise account of how contemporary writers have acutely reflected on the genealogies of their methods. While this book by no means offers a methodical narratological investigation of modernist legacies, it poses the question as to whether matters of technique have often been neglected within contemporary fiction studies in favour of the allegorisation of plots or the recruitment of novelists' thematic concerns to serve timely theoretical ends. We should be in a position now to start combining the history of how postwar fiction has evolved with closer analyses of the modes that this evolution has at once inherited and generated – a synthesis of historicism and formal analysis that can include both pragmatic *and* affective perspectives. Indeed, as Isobel Armstrong reminds us, '[t]he aspiration to form is a *sensuous* state'.[42] Additionally, she points out that our attention to art as 'a shaping of the *process* of shaping' demands some combination of linguistic or structural categorisation and our more involved, aesthetic intuitions, if we are to make sense of why certain narrative strategies move us emotionally in the ways they do.

In the chapters to come, I follow Armstrong's cue that the 'aspiration to form is a struggle brought to consciousness', a drama of 'perpetual remaking' that's staged within the work itself, just as it prompts us to reflect on the difficulties of reading that work. As Armstrong notes, art 'does not consist in achieved form, which would become finitude, but in the experience of making form, an experience distributed across makers and perceivers'.[43] To regard form not as a systematically produced artifice, but as an experience to which the writer contributes imaginatively and with which the reader interacts interpretively is to provide an alternative model for comprehending the continued validity of modernist aesthetics. The potential for thinking about modernist form in this way as a performative process rather than a means to an end is brought into sharp focus by the writers in this study. As we will see, their work evinces a common aim: to turn the innovative composition of fictional worlds into an emotionally and ethically implicative process, an aim that bespeaks their objective, in Toni Morrison's words, 'to have the reader work *with* the author in the construction of the book'.[44] Because they seek not merely to simulate the experience of the material world but also to stimulate new interpretations of it, their strategies for remaking form into a process of participatory engagement both defines what modernism means to contemporary novelists and underlines why it still matters.

LATE MODERNIST INSTITUTIONS AND POSTMODERN INTERRUPTIONS

Late-twentieth- and twenty-first-century writers have found it unsatisfactory, let alone desirable, to summon and redeploy modernist tactics for aesthetic ends alone. More than any simple act of artistic homage, their dialogues with modernism evidence instead politically urgent responses to the legacies of *post*modern metafiction, whose reigning paradigm of self-referential parody presented a futile loop from which all the novelists in this book have in their various ways wanted to escape. However successful their escape has been, though, we cannot simply sidestep the reasons for them doing so. In other words, '[w]hat, after all, is the place of postmodernism in all this?' It is a question Andreas Huyssen posed towards the end of *After the Great Divide* (1986), trying to explain as he did the avant-garde's 'energetic come back' in the 1970s, without suggesting that this should 'point to the exhaustion of cultural resources and creativity in our own time', but rather present 'the promise of a revitalization in contemporary culture'.[45] In this section, I will offer my own response to that question, bearing in mind this book's motivations to reassess contemporary writers' relations both to their immediate and to their earlier twentieth-century pasts – whether artistic or institutional. I don't mean to suggest that my selected novelists collectively represent 'attempts to shift into reverse', as Huyssen puts it, 'in order to get out of a dead-end street where the vehicles of avant-gardism and postmodernism have come to a standstill'.[46] The picture I paint is rather more pragmatic. Despite the varying degrees to which they either draw or else depart from modernist predecessors, the writers considered in this book – as dissimilar as they might seem – are united by a practical attitude towards upholding an attention to craft in the face of fiction's dissolution into narrative self-reflection. We may classify them as 'late modernists', but the term is imperfect because it insinuates that they are sifting through the relics of high modernism and its residual goals. Late modernism does have a certain currency, if we use lateness to capture the arc of an account in which contemporary fiction takes forward the trailblazing practices of early-twentieth-century writers in a new yet belated manner – belated by virtue of the way it reveals how postmodernism marked for a certain generation of novelists merely an interruption, a temporary delay in all that modernist aesthetics had still to achieve.

Following my consideration of the participatory nature of form, my second, and perhaps most historically significant, strand for *Modernist Futures* takes up the issue of why writers should want to identify with modernist aspirations after postmodernism. Even John Barth, sometime proclaimer of the novel's exhaustion, would highlight at the dawn of the 1980s the vitality of aesthetic formations lampooned by metafictionists of the 1960s and 1970s. Addressing postmodernism as though it were already on the wane, Barth conceded that the 'term itself, like "postimpressionism" is awkward and faintly epigonic, suggestive less of a vigorous or even interesting new direction in the old art of storytelling than of something anticlimactic, feebly following a very hard act to follow'.[47] That 'act' was, of course, the example set by modernism. A compelling reason for me to write this book has been to give recognition to the ways in which contemporary novelists have in fact dealt so effectively with postmodernism's 'anticlimactic' mood by reinvigorating the very methods it sought to parody, to exaggerate and, *in*effectively, to replace. As I have implied, Coetzee, Kundera, Morrison, McEwan, Ondaatje and Roth have held little affinity with that compulsion to foreground the mechanics of writing for metafiction's sake.[48] Indeed, they may be taken as a representative of a considerably different concern with the responsibilities of the novel and the responsiveness of the reader who interacts with it, a concern made manifest as an abiding conviction that innovation should enable the critical work that fiction can direct at the world rather than at itself. In place of postmodernist fiction's self-referential deliberation upon the failures and fabrications of illusionism, the novelists in this book 'demonstrate alternative values', as Charles Altieri has called them, 'defined by exemplary adjustments in the sensibilities produced by attention to formal structures'.[49] Sometimes these authors highlight for the reader that formal 'attention' at work – as McEwan does with his ideal vision of paragraphs that comment on their own creation; or as Morrison does by encouraging her readers to participate in the affective world of her narratives, oblique and linguistically demanding though they can. Yet these writers do so rarely in a way that lauds self-consciousness as the motivating theme or as the sole reason for us to find their storytelling important.

In light of these novelists' various, perhaps conflicting, backgrounds, some readers may find their alignment with each other unusual or at best partial. By virtue of their contrasting idioms and ambitions, however, each writer can be understood in terms of a common endeavour to reconsolidate fiction's formal integrity and ethical accountability as it survives the vanities of postmodern self-reflexivity, an endeavour that tests the way we recognise the consequences of that survival. As such, these writers compel us to wonder what's politically left of the postmodern after the closing decades of the twentieth century, when the 'oppositional agendas' of postcolonial and feminist intellectuals, writers and activists became 'deeply suspicious', as Linda Hutcheon admits, 'of the postmodern's lack of a theory of political agency'.[50] The formal correlative of this suspicion can be witnessed in the way contemporary novelists have increasingly moved beyond metafiction – postmodernism's primary vehicle for defamiliarising, if not undermining, the aesthetic claims of modernist fiction as much as the ideological claims of collective oppositional discourses. One couldn't deny that Coetzee, Kundera, McEwan, Morrison, Ondaatje and Roth have each, at one or other point in their career, invoked strategies of self-conscious narration. When we read them historically, however, their acquaintance with metafiction looks less like a lasting fidelity than a passing phase, whose temporariness suggested that such writers were well aware that postmodernism's interrogation of 'truth-claims and its denaturalizing and demystifying impulses had been compromised by its very institutionalization'.[51]

Modernist Futures contends that we can therefore take account of the cultural and historical reasons for modernism's continuation by focusing on novelists who intersected with this discrete phase of disillusionment with postmodernism, who refused its mandate that 'values are not permitted to be grounded' (in Hutcheon's phrase), and who departed from a terrain 'where no utopian possibility is left unironized'.[52] Such an account needs to be attentive to the political ramifications of modernism's legacy as it enables these novelists to exercise certain forms of critique to which we may in turn provide ethical forms of response. In the following chapters, writers thus invite us to analyse correspondences between the politics of style and the ethics of reading, since these exchanges help us to explain why it is that modernist strategies remain so vital to the novel today. This is not to argue that such innovators simply disavow the impact of postmodernism in favour of some nostalgic recuperation of models of composition drawn from an age before writers become self-parodic. That would be to mistake the formal integrity of modernist fiction as the antithesis of self-reflexivity, when in fact the 'modernist novel', as Pericles Lewis reminds us, 'through the difficulty and self-consciousness of its literary style, characteristically calls attention to the problem of its own interpretation'.[53] Indeed, one of the motivations for my selections has been to pinpoint writers whose reinvestment in modernism has enabled them to rethink the very role that rhetorical reflexivity might play in narratives that provoke our ethical engagement, insofar as their fiction may produce moments of intense absorption in and indignation towards episodes of oppression, trauma or disempowerment, while also 'call[ing] attention', in the fashion Lewis notes, to the virtuosity by which the critical effects of such episodes are achieved. In sum, each of the writers I have brought together stages some degree of formal self-reflection but without undermining our affective involvement in the personal and collective experiences he or she plots. As we shall see, it is this double capacity for immersing the reader and at the same time reflecting on modes of address and perspective, which offers a supple medium for contemporary writers as they remobilise modernist narrative practices after the postmodern. The novelists who appear in this study do so, firstly, because they exemplify the spectrum of formal and thematic concerns across which that medium can be employed; and secondly, because their work embodies a disposition towards valuing techniques tested throughout the modernist period, precisely for the reason that those techniques facilitate the kinds of cultural, philosophical and emotive work that they want their writing to perform.

When getting to grips with these larger scale transformations from modernism to postwar postmodernism, and onward again into the last decades of the twentieth century and the rise of what I am calling the novel's modernist future, we're led to interrogate ingrained habits of periodisation as well as the very terms of analysis – aesthetic, historical and socio-political – that accompany them. Our questioning of stock terminology should especially be directed to the way we frame writers who appear unequivocally postmodern, with reputations like those of Angela Carter, Peter Carey and Don DeLillo, who are famed for dramatising the contingency and relativity of historical knowledge. As Andrzej Gasiorek reminds us, even figures such as Julian Barnes and Salman Rushdie, 'far from acceding to postmodernist scepticism, contend not only that veridical accounts of the world are possible but also that they are *necessary* if various forms of oppression are to be opposed by rational critique and if the transformation of society is not to recede from view as a political desideratum'.[54] This gestures to the contention that while '[r]eality demands to be interpreted … it does not license the free play of just any vocabulary', a contention that has not only revealed a 'serious purpose' underlying the linguistic brio of many supposedly postmodern novelists,[55] but has also redirected the instincts of thinkers who have built their reputations from endorsing postmodernity's relevance for understanding contemporary culture. Fredric Jameson is the most prominent case in point here. With a change of heart from his earlier portraits of postmodernism as fatally numb to modernism's legacy and complicit instead with the voracity and cynicism of corporate culture, in *A Singular Modernity* Jameson indicates the 'dependence of the postmodern on what remain essentially modernist categories of the new'. As he goes on to explain, this is not an 'insignificant contradiction for postmodernity, which is unable to divest itself of the supreme value of innovation (despite the end of style and the death of the subject)'.[56] In a similar vein, Caroline Levine has elucidated the contradictions underlying postmodernism's supposed rupture from early-twentieth-century literary culture, suggesting that controversies over postmodernism's 'impossible' 'attempts to escape institutionalization' in fact 'tend to extend the logic of the avant-garde, rather than to disrupt it'.[57] While articulating their own distinctive and often contrasting allegiances to the artistic and political 'value of innovation', as Jameson calls it, the writers at the centre of this book speak directly to this notion of late modernism as an ongoing, undisrupted phase, one from which 'postmodernism attempts radically to break, imagining that it is thereby breaking with classical modernism'.[58]

'Late modernism', however, has itself faced definitional hurdles. If it's not used as an endlessly expansive and nimble category, applicable to any phase of post-high-modernist writing, it becomes, by contrast, too narrowly confined to the immediate aftermath of 1922, associated with writing leading up to the Second World War. This latter, contracted version of late modernism is the one that Tyrus Miller offers in his influential yet somewhat monochromatic account of the sardonicism of interwar fiction:

> In their struggle against what they perceive as the apotheosis of form in earlier modernism, late modernist writers conjured the disruptive, deforming spell of laughter. They developed a repertoire of means for unsettling the signs of formal craft that testified to the modernist writer's discursive mastery. Through a variety of satiric and parodic strategies, they weakened the formal cohesion of the modernist novel and sought to deflate its symbolic resources, reducing literary figures at points to a bald literalness or assimilating them to the degraded forms of extraliterary discourse. They represent a world in free fall, offering vertiginously deranged commentary as word, body, and thing fly apart with a ridiculous lack of grace.[59]

The scene of swirling satiric fervour that Miller frames is deceptive in its description, partly because of the enumerative manner of his critical style. It feels as though we are being offered a complex, multifaceted view of late-modernist writing, when in fact he is reducing it to monotony: the monotony of the retrogressive task of negating high-modernist artistry. In Miller's view, mid-century novelists could only reconcile themselves with the 'mastery' of their near predecessors by defaming it. Despite his effort to provide a more precise account of how diverse high modernism's influence was, Miller's picture of that struggle against form ends up condemning a whole generation of writers to a climate of anxiety – the scene of a contest that can be settled only when the resources inherited from high modernism are outdone.

We need a more multifaceted view of postwar literary history than this vision of the rivalry over 'degraded forms' can provide. To get a palpable sense of how late modernism evolved and survived alongside the very postmodern aesthetics that sought to displace it, we would do better to look to novelists rather than theorists. Pertinent here is an institutional story about the relation of modernism and pedagogy. I am not so much concerned with rehearsing complaints against the New Critical cherishing and entrenchment of modernist poetics, as with the curricular expansion of writing programmes that many of the practitioners working under the banner of New Criticism provoked – even if, as Tim Mayers reminds us, the movement 'also effectively worked to disenfranchise many creative writers from the act of criticism'.[60] Whatever other constrictions novelists in higher education face in their attempt to write their own criticism, the success of creative writing itself, nowhere more so than in the North American academy, is indisputable. Documenting the reasons for that success is beyond the scope of my discussion here; nor do I want to spot causal links between creative writing pedagogy and the literary-critical categories by which we trace modernism's later twentieth-century influence. More useful for our purposes will be to survey the conditions under which modernist techniques have themselves been subject to institutional incorporation by being disseminated across what Mark McGurl has called the 'Program Era', and in a fashion that affects the way writers choose to reactivate modernist methods.

Despite those attempts, tacit and overt, by New Critical formalism to elevate modernist style, the heterodox impulses that drove modernism to cross new frontiers in the first place were hardly immune, as McGurl reminds us, from becoming 'wholly respectable' beyond the middle of the century, 'sitting there fat and happy on the college syllabus'.[61] To this extent, the university would 'become the primary custodian' of a 'late modernist "literariness"' that embodied new tensions between personal inspiration and progressive education, craftsmanship and coursework.[62] This seemingly contradictory intersection of creativity and the curriculum was a productive one for the scene of fiction-writing instruction; and the programme came to operate as the disciplinary site of that 'ongoing struggle' in postwar fiction 'between the compositional values of self-expression and self-discipline' – the latter being inherited, as McGurl notes, from none other than 'the Jamesian tradition of narrative decorum'.[63] Seductive though he is as a role model for conscious artistry, James was quickly joined in the classroom by other modernist figureheads. Divided criteria of a qualitative kind emerged: to follow the verbal restraint and condensation of Hemingway, or the baroque syntax showcased by Faulkner. This is where the pedagogical, not to say personal, implications of modernist style are most apparent, observes McGurl, adjudicating the alternative and equally attractive options that the tutee is compelled to negotiate. In precisely this regard, Faulkner 'came to symbolize the value not of *craft* but of sublime *genius*, licensing the students of the Program Era to – linguistically speaking – *let it fly*.[64]

But not all students are alike. What is interesting in the case of Faulkner's influence is that his 'maximalism', as McGurl labels it, can inspire its modal opposite. As we will see in Chapter 5, Toni Morrison's commitment to economy exemplifies this process of turning-the-tables on the 'sublime genius' of Faulkner's run-on sentences, as she makes spareness into something elegant by upholding her belief that 'you should never satiate'.[65] In fact, Morrison's example shows that we shouldn't take the institutional absorption of modernist imperatives at face value. While McGurl argues that 'the beauty of literary minimalism is in its artful unwillingness to *conceal the concealment* of its own dependency and weakness', having as it does 'the ironic advantage of revealing the systematicity of creativity in the Program Era in its starkest form',[66] I will be providing a rather different take in Chapter 3 where we turn to Coetzee, just as I give minimalism a reprieve when considering Morrison's use of concision. Coetzee's unadorned fiction requires us to read minimalism not as a symptom of 'retreat or self-concealment',[67] but as a method with a distinct – and not exclusively North American – lineage that reaches back to the impressionist principles of Ford, and forward again (when traced through Coetzee's later modernist influences) to Beckett's tense yet verbally shorn narration. Undoubtedly the U.S. model of the writing programme represents a remarkable social and intellectual shift in the application of the high-modernist ethos of individual virtuosity. Yet the institutional mediations of creative writing – like the maligned vocabulary of New Critical appreciation with which the programme's terminology of craft had intersected, before superseding it – cannot pretend to tell the whole story of how contemporary writers extend the procedures and aspirations of modernist fiction.

When prestigious novelists take up established positions within the academy, they add to the reputation of their host institutions, and they show that becoming a renowned literary innovator brings with it a degree of cultural capital. In this sense, reviving modernist aesthetics could uncharitably be deemed to be the first step on the road to fame (or at least respect) in the eyes of scholarly peers, regardless of how unpalatable experimental fiction might be to the book-buying public. Equally, though, the charisma acquired by writers employed in higher education is something they don't necessarily choose for themselves but rather assume in the eyes of their students. In short, how writers choose to identify their own style or voice may not automatically match up with the identity attributed *to* them by those who respond to the way they write, or by those who learn from the traditions that writers endorse in the classroom. If this is so, we ought to ponder the proposition that a writer might see no complicity between what she does and how she teaches; or, likewise, between how she chooses to inherit devices from modernism and the exhaustive study of modernism's cultural heritage carried out by her neighbouring literary historians. Certainly, Hungerford makes a brilliant case for renaming the contemporary as 'long modernism', precisely because 'the second half of the twentieth century sees not a departure from modernism's aesthetic but its triumph in the institution of the university and in the literary culture more generally'.[68] At the same time, however, it is easy to overestimate the cross-contamination between this institution of teaching, reinterpretation and publication that now houses modernist literature in the academy and the experimental ambitions of contemporary writers who happen also to be employed there. With respect to this study's aims, I am mindful of such distinctions between the *disciplinary influences* of modernism's critical formation (as scholars from discrete fields, each with their own distinctive political and interpretive priorities, reassess twentieth-century fiction in ways that 'influence' the canonisation of contemporary writing) and those *artistic influences* that writers savour and incorporate for themselves. This is not simply to recognise the crude fact that many established writers have never taught consistently in higher education or else have shown reticence towards the disciplinary formation of the programme, a reticence expressed from time to time by McEwan, for instance, who admits that he had 'comparatively little contact' with Malcolm Bradbury or Angus Wilson,[69] his supervisors in the 1970s on the soon-to-be-famous fiction-writing programme at the University of East Anglia. It is also to acknowledge how those novelists from my corpus who *have* taught – Coetzee at Cape Town, Morrison at Princeton, and Ondaatje in Ontario at York University as well as Glendon College – regard their creative work as radically separate from their pedagogical objectives.

Morrison, for one, is resolute in this respect. Making a novel 'has to be very private and very unrelated', she confirms: 'When I write, I can't read other people I like', and 'I have to feel as if it's being done almost in a very separate womb of my own construction. Wholly free. And because it's the only activity at all that I engage in wholly for myself. It's the one place that I can't have any other interference of that sort'.[70] These preconditions have led her to 'suspect that full-time teaching would get in the way of writing', insofar as 'you have to think in a certain way about the literature you're teaching', where ultimately any 'critical stance' she adopts in the seminar room makes her 'too self-conscious' back at the writing desk.[71] Similarly, for Ondaatje, too, we need to take into account that he 'doesn't like talking about his work' at all. And oddly enough, his quibbling on the phone with Cary Fagan in the 1990s about the very idea of being interviewed occurred, in this instance, just after he finished teaching at Brown University – his wife, Lynda Spalding, had been Brown's writer-in-residence – where presumably he talked a good deal about what it means to carry out that 'work'.[72] Like Morrison, though, Ondaatje feels that 'the best writing comes when you're not self-conscious, and to think that there's somebody out there listening for something becomes pretty ominous'.[73] We could hardly imagine Ondaatje and Morrison shying away from the seminar room; but they are scrupulous about dissociating their contribution to the discipline of creative composition from how their own novels 'grow organically', as Ondaatje describes it, without 'a scheme', however consciously crafted they might seem.[74]

If Ondaatje and Morrison express some caution about being too self-aware, however, this shouldn't be confused with the way they have dealt with the legacies of postmodernism, as though postmodernism alone is the proper originator of artistic self-consciousness. Indeed, we need only look to a self-proclaimed postmodernist to tell us so. Speaking of that 'self-conscious exploration of composition', Clarence Major sees that it epitomises what modernism made possible. While taking lessons in perspective from that period of transition between impressionism and Cubism delineated by Cézanne's career, Major also 'drew a profoundly romantic response' from Gauguin and was spurred to find a contemporaneous equivalent in fiction. To do so, he reached for Lawrence, Mansfield and Joyce, attracted to the 'kind of self-apparent urgency' and 'reflexive brilliance' of their most 'expressionistic' work.[75] Inspiring him to become 'more fascinated in technique' than 'by subject matter',[76] Major's awareness of the way compositional reflexivity predates postmodernism establishes a frame, for our purposes, for approaching writers in succeeding chapters who take modernism up on its promises. This is not to claim that Major is in fact a 'late modernist' after all, despite what his critics have said. It is to highlight, instead, a key methodological point for this book concerning how we go about relating the compositional to the political, while remaining alert to the role that heritage plays for novelists who reflect on technique but who prevent self-consciousness from compromising the integrity of their fictional worlds.

In his later work, McEwan has embodied these protocols more explicitly than most. In the same year his most self-scrutinising novel,

Atonement (2001), appeared, McEwan asserted that he is 'drawn to some kind of balance between a fiction that is self-reflective on its own processes, and one that has a forward impetus too, that will completely accept the given terms of the illusion of fiction'.[77] That 'balance' is one that unites the very different novelists I address. Drawing attention to writerly 'processes', Coetzee likewise sustains the simultaneously arresting 'illusion' of his disturbing plots. He engages a modernist heritage of stylistic obliquity and economy precisely in order 'to engage the reader ethically', as Derek Attridge puts it, challenging our preconceptions especially when his fiction – 'as in the case of modernist writing' in its early-twentieth-century contexts – purposefully seeks to 'resist the immediacy and transparency of language'.[78] And to give a final flavour of those instances of 'balance' addressed in this book, we can think of how Toni Morrison has, across her career, tried 'to blend' the 'artificial with improvisation'.[79] In achieving that synthesis she has satisfied the compulsion, as she describes it, to involve the reader in the very 'construction of the book',[80] but without curtailing our deep emotional response to those arresting scenes of racial dispossession, communal violence and personal sacrifice that readers find so haunting throughout Morrison's work.

Such strategies for combining narrative self-reflection and readerly involvement, whether difficult or pleasurable, are more overtly deployed by some novelists than others and with contrasting degrees of polemical force. Given that range of deployment, I have opted for author-led discussions that, taken together, showcase richly contrasting thematic and stylistic commitments. An upshot of their mutual differences, however, is that they show the varied contours along which modernist continuities flow. As we shall see, this variety in purpose and technique suggests that it is not simply the case that 'the two ends of the twentieth century hail each other like long lost twins', apposite though Tom Gunning's simile is for the transhistorical conversation this book convenes between modernist and turn-of-the-millennium fiction.[81] Those twins have been together all the time, as it turns out, even though postmodernism intervened for a considerable time in their kinship – a kinship that has often been mistaken for more anxious versions of influence.

'GETTING BEYOND INFLUENCE': ON IMPIETY AND ADAPTATION

'[S]omething had changed', recalled Peter Carey in 2006, reflecting on the moment he turned from short-fiction to the novel; but why did that change come about? 'Age, experience, a simpler form, practice, reading, influence, getting beyond influence'.[82] In Carey's account, influence is something that writers grow out of, a phase in the initiation process through which they find their own voice. The implication here is that 'experience' has shown how not to fall under the influence of figures like Jorge Luis Borges and García Márquez, whose allure Carey now sees, with 'age', as having been inescapable for his younger, short-story-writing self. We can only surmise that the *effects* of literary influences need to be felt before they can be relinquished. Milan Kundera also elaborates on this procedure of engagement and relinquishment, less in terms of succession – whereby a writer moves from identification with forebears to the recognition of her own individuality – but as an ongoing dialectic. In *The Curtain*, his stringent yet probing manifesto on technique from 2007, Kundera declares the 'novelist's ambition is not to do something better than his predecessors but to see what they did not see, say what they did not say'.[83] Some sixty pages later, Kundera expands this notion intriguingly. He points to the insights we gain when writers themselves speak about their own practice in conversation with their predecessors. Novelists reflect as assiduously on method as they do on thematic materials, a process in the early stages of composition that opens the seeming privacy or hermeticism of the creative act to an expansive heritage:

> According to his criteria of values, he will again trace out for you the whole *past* of the novel's history, and in so doing will give you some sense of his own poetics of the novel, one that belongs to him alone and that is therefore, quite naturally, different from that of other writers. So you will feel you are moving in amazement down into History's hold where the novel's *future* is being decided, is coming into being, taking shape, amid quarrels and conflicts and confrontations.[84]

Modernist Futures shares something of Kundera's desire to enter that 'hold', that laboratory of style, where new formal priorities are being 'decided'. I'm not implying that we try to understand contemporary writers simply by who, and what, they admire, as though we can only know style by its remains. I am suggesting, however, that we reflect on our own interpretive stance on affiliation and inheritance, with the view to asking why the recapitulation of modernist aesthetics might or might not be important to understanding a writer's own sense of where tradition and innovation coincide.

This question of how we decipher influence is often caught between binary alternatives: between, on the one hand, that melodramatic battle of artistic egos, where the inheriting writer is afflicted, in Harold Bloom's famous diagnosis, with 'immense anxieties of belatedness';[85] and, on the other hand, the rule of critical common sense that holds that 'if one is attuned to the effect', as Henry Widdowson claims, 'all texts reverberate with the echoes of other texts. All uses of language have a history of previous uses'.[86] Both approaches generalise the formal *substance* of influence as writers negotiate it, in order to preserve the freedom with which readers can invoke vague terms like 'association' or 'echo' for pinpointing the nature of creative debt. Widdowson himself admits that readers are 'free to conjure up all manner of intertextual associations' and 'resonances' that 'come not only from the countless times ... words have been used in reference, but also from our experience of other literary texts'.[87] Again, the emphasis is on the reader to spot connections, rather than taking it from the compositional viewpoint of the writer who, in interview, may disqualify our notions of where her allegiances lie. As Paul Fry has remarked in a recent reappraisal of the high-modernist lineage of *The Anxiety of Influence*, the 'Bloomian thief steals origins, Eliot's thief steals mannerisms, yet the question remains between them how, if not via words, the thief is to be detected'.[88] If Fry is right to point out 'that novelty does not just happen when it appears but is a phenomenon whose emergence as an influence is subject to delays, detours and bypaths of reception', how do we gauge the originality of writers so contemporary that their body of reception has only just accumulated, and whose influence upon a still younger generation of novelists has yet to be accounted for? Even if we follow Bloom's cue that 'criticism is the art of knowing the hidden road' leading from work to work,[89] then how do we approach the use of the past in *oeuvres* that are unfinished or that might be reaching that stage where, as Carey puts it, we find the writer 'getting beyond influence'?

An answer to this cluster of questions is offered by one of this book's key figures, a writer who in turn raises his own questions about influence and in the most unlikely of contexts – the acceptance speech for the world's most prestigious prize for literary distinction. As a one-time pragmatic literary-linguist, we would expect J. M. Coetzee to be an eloquent commentator on the very essence of originality. And so he is; except that he chose the occasion of his 2003 Nobel Prize speech to offer a most intimate yet characteristically oblique reflection on the very dialectic of inheritance and innovation that I will be tracing throughout this book. 'He and His Man' may be read as a deliberate, and doubly self-reflexive, attempt by Coetzee to hybridise Defoe's plots, as we see episodes from *A Journal of the Plague Year* (1722) reread by Crusoe. Coetzee adopts Robinson as his speech's focaliser, one who envisions from his writing desk the 'leaping and prancing' of people agonised by disease as 'allegoric of his own leaping and prancing when, after the calamity of the shipwreck and after he had scoured the strand for sign of his shipboard companions and found none, save a pair of shoes that were not mates, he had understood he was cast up all alone on a savage island, likely to perish and with no hope of salvation'.[90] This affinity between the traumas of Defoe's chronicle and his own leads Crusoe to ponder the artistry of *Plague Year*, entering into dialogue with the very texture of the text in an effort to discover why it ignites his imagination as vividly as it does: 'How then has it come about that this man of his, who is a kind of parrot and not much loved, writes as well or better than his master? For he wields an able pen, this man of his, no doubt of that'.[91] However allegorical Crusoe deems Defoe's fiction to be in relation to his castaway experiences, it is at this point that Crusoe's meditation on 'his man's' rhetorical flair begins to allegorise Coetzee's *own* scrutiny of fidelity and singularity, piety and virtuosity – the interaction of engagement and self-differentiation that characterises Coetzee's negotiation of influences (those prominent yet contrastive personas of Ford and Beckett), the same sort of a negotiation that each writer in this study undertakes.

As his speech unfolds at this meta-compositional level, Coetzee reconstructs the idea of the precursor as a figure who expresses 'a touch of fellow feeling for his imitators', knowing that 'if the young are to be forbidden to prey upon the old then they must sit forever in silence'.[92] In place of *he* and *his man*, then, we're invited to read *contemporary writer* and *modernist forebear*. If we do so, though, ultimately '[h]ow are they to be figured?', asks Coetzee: 'As master and slave', as Harold Bloom would have it, where the descendent captures and controls his powerful precursor, even though, as Roth's fiction will reveal in Chapter 1, to adopt Conrad's famous maxim to make the reader see need not presuppose an enslavement to imitation?[93] 'As comrades in arms',[94] just as Morrison's own admiration for Faulkner, Zora Neale Hurston and James Baldwin suggests, encouraging her as they do to write 'at the top of [her] form' when envisioning alternatives to scenes of discrimination, communal fortitude and racial injustice?[95] 'Or as enemies' and 'foes', an antagonism that McEwan dramatises in *Atonement* where he indicts the indulgences of Briony Tallis's high-modernist embellishments, only subsequently to reassert his attraction to the urban novel-of-consciousness, as *Saturday* (2005) orbits Bloomsbury while making no attempt to conceal its allusions to the one-day narratives of Woolf and Joyce?[96]

Coetzee invites us to hear the broader resonance of these questions, while at the same time acknowledging how those choices between kinships and contenders, 'comrades' and 'foes', imitation and individuality, represent extremes that have little bearing on the way formal inventiveness comes about – extreme alternatives that may, when recycled as critical terms, weaken our grasp of the specificity of a novel's ingenuity. As Coetzee implies, the binaries that separate forbear and inheritor perpetuate inelegant scenarios for making sense of the working relations that exist between modernism and contemporary writers. Instead, such relations are always in motion; and for the interactive way they operate for the writers in this book, Coetzee himself goes on to provide an especially appropriate maritime analogy:

If he must settle on a likeness for the pair of them, his man and he, he would write that they are like two ships sailing in contrary directions, one west, the other east. Or better, that they are deckhands toiling in the rigging, the one on a ship sailing west, the other on a ship sailing east. Their ships pass close, close enough to hail. But the seas are rough, the weather is stormy: their eyes lashed by the spray, their hands burned by the cordage, they pass each other by, too busy even to wave.[97]

In a scene of work where skill and full attention are consciously put to the test, Coetzee pictures the writer as consumed in the process, a process that overtakes any opportunity for explicit acknowledgement of artistic affinities. Precursor and heir are both immersed here in the urgency and necessity of the undertaking, pursuing themes and methods that may well move 'in contrary directions' but that nonetheless mark a comparable endeavour. In this manner, their techniques 'pass close' to each other: 'close enough' for us to hear semblances between their styles, especially in the compositional stages of shaping and revising, even if, in their finished form, their fictions 'pass each other by'.

Encapsulated in this remarkable peroration to Coetzee's Nobel speech is a scenario that echoes throughout this study, as it brings together writers whose modes of working resonate with priorities that they don't passively inherit from modernism, like period-souvenirs, but that revitalise modernist aesthetics for tackling a new spectrum of artistic, cultural, ethical and political demands. Despite the commotion of the scene, Coetzee could be seen as dramatising a moment of piety, a condition that Michael Roth has defined as 'the turning of oneself so as to be in relation to the past, to experience oneself as coming after (perhaps emerging out of or against) the past'.[98] Granted, we can appreciate piety's relevance here, as each of the novelists studied gestures to the vital presence of what has gone before, pointing in turn to modernism's presence within, and *as* a precondition of, new circumstances of creativity. Those same writers would surely agree that we ought to 'acknowledge the importance of something in the past', just as 'we acknowledge the claim that that thing has on us'. They might also agree that piety thereby facilitates a deeply ethical 'refusal simply to *use* the object or to forget it'.[99] Indeed, my contention will be that for those novelists who navigated the aftermath of postmodernism, the *prospect* of the unrealised potentialities of modernist fiction exists not simply to be used but to be continually tested, redesigned and remade. Piety, however, doesn't quite do justice to their dialogues with tradition. For I aim also to reveal how contemporary writers are responding *actively* to the past in a fashion that this notion of piety – with its connotations of devoted acknowledgement and reverential fidelity – cannot quite encompass. 'We moderns', exclaimed Gertrude Stein, 'must create a complete tradition and live into it, for we do not follow teaching'.[100] The writers I have addressed can be seen to be moving forward still with that task of completion, even if the irreverence that Stein cherished is now dialectically connected to a process in which artistic inheritance and infidelity coincide. Without denying the influence and magnitude of historical modernism, contemporary novelists are demonstrating more audacious means of negotiating its legacy, making us all the more 'aware', as Toni Morrison put it in *Playing in the Dark*, 'of the writer's notions of risk and safety, the serene achievement of, or sweaty fight for, meaning and responsibility'.[101]

To plot that audacity both inside and outside the fictional text requires an agile methodological framework that can draw, without preconceptions, on alternative kinds of evidence. In addition to essays, reviews or even speeches of the sort we have just analysed from Coetzee, another important extra-literary resource for *Modernist Futures* is the author-interview. 'The interview form is characteristic of the age', declared Joe David Bellamy, introducing his conversations more than three decades ago with such pyrotechnic experimenters as Barth and Barthelme. 'In the immediacy of its appeal', he reckoned, 'to our voracious appetite for personality and glamour, for human contact, for character revelation, for getting-it-from-the-horse's-mouth, it has become a mainstay of *Playboy* and *Rolling Stone*'.[102] It has also become a mainstay for scholars of contemporary fiction who wish to reintroduce matters of motivation and inspiration back into their portfolio of terms, instead of leaving all artistic intentions in doubt or refuting them outright. As Bellamy observes, interviews 'may also provide insight into the nature of a particular writer's sensibility – that smoggy area of aesthetic distinctions least apt to be revealed by traditional analytical methods'.[103] Shrewd and well-intentioned though Bellamy's defence of interviews may be, he tends to rehearse the polarisation between critical analysis and authorial sensibility, when what we need is a means of combining interpretive methods with that sensitivity to artistic motivations. Kundera seems to suggest so as well, offering his own impression of how we should treat the information that writers disclose:

> A novelist talking about the art of the novel is not a professor giving a discourse from his podium. Imagine him rather as a painter welcoming you into his studio, where you are surrounded by his canvases staring at you from where they lean against the walls. He will talk about himself, but even more about other people, about novels of theirs that he loves and that have a secret presence in his own work.[104]

In each of the following chapters, I have heeded Kundera's advice when engaging with novelists' interviews and essays. Something analogous to that intimate acquaintance with the writer 'in his studio' can be facilitated either by conversations with novelists or by the commentaries they provide on 'other people'. These materials, however, also help us to gauge how that 'secret presence' of past works in a novelist's own has got there, and why that act of appropriation occurred in the first place – if, indeed, appropriating modernism is what that writer has wanted to do.

We need to provide alternatives, then, to the oppressive jurisdiction of influence, as Stein mocked it in *Three Lives*, when it is viewed as 'a steady march' from past to present from which the contemporary writer can 'never break away'.[105] Here the term *appropriation* deserves some elucidation. Recently, the expanded field of adaptation studies has provided its own critique of the hegemony of source texts. Calling for fluid conceptions of influences and their effect on subsequent creations, these critics have replaced accounts of straightforward borrowing with more open-ended notions of appropriation. For instance, what Julie Sanders finds useful about appropriation as a critical category is the way it helps us think more flexibly about the compositional *cooperation* of allusion and re-creation, inheriting and renewing. In this framework, we are able to observe how artistic precedents are regenerated, their initiatives redeployed, and their styles not simply mimed but reanimated for the markedly different characterological, descriptive or political concerns of the appropriating artist. Sanders's recommendation for studying adaptation is equally applicable for our purposes of charting modernism's continuance in contemporary literature without recourse to 'a static or immobilizing discussion of source or influence'.[106] In place of causal diagnoses of artistic affinities, we need a 'more active vocabulary' that works beyond preconceived ideas about the dominance of canonical originators.[107] Such a vocabulary for tracing how traditions are reformulated allows us to examine formal legacies without assuming that the inheritors in question are either fixated in their fidelity to past masterworks or anxiously trying to out-write them.

One has to tread carefully, of course, when using authors' interviews and essays to substantiate our understanding of how they might alternatively adapt, appropriate and transcribe modernist procedures, while also alluding or paying homage to identifiable modernist texts. There are two caveats, then: firstly, there is the risk that such interviews will simply assume the position of an authenticating 'source-text' that overly deterministic ideas of influence uphold and which the more supple notions of adaptation and appropriation seek to complicate; and secondly, we have to concede that writers' answers are guided by the questions asked, and even the most conversational (and confessional) novelist might not be able to sidestep the interviewer's insinuations. Peter Carey himself has drawn attention to these issues, remarking that interviews often compel writers to pin down definitive inspirations that in practice have a more diluted impact on their craft. When asked in 1986 whether he saw himself as a successor to Borges, Carey replied: 'Is what I am saying the truth? Was this really the attraction or am I simply trying to build an answer that will make us both happy?'[108] The question arises as to how we use such interviews to substantiate a commentary, like the one that unfolds in this book, whose concerns are more politico-aesthetic and literary-historical than they are biographical. Leaving aside the issue of whether or not we should treat writers' self-reflections as 'evidence' in the first place, the recent work of narratologists like Robert Walsh suggests that it is misguided to reject notions of authorial compulsion or esteem, even if many early plans never eventually make it into a novelist's published work. To any genetic critic, this would sound like an obvious point; but to accommodate an analysis of intentionality alongside that of influence is important when encountering writers who are still living, producing and commenting on their work, while also talking about the literary movements they inherit and whose impulses they extend. In these cases, Walsh proposes an 'idea of creativity as mediation, as expressed in the comments of novelists themselves upon their experience of the narrative imagination – bearing in mind that these comments also contribute in their own right to the communicative context of their fiction'.[109] In more insidious respects, that context may well give writers the chance to speak about their place in an ongoing tradition, thereby acquiring some prestige by flagging-up the heritage with which they are aligning their work.[110] This caution aside, however, I share Walsh's sentiment that artistic ambitions are not simply arbitrary or deceptive but provide another layer for critical evaluation, providing a form of contextualisation that is as legitimate as any cultural or historical one. In this sense, I concur with Michael Wood who, in an elegant discussion of Yeats and form, has warned that 'there is something wasteful and disagreeable about not wanting to know what writers think they are doing, and about the accompanying assumption that critics know better. It doesn't seem implausible that writers often achieve what they intend and that their intention has something to do with their achievement'.[111] Taken together, Walsh and Wood offer a useful reminder that the idea of being able to situate writers against their own essays and interviews is a genuinely worthwhile endeavour – even if what we discover is that contemporary novelists are often, if not especially, eager to ring-fence their style and define their impulses as unique.

'A BRIDGE WITH THE PAST': DIALOGUES AND DEPARTURES

Speaking before an undergraduate audience in 1957, William Faulkner was candid about working in conversation with what has gone before. Literary-historical landmarks need not be insurmountable, he implied; they are catalysts for each generation of emerging experimenters, spurring new writers to make their own advances in the afterglow of past achievements:

I think that the writer ... is completely amoral. He takes whatever he needs, wherever he needs, and he does that openly and honestly because he himself hopes that what he does will be good enough so that after him people will take from him, and they are welcome to take from him as he feels that he would be welcome by the best of his predecessors to take what they've done.[112]

Faulkner points here to a process of aesthetic inheritance in which the precursor is not so much abandoned or hidden, as 'openly and honestly' reprised. Pre-existing traits are woven in the very fibre of what's new. Faulkner implies that, as a writer, what you inherit depends on the *way* you use it, since the most formidable influences need not compromise the individuality of your own experimental aims. Echoing Faulkner fifty years later, New York-based novelist Siri Hustvedt sees that the issue isn't one of straightforward influence, for 'every writer takes from the past. It is how it happens', such that '[my] love for Henry James doesn't make me want to fight it out and get *over* him'.[113] In a deliberate refutation of the

Bloomian vision of conflict between virtuosic inheritors and their equally virtuosic forebears, Hustvedt prefers to see heritage circulating within the here-and-now, inviting contemporary writers into a scene of 'literary mingling'.[114] We are back to the prospect of conviviality with which this Introduction began, which allows us to see how contemporary writers work 'in dialogue', as Laura Marcus terms it, 'with the structures of modernist fiction'.[115]

To observe how novelists participate in these dialogues, even as they manoeuvre towards new departures, is a task I attempt in the following chapters by zeroing-in on key transitions across each writer's *oeuvre*. If certain modernist interlocutors stand prominently at the other end of those dialogues, I have nonetheless avoided the overly schematic pairing-off of precursors and legatees. The writers I consider are not simply 'pursu[ing] the narrow path of aesthetic duty' of the sort that James, in E. M. Forster's view, encouraged all heirs of the art-novel to do.[116] As a result, this book makes no bid to offer a systematic survey of which novelists today have been influenced by which modernists. Indeed, there are many early-twentieth-century writers, artistic developments and period-specific phases (Surrealism and Vorticism being the most glaring absences) for which I have not included late-twentieth-century inheritors. Among those excluded is Forster himself, not because he is formally uninventive, and certainly not because '[t]here's something middling about' him, as Zadie Smith has argued.[117] Curiously enough, in light of her own homage to *Howards End* in *On Beauty* (2005), Smith sounds as unflattering towards her own work here as she does about Forster's. More perceptive is her later remark that Forster 'didn't need anyone else to be like him. Which would appear to be the simplest, most obvious principle in the world – yet how few English novelists prove capable of holding it!'[118] It would hardly be true to say that nobody wants to be 'like' Forster these days, not only after *On Beauty*'s tale of prejudice and accountability, but also because Forster's ethics of connectedness, along with his own 'insider-outsider' status, as Paul Armstrong calls it,[119] reverberate through such admired narratives of nationhood as Ishiguro's *An Artist of the Floating World* (1986) and *The Remains of the Day* (1989), as well as Timothy Mo's *Sour Sweet* (1982). Just as Joyce, therefore, will appear largely in the background when compared to my more explicit analyses of McEwan's and Coetzee's conversations with Woolf and Ford, respectively, so Forster's absence is a matter of selection rather than qualitative discrimination. What motivates my selections, as I indicated previously, is the extent to which each writer chosen enriches our understanding of that 'balance', as McEwan called it, between narrative self-reflexivity and formal integrity, between pushing back the frontiers of artistry and ethically engaging the reader. The bolder argument underpinning this book is that only by scrutinising those contemporary novelists who have consciously negotiated that balance in the wake of postmodernism can we develop a more nuanced portrait of the future of novelistic innovation and the roles that modernism's reanimation plays in shaping that future.

Those earlier twentieth-century modernists who *do* appear in this study, then, are selected because they matter to the formal and political aims of some of the most singular writers of our age. Rather than being the object of mimicry or pastiche, these precursors have been re-engaged in the very warp and weft of contemporary narrative. From the more expected appearances of James and Conrad in discussions of impressionism's afterlife or the equally inevitable pairing of Faulkner with Morrison (whose interaction has now become for Faulknerians a significant sub-discipline in its own right), to the far more neglected legacy of Ford for such a seemingly contrasting prose-stylist like Coetzee – these figures make their appearance alongside essays and interviews in which contemporary writers testify to their impact. These dialogues are thus substantial rather than speculative. I have chosen contemporary fictions that tangibly register modernism's impact at a compositional level, even if (as is often the case) we see them 'getting beyond influence' altogether. My readings are based not in theoretical conjecture, but on the authority of writers who have reflected deeply upon the very historicity of their craft and its ethical implications. What Rob Nixon says of V. S. Naipaul's affinity with Conrad as a precursor applies to many of the anterior affiliations analysed in this book: when a modernist predecessor is seen by a contemporary novelist 'as neither an invented nor a chosen starting point but a natural one'.[120]

Is there surely not a difference, though, between a writer whose dialogue with the past is strategic and one for whom it seems inevitable? Are there novelists who combine or negotiate between 'chosen' and 'natural' precedents? Pondering such questions in relation to the shifting attitudes towards experimentalism in postwar fiction, David Lodge saw that fiction had reached not a turning point after the social realist reaction against modernist subjectivism in the 1950s, so much as an intersection of diverging aims that spoke directly to the novel's undecided future. Hence Lodge's talismanic image: that of the 'novelist at the crossroads', a figure poised at the junction of personal priorities and lines of shared inheritance. As Lodge argued, 'the novelist is constantly divided between two imperatives – to create and invent freely, and to observe a degree of realistic decorum'.[121] What he implied was that the genuinely daring move for novelists approaching the 1980s would be to reconcile the perceived antagonisms between the social realism they inherit from Sillitoe's generation of the 1950s, and the rise of a new avant-garde heralded in the 1960s and 1970s by John Fowles, Christine Brooke-Rose and B. S. Johnson. Lodge concluded that his generation seemed to 'be living through a period of unprecedented cultural pluralism which allows, in all arts, an astonishing variety of styles to flourish simultaneously. Though they are in many cases radically opposed on aesthetic and epistemological grounds, no one style has managed to become dominant'.[122]

Such proclamations about a cultural climate with no consensus on which direction the novel should go were, in significant respects, influenced by binary understandings of realist and experimentalist impulses. Lodge's work in stylistics did much to dispel that binary, arguing as he did for a more complex view of the polyphonic mix of mimetic and metafictional modes – anticipating by more than a decade his eventual allegiance to theories of heteroglossia, after Bakhtin became popular in the British academy through the 1980s. Even then, however, when novelists like Angela Carter, Graham Swift and Salman Rushdie were writing the fictions that would make them famous for blending historical, phantasmagorical, and metadiegetic registers, discussions about what novelistic innovation was actually *for* were still susceptible to the image of the writer at the crossroads, where socially responsible realist fiction clashes with the self-indulgence of neomodernist experiment. In the same year *Money* (1984) first appeared, though, we find Martin Amis acknowledging that novelists cannot stay standing those crossroads forever. Someone who would repeatedly uphold the modernist conviction that 'style is absolutely embedded in the way you perceive',[123] Amis adopted Lodge's plea to find a confluence between seemingly incompatible imperatives: 'realism and experimentation have come and gone without seeming to point a way ahead. The contemporary writer, therefore, must combine these veins, calling on the strengths of the Victorian novel together with the alienations of post-modernism'.[124] Ten years later and Jeanette Winterson, despite being so formally and thematically different from Amis, repeats his call to 'combine' heritage with alternative conceptions of what is new by *not* 'refusing tradition its vital connection to what is happening now'.[125]

How novelists might productively utilise, rather than dismiss, the modernist legacy 'for what is happening now' was one of the subjects addressed by a symposium on the 'state of fiction', hosted in the late 1970s by the short-lived journal *The New Review*. In the generational mix of its contributors, this issue reflected a decade of mingling, often conflicting, compulsions. Writers were deliberately juxtaposed: John Braine sat alongside Christine Brooke-Rose, and Ian McEwan claimed that 'the artifice of fiction can be taken for granted' just lines before Olivia Manning condemned *Ulysses* as 'a monster' who, 'like all monsters', is 'without progeny'.[126] As D. J. Taylor recalls, those novelists contributing to *The New Review* issue were 'in no doubt that experimental fiction, whatever that was, had been tried and found wanting. But they were in no doubt either that the ordinary novel, the sort of book that gets discussed in newspapers, that people buy or borrow from the libraries, was somehow failing to do its job; that a gap existed between fiction and the environment it attempted to describe'.[127] It is precisely this gap that those novelists who established themselves in subsequent decades have sought to shrink, but not in a way that would make their work any more palatable for the kind of local-library member who Taylor quaintly imagines. This is why I have concentrated on that distinct generation of novelists who worked in the wake of 'high' postmodernism's fallout in the 1970s and 1980s: it is they who developed particular responses to the relevance of modernist experimentalism and who have continued to reconsider what it takes to negotiate between the self-reflexivity that serious 'literary fiction' has inevitably acquired and the ability, as Winterson identifies it in Stein, 'to make a bridge with the past that is both conscious and liminal', something that 'only *new* work can do'.[128]

Critically speaking, then, Lodge was ahead of his time: paving the way to a kind of commentary that could be sensitive to how aesthetic and ideological concerns associated with, and facilitated by, past methods can be revitalised *through* the contemporary novelist's own virtuosic self-advancement. With this fluid model of the mutual articulation of heritage and innovation, Lodge suggests that it is more productive to think of new fiction as 'a new synthesis of pre-existing narrative traditions, rather than a continuation of one of them or an entirely unprecedented phenomenon'.[129] Despite the interiority often associated with that impulse to experiment, 'there are', he says, 'formidable discouragements to continuing serenely along the road of fictional realism. The novelist who has any kind of self-awareness must at least hesitate at the crossroads; and the solution many novelists have chosen in their dilemma is to *build that hesitation into the novel itself*.[130] Lodge recalls here a practice of 'conscious artistry' of the kind that Ford had applauded in Conrad and James. It is a practice whose afterlives are traced in the following discussion through the work of writers who consciously reach for new stylistic horizons but without allowing that self-awareness to impose upon the emotional states and ethical situations they dramatise.

'CRITICALLY, CONSTRUCTIVELY, *RE*-CONSTRUCTIVELY:' READING MODERNIST FUTURES

It would be tempting, then, to paint a portrait of the millennial novelist still standing at the crossroads. In some respects I have done this already, by suggesting that the writers we'll be encountering are navigating a path between ironic or metafictional self-reflexivity, on the one hand, and the more realist demands of uncompromising observation and critique, on the other. Equally, though, I've also contended that we need a different language now for analysing how the very act of '[w]riting', in Don DeLillo's words, 'also means trying to advance the art'.[131] What we shall see in each of the writers here is not a case of indecision, or the incorporation of hesitancy into their political and stylistic concerns, so much as it is a range of serious reflections on the integrity of what they make. 'What writing means to me', asserts DeLillo, 'is trying to make interesting, clear, beautiful language', such that '[w]orking at sentences and rhythms is probably the most satisfying thing I do as a writer'.[132] It is a sentiment echoed by McEwan's fascination with 'shaping sentences and shaping paragraphs, and shaping parts of characters and making characters'.[133] Both DeLillo and McEwan seem to share Henry James's attraction to the unrealised possibilities of 'style', whereby he brought *to* that style, as Alan Hollinghurst points out, an 'awareness' equivalent to that which 'he brings to his characters and their situations'.[134] As an impressionist, James speculated that ways of knowing could be synonymous with ways of feeling, an equation that led him famously to hypothesise in 'The Art of Fiction' (1884) that 'impressions *are* experience'.[135] Despite the frequency with which he is labelled and treated as a postmodernist, DeLillo shares something of James's bold sentiment, attesting that '[o]ver the years it's possible for a writer to shape himself as a human being through the language he uses'.[136] In this claim, DeLillo also complements James's vision of the novel's futurity: just as James saw fiction's survival would be enabled by its 'free character', moving as it does 'in a luxurious independence of rules and restrictions',[137] so DeLillo believes that the novel 'hasn't quite been filled in or done in or worked out. We make our small leaps'.[138]

Making *modest* advances in the novel's philosophical reach and formal capabilities is hardly what DeLillo has become renowned for. Neither, for that matter, are the writers who appear in this book. What he implies, however, is that the only way is forward: to 'make ... leaps' means no longer standing at the crossroads. In this respect, DeLillo's conviction that fiction is not yet 'done in' not only allies him with James's futurology of the novel; looking further back still, it also reveals the remarkable prescience of Thomas Hardy's advice that 'the utmost which each generation can be expected to do is to add one or two strokes toward the selection and shaping of a possible ultimate perfection'.[139] The present study offers no speculations on who among the contemporary scene is getting nearest to achieving that perfection. But it does offer an account of how those procedures of 'selection and shaping' can be understood as incorporating modernist aims, though without suggesting that modernism's promise has been, in DeLillo's phrase, fully 'worked out'.

Two weeks into the second decade of the twenty-first century, three very different novelists gathered at London's Royal Festival Hall to discuss this issue of whether modernism is still being worked out in contemporary literary culture. Sometime metafictionist turned children's writer, A. S. Byatt, was joined by the author of the Nabokovian *Nowhere Man* (2002), Aleksandar Hemon, and the neo-Futurist creator of *Remainder* (2005) and *C* (2010), Tom McCarthy. As co-founder of the International Necronautical Society – a collective whose culturally oppositional manifestos and defence of conceptualism openly exemplify his avant-garde persuasions – one might have expected McCarthy to cheer modernism's persistence in contemporary culture. Instead of encouragement, however, came disappointment: McCarthy felt that postwar fiction was simply 'not on my radar' by virtue of the way it had dismissed 'the legacy of modernism'. Byatt, too, was campaigning on behalf of a heritage refuted by social realism and parodically dissected by postmodernism; and, like McCarthy, she regarded herself as fundamentally 'a modernist' committed to prospects of formal integrity where the future of the novel is concerned. Though McCarthy aligned himself with a lineage that stretched from Beckett to Kafka to Michel Houellebecq, Byatt saw her fiction as inheriting modernism 'via a different line' – one that reached back to Eliot and Matisse.[140] As the third respondent, Hemon again painted a different self-portrait. Although *The Question of Bruno* (2000) and *The Lazarus Project* (2008) both experiment with retrospective narration in ways that seem idiomatically linked to Conrad and Nabokov, Hemon has elsewhere expressed some caution about becoming overtly self-referential – whether the references in question are other writers and traditions or his own devices. Wary of the 'fundamentally postmodern ... idea' that 'language always refers to itself', his fiction takes a stand against 'watching thought evolve and meaning dissolve in the pressure chamber of abstraction'. If Hemon identifies with modernist fiction, it is because of its avoidance of ungrounded abstraction, drawn as he is (just as any impressionist would be) to evoke the exactitude of ordinary sensations pregnant with significance and affection: 'I'd rather eat a strawberry, smell my daughter's hair, or read a book that, against all postmodern odds, conjures up the intense experience of human life'.[141] In addition to highlighting such different trajectories along which the principles of early-twentieth-century writers have travelled to and been transcribed by those of the twenty-first, Byatt, Hemon and McCarthy confirm that modernist continuities cannot be homogenised just as novelists' strategies today must be particularised if we are to see how the promise of modernism survives within and because of them.

McCarthy vented his frustration at the state of contemporary fiction by claiming that, at best, it's 'the nineteenth-century novel with a few Joycean knobs on'.[142] In this book, I offer a more positive view of the vitality of modernist processes in late-twentieth- and twenty-first-century fiction, showing how the point of being a modernist today amounts to more than snatching frills from *Finnegans Wake*. Granted, influence *is* and must be a key factor in understanding how modernist aesthetics are redeployed for new politico-aesthetic ends, and the role that early-twentieth-century writers (and painters) play as interlocutors with our contemporary moment testifies to this. Such correspondences across literary-historical time, however, urge us to refine the distinction between modernism's achievements as a heritage to which writers simply allude and the more substantive function of modernist ideals as catalysts for enterprising if not unprecedented kinds of fiction.

This debate provokes us to consider what modernism was and what it still does, something I have devoted much of this Introduction to elucidating. As the institutionalisation of modernist principles through creative writing curricula invites us to observe, how we define what modernism means will continue to depend on whether we are looking at its legacies and possibilities from a critic's or a practitioner's point of view. One challenge I've faced in writing this book, therefore, has been to see whether those viewpoints – with writers' compositional ambitions or achievements on the one hand, and those political orientations or impulses of literary criticism on the other – are at all compatible and, where they are, to explore how their compatibility can enrich our understanding of the reasons for modernism's perpetuation.

Modernist Futures is thus motivated by the conviction that we ought to be able to engage with such matters concerning how tradition and innovation intersect for contemporary writers without fearing that an accompanying attention to form will sideline broader sociological or cultural considerations. Even Jameson has applauded the 'resuscitation of aesthetics' as a disciplinary turn that seeks to correct the tendency for 'various modernist forms of the sublime' to 'effac[e] aesthetic questions as swiftly as they began to emerge'.[143] Admittedly, the present study might not initially appear to sit well with the contextualising impulses of the New Modernist Studies, impulses that avoid lending primacy to style in retrospective analyses of modernism so as to discuss (as Pamela Caughie notes in her recent summary of the state-of-the-discipline) how to address 'industry-produced, mass-consumed, machine-made art that not only reflected modern culture but also taught its audiences how modernity might be experienced'.[144] As such, some readers will no doubt perceive that my focus on technique bypasses this otherwise valuable approach to modernism's economic conditions of production and transnational reception. Yet a more thorough comprehension of the interaction between 'technicist' understandings of how fiction operates and the new modes of attention it demands (by virtue of the conventions of reception it eludes), is surely the foundation for obtaining a firmer grasp of the novel's capacity for critical work – together with the role that modernist aesthetics played, and might still play, in enhancing that capacity.[145]

The discipline of modernist studies has become no less receptive to the timeliness of these interactions. I am reminded of the new directions recently mapped by Douglas Mao and Rebecca Walkowitz, who highlight precisely those 'questions pertaining to literary form' that scholars are starting to answer as they follow modernist afterlives into new geographical regions.[146] A growing body of work on modernism's extensions into late-twentieth- and twenty-first-century writing is being undertaken in ways that often seem peripheral to, or at least less urgent than, the 'transnationalist' impulse to expand the global ambit of early-twentieth-century literature.[147] By the same stroke, although Huyssen's remark almost a decade ago that '[m]ost modernist research' in the 'academy is still largely bound by the local' no longer seems fair,[148] it may be less of a misrepresentation to say that scholarship is still largely confined by period. I don't mean to suggest that the New Modernist Studies has deferred questions of modernism's continuity in favour of mapping its transnational scope, but rather to highlight that the mode of distant reading by which modernism's internationalisation is often analysed can lead to 'an abandonment', as Huyssen anticipated, 'of aesthetic and formal issues coupled with [an] unquestioning privileging of popular and mass culture'.[149] To read modernist legacies in a closer manner, as this book does, *through* the forms of their re-articulation, is not to endorse an elite vocabulary that privileges the hallowed autonomy of the modernist art-novel over the popular marketplace of contemporary fiction's consumption. On the contrary, it marks a first step towards redrawing the lines between creative practice and critical thought. Exploring such proximities of craft and interpretation allows us to foster rather than forego what Thomas Doherty has described as 'the intimacy of aesthetics with materiality', in order thereby to discover why some of the most virtuosic novelists of our time are realising what modernism can still become in response to new social actualities.[150]

The prospect of cultivating this intimate contact with formally innovative works – even in the methodical process of unpacking what they do and why they remain so meaningful to us – is one that Henry James pondered in a letter to Howard Sturgis in 1903. James admitted that 'I, as a battered producer & "technician" myself, have long since inevitably ceased to read with *naïveté*; I can only read critically, constructively, *re*-constructively, writing the thing over (if I can swallow it at all) *my* way, looking at it, so to speak, from within'.[151] Like James, we cannot opt for critically naïve readings, even if it were desirable to do so; and it would be to misrepresent the legitimate interventions of 'New Formalists' to suggest that they are tacitly endorsing an unselfconscious attention to aesthetic properties simply as a response to the era of postmodern scepticism.[152] The twofold imperative to read 'critically' and '*re*-constructively', as James usefully implies, *can* be squared with the demands of 'looking at' narrative fiction rigorously 'from within'. Similarly, to read a novel with the eyes of a 'technician' is not to neglect the force of its engagement with the world, but rather to observe how different writers' aims – sometimes economical, as we will see, at other times audacious – are indelibly linked to their ethical and political convictions. With this kind of approach we can start to see how modernism has enabled writers 'aesthetically', as Jahan Ramazani notes, to 'encode intersections among multiple cultural vectors'.[153] There is, however, another more curious, though no less crucial, upshot of modernism's bequest to writers and critics alike. Speaking to positions that are as important for rethinking the way we evaluate contemporary literature as they are for understanding its composition, this bequest illuminates a fruitful paradox. It is a paradox that's exploited to the full, as we will see next, by two leading writers who remake their modernist inheritance anew, setting the scene for demonstrating a logic of creativity that reaches across this book: namely, how tradition enables novelists to achieve what they have yet to do in the light of all that fiction hasn't quite done before.

CHAPTER 1

'Advancing along the inherited path': Making it traditionally new in Milan Kundera and Philip Roth

Among modernism's many paradoxical attractions to what has passed, one stands out more than most. Though we could accurately call it a commitment, or hear it repeated as an obligation expressed by artists themselves, it might best be posed as a question: how can experimenters draw upon tradition without undermining their own claims to originality? Though, undoubtedly, this was a conundrum that high modernism intensified, it was hardly unprecedented. When George Eliot insisted that we notice how 'each new invention casts a new light along the pathway of discovery, and each new combination or structure brings into play more conditions than its inventor foresaw',[1] she laid the groundwork for her poet-namesake who, half a century later in 1919, famously advised his generation of aspiring writers that 'existing monuments form an ideal order among themselves, which is modified by the introduction of the new (the really new) work of art among them'.[2] T. S. Eliot may have been reluctant to admit that, as an 'inventor' himself, he might not always foresee where new 'conditions' arise for genuine innovation. Invariably, Eliot was adamant that he *could*, and he took pains to identify himself with the rigour and insight of those who could acknowledge that tradition 'cannot be inherited', because 'you must obtain it by great labour',[3] precisely in order to suggest how difficult it was for the modern poet to be new. Nonetheless, even if the two Eliots may not have agreed on the extent to which writers are capable of predicting what sort of 'combination or structure' newness will assume next, they would surely concur that the measure of 'each new invention' is the way it challenges all prior expectations – sending a ripple through assumptions of what's currently possible for the artistic medium in question. For, 'after the supervention of novelty', insists (T. S.) Eliot, 'the *whole* existing order must be, if ever so slightly, altered'. In turn, 'the relations, proportions, values of each work of art toward the whole are readjusted' – a mutual adjustment that reveals what he pinpoints as 'the conformity between the old and the new'.[4]

Tautological as it might sound, understanding innovation in terms of this 'conformity' between invention and inheritance remains one of modernism's most appealing, if challenging, legacies for late-twentieth- and twenty-first-century writers. To that extent, Michèle Roberts represents the exception rather than the rule when she claims that if a novelist 'wants to produce good, original work, not just cosy re-hashes of what's gone before', he or she will have 'to accept internal chaos and breakage as part of the process'.[5] This rhetoric of fracture and rupture is familiar enough from long-standing accounts of high-modernist esteem. Among writers today, however, we are likely to hear of more hospitable models being proposed. As the late Carol Shields put it in 1996, formal or linguistic rupture should not be taken as the benchmark of success. Indeed, Shields had her own vision of where (George) Eliot's 'pathway of discovery' might usefully lead novelistic experiment. The 'project for the narratives of the next millennium', as Shields foresaw it, would be to ask 'why the rub of disunity strikes larger sparks than the reward of accommodation'.[6] In a similar plea for innovation as accommodating rather than overturning the past, Ian McEwan also regards what is new about emerging narrative forms as part of a literary-historical continuum. He suggests that our evaluation of inventiveness ought to be underpinned by our recognition of how and where contemporary fiction connects with its heritage. Echoing the dialectical logic at the heart of 'Tradition and the Individual Talent', McEwan observes that 'a work of literature produced now infinitesimally shifts our understanding of what has gone before',[7] a remark that is also consistent with Borges's often quoted view that an original writer's '[w]ork modifies our conception of the past, as it will modify the future'.[8]

This paradoxical idea, or ideal, of innovation's deep kinship with tradition, therefore, couldn't be claimed as the brainchild of high modernism; neither was that 'pathway of discovery' mapped conclusively or exhaustively by the pyrotechnic ambitions of early-twentieth-century fiction. In short, the ideal persists, and it's the purpose of this chapter to show how pervasively it does so by turning to two novelists descending from what seem like radically different lineages: Milan Kundera and Philip Roth. Despite a close friendship that is now several decades long – one that prompted Roth to serve until 1989 as general editor of the Penguin series 'Writers from the Other Europe' – he and Kundera can be identified in more obvious formal and biographical terms with nationally distinct heritages, just as they write in visibly contrasting narrative registers. Nevertheless, both novelists share the same belief in engaging with modernist aesthetics in ways that show how tradition and experiment productively coincide. In tune with the prevailing tenor of this book, this chapter isn't concerned with tracing modernist afterlives through the lens of influence, or with framing modernist legacies by detecting allusions or by tracking styles that are emulated down the decades. Rather, I focus on the perpetuation of a certain sensibility towards modernism's continuance (what T. S. Eliot would have called that 'historical sense' of the 'presence' of the past) as Kundera and Roth have adapted it – two writers who are themselves famed for remaining so inimitable.[9]

MAKING IT SERIOUS IN THE LEAST LIKELY WAY

No one more than Kundera would agree with the argument for modernism's continuing presence and relevance. For him, to be a modernist means not so much joining a movement as it does taking part in an ongoing activity. This implies that contemporary writers should proceed 'through new discoveries, advancing along the inherited path. As long as that is still possible. As long as the inherited path still exists'.[10] Discoveries achieved via, rather than in spite of, inheritance; progressions enabled rather than hindered by recuperation – these seemingly contradictory imperatives lie at the heart of Kundera's conviction that literary innovation is itself necessarily historical, or more precisely, self-historicising. 'Every novelist's work contains an explicit vision of the history of the novel', he declares in an epigraphic note to the 2000 edition of *The Art of the Novel*, a manifesto for understanding novelistic development as something in perpetual flux rather than as a succession of monuments: 'The *sequence of discoveries* (not the sum of what was written) is what constitutes the history of the European novel'.[11] So it follows, as Kundera contends in *Testaments Betrayed*, that one of modernism's key provisos was, and still is, that investment in the power of 'rehabilitation'.[12] As I understand it, Kundera is directing us here, a decade after *The Art of the Novel*, to a conception of modernism implicitly based on the Latin meaning of *habilitare*: to be made able. Enabling the novel's ability to remake itself is the task he expects modernism to aid, a task that in turn ensures the relevancy of the modernist project for late-twentieth-century fiction. To habilitate form, suggests Kundera, is 'to *redefine* and *broaden* the very notion of the novel', which at the same time is 'to rethink and remake the scale of values of its *whole* history'.[13]

Entertaining craft on this scale characterises one of the ways in which Kundera and Roth set about valuing modernism's achievements in retrospect. In other words, they share the 'inclination to reread and reevaluate', as Kundera calls it, that is 'common to all the great modernists' – an inclination whose manifestation as a way of working, as conscious artistry, became the 'mark that distinguished great modern art from modernist trumpery'.[14] Sentiments Roth and Kundera hold in common, however, lead them also to value a particular *version* of modernist fiction which inspires in them both a creative irreverence that departs from any loyalty to traditional fictional modes. For just as Kundera sees that writers of the 'post-Proust period' freed composition and 'reclaimed the right to digression' while they, thematically speaking, 'breathed the spirit of the non-serious and of play into the novel',[15] so Roth reflected – aptly enough in the same year he released another kind of retrospective, his first extended meditation on literary and familial history in *The Facts* (1988) – that modernism's bequest was precisely this: to strive to be unserious in a fashion that modernist writing is not often assumed to be. In Roth's view, to endorse modernism's continuance is to do something more than appeal to early-twentieth-century fiction as a talent pool from which tried-and-tested devices can be retrieved and reused:

The lesson of modernism isn't encapsulated in a technique that's 'Joycean' or a vision that's 'Kafkaesque' – it originates in the revolutionary sense of seriousness that's exemplified in the fiction of Joyce, Kafka, Beckett, Céline – even of Proust – fiction which to an unknowing reader probably bears the earmark less of seriousness than high eccentricity and antic obsession. By now the methods of these outlandish writers have themselves become the conventions of seriousness, but that in no way dilutes their message, which isn't 'Make it new', but 'Make it serious in the least likely way'.[16]

Despite Roth's admission that Henry James's *The Portrait of a Lady* remained 'a virtual handbook during the early drafts of *Letting Go*',[17] the picture he paints here reveals modernism's 'lesson' to be a far cry from functionality, because it bespeaks a 'message' more so than it provides a mere crutch for latter-day novelists seeking technical solutions for sprucing up their style. According to that message, modernist fiction's hallmark obliquity – and the difficulty that can characterise the interpretation of oblique narration – has, in time, turned into the very thing its pioneers strove to avoid: a convention. Roth contends that the 'seriousness' of Joyce's neologising diction, or the stark economy of Kafka's and Beckett's language, have become features that are no longer 'revolutionary' because they meet a familiar (and institutionally taught) set of expectations about how far modernism transformed the novel. It's not that these features no longer elicit surprise from readers today, so much as their absorption within the pedagogical and scholarly field that modernist studies has become can distract us, as Roth implies, from appreciating the extant work of modernism in helping the contemporary novelist to acquire 'a voice and a subject of one's own'.[18] Crucially, for Roth, this task involves a conception of originality that is bound up with surprise, experimenting with the lessons of tradition 'in the least likely way'. Distinguished both from the pastiching of modernist innovation and from the exercise of stylistic difficulty for its own sake, the strategy Roth has in mind 'entails making fiction that may well prompt the writer's first readers to think, "But he can't be serious," as opposed to, "Ah, this is very serious indeed"'.[19]

To experiment without solemnly or stridently demonstrating it; to maintain a lightness of touch that holds the reader's judgement in suspense before a narrative that never quite seems as serious as it might otherwise aspire to be – these twin objectives encapsulate Roth's response to those high-modernist precursors he names. It's a response that likewise shares Kundera's sense that 'novel form is almost boundless freedom', while going some way to reinforcing his concomitant concern that fiction 'has missed out on that freedom' to the extent that writers have 'left unexplored many formal possibilities'.[20] One such possibility, uniting both these novelists, draws on Roth's implication that the comic and the experimental live in close proximity to one another. This coexistence becomes apparent in much of Roth's audacious late work, where the 'astonishing farce of misperception', as Nathan Zuckerman describes it in *American Pastoral* (1997), offers a generic framework within which to reactivate for ironic (and indeed at times seemingly farcical) ends modernist fiction's concern with how characters make ethical judgements on the basis of sensory impressions.[21]

'No one writing in fiction in English today', Jay Halio recently proclaimed, 'has as great a mastery of the varieties of comedy as Philip Roth'. What Halio calls 'deadly farce' joins an 'arsenal' of devices which showcase Roth's 'use of comic juxtapositions, antic dialogue, and mimicry', none of which are employed 'merely to arouse laughter' but rather to highlight 'an awareness of human frailty'. As Halio correctly concludes, '[u]nderneath' Roth's 'comedy ... almost invariably lies a serious intent',[22] pointing to a model for deciphering how seriousness shimmers beneath the surface flair of narratorial irony and rhetorical play. A two-tiered model, it significantly resembles what decades of Conrad scholars have taught us about the distinction between the events Marlow recalls and the lexical embellishments he tacitly or unconsciously employs to facilitate those recollections: the same model that Nathan too becomes acutely aware of in *American Pastoral* when, despite his own perceptiveness and verbal felicity, he fails to grasp '[w]hat *was* the Swede's subjectivity'.[23] Nothing could be more serious than Roth's point about the vacancy that might lie beyond the 'natural physical refinement of a star' that Swede Levov emblazons. Yet the interiorised self-questioning – which is itself provoked by Nathan's observations of that 'refinement' – sets up a comedy of cognition that periodically intervenes in the prevailing seriousness of his documentation of the Swede's tragic fall. Caught in a confessional conversation in which 'all this giving' in fact

> gave nothing and gave away nothing, I had no idea where his thoughts might be or if he even had 'thoughts'. When, momentarily, I stopped speaking, I sensed that my words, rather than falling into the net of the other person's awareness, got linked up with nothing in his brain, went in there and vanished.[24]

What could be construed as yet another allegorisation by a contemporary writer of James's claim in 1884 that 'impressions *are* experience'[25] actually reads less like a homage to the mental conundrums once dramatised by literary impressionism than as evidence of Roth's continuation along its formal path. Which is to say that just as perception and misrecognition were key thematic resources for the likes of James, Conrad and Woolf, so have they been for Roth's self-analysing narrator, who for much of his career – and much of Roth's corpus since Nathan Zuckerman's first appearance in *The Ghost Writer* (1979) – has been fascinated by 'falling into the net' of another's consciousness. This preoccupation, condensed epigrammatically in the previously mentioned episode from *American Pastoral*, not only allows Roth to explore the question of '[w]hat sort of mental existence had been' experienced by the subject whose life story anchors the novel;[26] it also allows him to embrace Conrad's famous belief in 'the power of the written word to make you hear, to make you feel', and 'before all, to make you see'.[27]

In his most recent work to date, *Nemesis* (2010), Roth adopts this injunction, or rather its obverse – the fatal inability to see a situation for what it is – and deploys it to serve the novel's tragic arc. *Nemesis* tracks the central character, Bucky Cantor, the muscular Jewish athlete who is in his prime when the novel begins, but who finds himself in the midst of a devastating polio epidemic sweeping through Newark in the penultimate year of World War II. Bucky seems blinded by his own devotion to the duty and loyalty he expects of himself as playground director, helpless to prevent growing numbers of children from contracting a disease that paralyses and kills with horrendous speed. As he battles with the decision of whether to keep the playground running in the face of infection, we learn that Bucky has been excluded from military service owing to poor eyesight. Without pushing this visual metaphor too far, Roth gradually insinuates that Bucky fails to look steadily at the prospect of whether he could be the primary carrier of the disease as it starts to ravage the community around him.

So far, so pathetic. Yet Roth is keen on conjuring something else in this novel, apart from the inward distress of Bucky's morally fraught debates with his conscience about his responsibilities towards the community he serves. At the level of its narration, *Nemesis* represents a departure from prioritising the rendering of consciousness, as though Roth isn't content with the more familiar modernist tactic of 'falling into the net' of his protagonist's mentation. Instead, he has chosen a mediator for this tragedy of heroism: while events at least appear at the outset to be focalised by Bucky, that focalisation is in fact a Zuckermanesque simulation by the narrator Arnie Mesnikoff, who was himself present at Bucky's playground at the time of the outbreak and who subsequently, we later learn, became a polio casualty himself. What Roth is trying to 'make you see' with the help of this mediating figure is not simply an interior account of Bucky's reflections, though Mesnikoff does offer that when he homes in on Bucky's agonising ethical decision of whether to leave Newark for the safety of the Poconos, where he is awaited by his beloved Marcia at the Indian Hill summer camp that offers a pastoral refuge for them both. Rather, Mesnikoff's refracting narrative voice opens a certain distance between his voice as a chronicler and the subject of the chronicle, a distance that distinguishes *Nemesis*'s register from the extensive psychological commotion produced by Zuckerman's ventriloquism in Roth's epics of the 1990s. Restraining that kind of intense reproduction of interiority displayed in *American Pastoral* and *The Human Stain*, Roth offers a more action-led approach to his character's behaviour in *Nemesis*. Inflected by Mesnikoff, it's an approach that substitutes surface mannerisms for Bucky's mental turmoil, while tracking unfurling events in a tenor redolent of an adventure yarn:

> He'd never been to the Pocono Mountains before, or up through the rural northwestern counties of New Jersey to Pennsylvania. The train ride, traversing hills and woods and open farmland, made him think of himself as on a far greater excursion than just travelling to the next state over. There was an epic dimension to gliding past a landscape wholly unfamiliar to him, a sense he'd had the few previous times he'd been aboard a train – including the Jersey line that carried him to the shore – that a future new and unknown to him was about to unfold. Sighting the Delaware Water Gap, where the river separating New Jersey and Pennsylvania cut dramatically through the mountain range just fifteen minutes from his stop at

Stroudsburg, only heightened the intensity of the trip and assured him – admittedly without reason – that no destroyer could possibly overleap so grand a natural barrier in order to catch him.[28]

Bucky's childlike wonder provoked by the sublime topography is matched here in pace and register by the equally childlike impetus of what, in Mesnikoff's reconstruction, is pictured as an 'epic' escape from an indiscriminate 'destroyer'. To be sure, we're gunning for Bucky by this stage, gripped more by 'the intensity of the trip' than by psychological introspection. Ancillary information about the exceptional nature of this journey also belies the extent to which details about character are externally imported, confirming that this is the stuff of a faithful chronicler rather than a focalising consciousness:

> This marked the first time since his grandfather's death, three years earlier, that he would be leaving his grandmother in the care of anyone else for more than a weekend, and the first time he'd be out of the city for more than a night or two. And it was the first time in weeks that thoughts of polio weren't swamping him. He still mourned the two boys who had died, he was still oppressed by thinking of all of his other boys stricken with the crippling disease, yet he did not feel that he had faltered under the exigencies of calamity or that someone else could have performed his job any more zealously. (*N*, p. 141)

What we are given here is an aerial view of Bucky, a view that tracks back to indicate how this journey is a 'first time' in more than one respect. Even when matters of interiority are raised ('thoughts of polio weren't swamping him'), we are not presented with an insight into the mind of someone released from the barrage of guilt-ridden reflections on what he's doing and why he's leaving, but rather a matter-of-fact observation that such reflections no longer beset him. Mental processes are thus reduced to a mere mention: that 'he was still oppressed by thinking' back to polio's playground victims is duly noted; yet it isn't a sensation of that oppressive thought that's conjured for the involved reader, only the fact that such a guilty reflection on moral culpability has been registered and processed. I wouldn't want to imply that this kind of externalism makes Roth's ambition any less modernist. Pertinent here is Dorothy Richardson's comparison between Proust's 'reconstruction of experience focused from within the mind of a single individual' (a tactic that Roth developed so effectively with the invasive and vicarious Zuckerman) and the Jamesian strategy of 'keeping the reader incessantly watching ... through the eye of the single observer'.[29] Both approaches to focalisation would be applicable to *Nemesis*, except for the fact that what keeps us 'incessantly watching' in this novel is the way felt experiences are reconstructed not so much through the perceptions of the character who participates in the world of immediate actions, as through 'the eye' of an external and self-effacing documenter.

Yet Roth's choice of this externalised voice has a critical point to it. By opting for a narrator who is less interested in unstitching the fabric of Bucky's consciousness than in giving a portrait, from the outside in, of a man whose heroic self-image leaves him bereft of ethical and emotional reflexivity, Roth delivers a version of what Kevin Bell calls 'modernism's critique of the cultural pressures exerted on individual subjectivity to abandon the ongoing experimentality of its own experience and to abdicate its own potentiality'.[30] Roth's adaptation of the subjective method Richardson admired and practiced, and which lay at the heart of Conrad's endeavour to make his readers see the world of the senses in the instant of their reception, thus helps us to understand the political implications of narrative timbre in *Nemesis*. It also might help to explain why, in the aforementioned episode, Roth chooses to render the boyish thrill of narrow escape, instead of the complexities of ruminative cogitation that so powerfully extended (in his earlier work) the stylistic resources of modernist subjectivism into the realms of ethical decision making.

In such instances, the question arises: What is it that Roth is trying to make us feel and make us see, by employing a narrative discourse that operates more at the surface than at the sensory depths of what Bucky is feeling and seeing? One answer could be that Roth is, in fact, upholding the very modernist use of free indirect discourse as a means of emulating the most idiosyncratic elements of a character's mindset. Mesnikoff's somewhat brisk, two-dimensional narration might be judged as a rather immature attempt at free indirect style, a caricature of interior thought by a homodiegetic narrator who is more concerned with causality than with craft, as he tells us about the tragic imminence of events rather than showing the decisions of those involved in them with more obliquity and ambiguity. That same register, however, in all its unreflective directness, could equally be construed as a fitting correlative to Bucky's own two-dimensional sensibility, driven as he stoically is by loyalty and heroism, a man who, as Mesnikoff later summarises, is 'haunted by an exacerbated sense of duty but endowed with little force of mind' (*N*, p. 273). According to this second reading, Roth's choice of an economical narrator who is still in awe of his sometime javelin instructor – to whom he periodically refers throughout the novel as 'Mr Cantor' – is precisely a way of reciprocating stylistically the perspective of this unselfconscious hero who, in Mesnikoff's retrospect, 'was largely a humorless person, articulate enough but with barely a trace of wit, who never in his life had spoken satirically or with irony, who rarely cracked a joke or spoke in jest' (*N*, p. 273).

The point of drawing attention to this novel's capacity to embody in mode the mentality of its morally compromised then devastatingly crippled protagonist is not simply to provide a defence of a side to Roth's prose that can occasionally be so restrained as to seem tedious. The purpose is to highlight instead how Conrad's famous injunction has been adapted so as to continue what Bell describes as modernism's critique of 'automized systems of valuation and identity [that] prop up a culture that ultimately bends our lives toward sameness and satisfactions that we ourselves do not request or create'.[31] By switching back on the political mechanism of Conrad's proviso, Roth makes us feel and see so vividly in *Nemesis* the constitution of someone who cannot adapt to change because he is forever subject to his own negative laws of valorous self-vindication. A figure whose actions are programmed, as though for an automaton, by that 'exacerbated sense of duty' inherited from his father's generation, Bucky tries to repossess the very prototypes of obligation that he'll never cultivate as his own. Spotting this double-bind, Mesnikoff sounds condemning indeed when concluding that for Bucky '[n]othing he does matches the ideal in him', so much so that he 'never trusts his limits because, saddled with a stern natural goodness that will not permit him to resign himself to the suffering of others, he will never guiltlessly acknowledge that he has any limits' (*N*, pp. 273–74). This perorating condemnation, however, feels warranted once we remember what kind of reading experience we've just endured: provoked as we are by the two-dimensionality of Roth's register, a register that renews the political force of a vital component in Conrad's aesthetic. Roth makes us see how stoicism operates ideologically when it becomes not so much an individual's trait as a mark of the cultural inscription and enslavement of individuality – a critique he achieves by simulating for us, at the very level of style, Bucky's refusal 'to resign himself' to the possibility of his own mortal limitations.

INNOVATION AFTER 'ESTABLISHMENT MODERNISM'

Linking a figure like Conrad with an heir as eminent as Roth can tell us a great deal about the adaptability of specific aesthetic principles as they are transferred across time and into new cultural contexts for political critique. In the course of making such links, it is tempting to listen to Roth recalling how he re-encountered 'Conrad's presence' throughout the spring and summer of 2006, spending 'most of my evenings' in a routine of 'rereading ... with great admiration as, during day, I was writing *Exit Ghost*'.[32] But we should be mindful of turning transhistorical affinities into cause-and-effect explanations for how Roth inherits modernism, however valuable it is to make such comparisons between his and Conrad's respective approaches to narration. We have already seen how careful Roth is to make the distinction between simply reusing modernist devices and the more challenging work of absorbing modernism's 'message' while 'finding a voice and subject of one's own'. To put it another way, it's important to acknowledge Roth's artistic individualism, especially when tracing moments when he most loyally envelops an identifiably modernist strategy. This same difference between inheriting modernism and moving forward along an inherited path – between making inroads back to modernism and shining 'new light' (to recall George Eliot) 'along the pathway of discovery' – also allies Roth with the equally complex, if not more dissident, relationship to modernism sustained by Kundera. Like Roth, Kundera is mindful of the institutionalisation of literary innovations that had once appeared so radical. As he complains in *The Art of the Novel*, 'in the second half of this century, we must reckon with the modernism of fixed rules, the modernism of the university – establishment modernism, so to speak'.[33] There's an echo here of Roth's point about the conversion into convention of what had been critically elevated as inventive; moreover, we sense again a gesture to James. Offering a more solemn acknowledgment of the Master than Roth, Kundera worries that the modernist legacy has fallen into propriety, living on as nothing other than a series of respectable 'rules'. Kundera implies that James was being too optimistic in his *fin-de-siècle* prophecy about 'The Future of the Novel', where he expected fiction to survive whatever the new century might hold simply because it 'moves in a luxurious independence of rules and restrictions'.[34]

Roth and Kundera are equally watchful, then, of how their own incorporations of modernist aesthetics might contribute to the stultifying institutionalisation of modernism as a set of 'fixed rules', packaged into conventions of the kind that are more readily studied than they are practised. In turn, both writers are aware that the greatest justice they can do to their modernist heritage is to *depart* from it, in order to advance in spirit rather than by the letter along a path of invention that modernism had established. Aptly enough, this resolution has led Roth and Kundera to promote various forms of infidelity, whereby their fictions dissent time and again from one mode in order to reoccupy another.[35] In Roth's case, the infidel's influence can be spotted in what Hermione Lee calls the 'zig-zag process' overarching his career, whereby he has moved back and forth from large-scale political realism to the novella's crystalline contraction, the stylistic upshot of which is a marked 'antithesis between high seriousness and vaudeville knockabout'.[36] In the case of Kundera, the rebel in his register is more vocal still: 'I dream constantly of some great unexpected infidelity',[37] pointing to the degree of disengagement that has become his ideal means of relating to modernism. We hear once more the rebellion against encroaching conventionalism, for to keep the modernist project alive is 'to rid the novel of the automatism of novelistic technique'.[38] Counteracting the technical legislation of 'establishment modernism', Kundera proffers a dual alternative for the novel that seeks not only to exploit its 'boundless possibilities' but also 'to make it dense'.[39]

With the same gesture as Roth of alluding to Pound's famous injunction – if only to revise Pound's plea for newness alone – Kundera understands density here as curiously synonymous with 'clarity'. To be dense means maintaining a novel's 'shape', ensuring its 'architectonic' coherence even in the process of opening it up to multiple registers.[40] It was from his musical training that Kundera learned how such 'formal diversity' can be 'balanced by a very strong thematic unity'.[41] In particular, by studying Beethoven's 'determination to transform that assemblage [of symphonic movements] into a true unity',[42] one can illuminate correlations between the integrity of musical composition and the kind of interaction between content and form, felt perception and representation, advanced by modernist fiction. For Kundera, this aspiration involves more than simply drawing a 'comparison between the novel and music'; it is instead a model for conceiving of novelistic innovation as a matter of variation, based on the variant structure of a symphony's progression. To 'compose a novel' along these lines, he remarks, 'is to set different emotional spaces side by side – and that, to me, is the writer's subtlest craft'.[43]

Sustaining that subtlety sees Kundera synthesising periods in ways that might seem contradictory. While keeping with the principles of classical symphony at a structural level, he then exploits at a thematic level what Carlos Fuentes – identifying Kundera as 'the other K of Czechoslovakia' – calls the 'estrangement and the sense of discomfort with which Franz Kafka flooded, in luminous shadows, the world that already existed without knowing it'.[44] With similarly estranging results, Kundera's narration works in an exteriorised fashion, because he is more committed to documenting the effects of discomfiture from outside the individual in question rather than (in the version of novelistic subjectivism that reached from James to Woolf) from the inside out. This externalism is maintained by Kundera's technique of *parabasis*, as he interjects to outline precisely what we might pay especial attention to within scenes that place the self under existential scrutiny. As Fred Misurella remarks, in Kundera's work '*parabasis* furnishes a practical novelistic method of having things two ways (serious yet playful, tragic yet comic, meaningful yet meaningless, and, to use one of his own contradictory couplings, heavy yet light) with narrative tone and theme working as the glues that hold opposites together'.[45] In *The Unbearable Lightness of Being* (1984) Kundera goes as far as to imply that character-creation is also a partly 'meaningful yet meaningless exercise'. Likening it to dreaming, characterisation remains to him a hypothetical, 'aesthetic activity, a game of the imagination, a game that is a value in itself'.[46] Such game-playing is what we might expect from Nathan Zuckerman too; except that unlike the ever-shifting provenance of Roth's free indirect style, Kundera makes no attempt to hide the fact that the interjecting voice is an authorial one, not that of an alter-ego, like Nathan, who happens to enjoy impersonating the verbal idiosyncrasies of others whose consciousnesses he invades and ventriloquises. Taking a deliberate stand against the qualities of perspectivism and obliquity that Roth inherits from James, Kundera aligns himself with a tradition of narratorial intrusion belonging to Robert Musil, Hermann Broch and Witold Gombrowicz, none of whom 'felt', according to Kundera, 'the least discomfort at being present as a mind in his novels'.[47] In *The Unbearable Lightness of Being*, Kundera is thus unhindered when it comes to employing *parabasis*:

And once more I see [Tomas] the way he appeared to me at the very beginning of the novel: standing at the window and staring across the courtyard at the walls opposite.
   This is the image from which he was born. As I have pointed out before, characters are not born like people, of woman; they are born of a situation, a sentence, a metaphor containing in a nutshell a basic human possibility that the author thinks no one else has discovered or said something essential about.
   But isn't it true that an author can write only about himself?[48]

Kundera assumes an elevated, prospect-view over the scene and Tomas within it, while giving himself the freedom to suspend the novel's onward diegesis and to remind us of his hero's spatial placement within the plot. It appears he wants to ensure we appreciate in geometrical terms the potential significance of where Tomas exists now in relation to 'the very beginning of the novel'. In that sense, the episode takes on a decidedly mechanical function: emotional employment is stalled and events are reduced to diagnosis. This move from elaborating Tomas's emotions to 'containing' them 'in a nutshell' is matched in tone, as the centrepiece 'image' here is viewed forensically by the narrator from above. There is no attempt at focalisation; that's because Kundera is not interested in probing Tomas's introspection. He seems even less interested in allowing his style to emulate – as we might expect a literary impressionist to do – the undulations of perception. Instead, we are offered a seamless demonstration of Kundera's insistence from *The Art of the Novel*, echoed in the previous passage, that '*both* the character *and* his world must be understood as *possibilities*'.[49] It is, however, exactly this kind of forward-looking enthusiasm for what can possibly be done in fiction that's part of what makes Kundera look back. As an experimental traditionalist, he treats 'learned arguments that the novel has exhausted its possibilities' to a lesson in heritage. He holds 'precisely the opposite feeling' about the fate of fiction, which leads him to envision its future by orienting toward the past, showing – as he did in conversation with Roth – how 'in the course of its history the novel missed many of its possibilities'.[50]

Just to be clear: Kundera's work can hardly be said to carry on the Jamesian tradition that might, at first glance, seem to feed into the values and hopes behind his reflections about novelistic aesthetics. Admittedly, Kundera's claim that '[t]here is enormous freedom latent within the novelistic form' strongly reminds us of James's consistent opinion of fiction's elasticity and unruly vitality; and his pitch to Roth that 'the synthetic power of the novel is capable of combining everything into a unified whole' recalls James's conception of fiction's organic integration, where 'the idea and the form' for any novel should act like a 'needle and thread'.[51] These are theoretical models of Kundera, though, and often no more than that. Where his own hands-on procedures are concerned, he remains far more idiosyncratic – so much so that he also should be distinguished, for our purposes, from Roth's way of working in what some critics have called a distinctly 'satiric modernist tradition' that owes more to Joyce, Chekov and, to some extent, James, than Kundera's work ever has.[52]

If Kundera's comedy, at this modal level, affiliates his fiction with late modernist sardonicism of Kafka and Beckett, thus setting it apart both from Roth's early modernist satire and from his impressionist interest in the acrobatics of characters' inner thoughts, then there are further differences at the level of narrative voice. Kundera's penchant for *parabasis*, for example, would be heresy in the eyes of that 'conscious artist' who Ford Madox Ford promoted for his generation, and on whom so many writers, experimental or not, modelled themselves. For Ford, what sets the modern novelists apart is precisely the way they conceal their narratorial position; they should never 'obtrude their personalities: they state as well as they can the definite facts of a story, leaving to the reader the task of adopting what moral attitude he will towards a given set of circumstances'.[53] The contrast couldn't be more apparent: the virtues of depersonalisation, as James and Ford variously promoted it, sit at the opposite end of the stylistic spectrum to Kundera's endorsement of what he describes as 'an essayistic art that is specifically novelistic', where the narration 'limits itself to a hypothetical, ludic, or ironic point of view'.[54] Given these antinomies in technique, it would be tempting, and no doubt credible, to conclude that the modernist aesthetic Kundera extends is hardly close to what Woolf had in mind when she asserted that 'a novel is an impression not an argument' – reiterating, as she acknowledges, Thomas Hardy's Preface to *Tess of the D'Urbervilles*, where he exhorts fiction's obliquity to admonish himself from being held accountable (because his very style is irreducible) to any political standpoint.[55] Following these distinctions, it would also be tempting to take Kundera at his word and rehearse the view that what he inherits is an *existential* modernism, not the psychological one that was, as Mark McGurl has shown, by far the most dominant strand and source of literary prestige in the wake of Henry James.[56] To opt for this conclusion, however, would be to miss the opportunity for noticing surprising affinities (as I will do in the following section) between Kundera's vision of the novelist as 'neither a historian or prophet' but as 'an explorer of existence' and precisely the kind of impressionist writer whom he, unlike Roth, so resolutely defines himself against.[57]

'THE ANTERIOR EXPERIENCE OF THE NOVEL':
MODERNISM AS A USABLE PAST

For Kundera, the novel-form is above all 'an investigation of human life in the trap that the world has become'.[58] On the basis of this view, it appears that he holds more in common than he might admit with James's assertion that the '[n]ovel is in its broadest definition a personal, a direct impression of life'.[59] Likewise, throughout his mature work, Conrad too demonstrated how impressionist narratives could depict psychological states without compromising the work of existential inquiry and philosophical argumentation. A late work like *The Shadow-Line* (1917) most vividly enacts the answer to Kundera's question: 'What lies beyond the psychological novel'?[60] Conrad anticipates Kundera's claim that '[t]o apprehend the self in my novels means to grasp the essence of its existential problem', precisely by showing how there *can* be a 'nonpsychological means to apprehend the self', even with a mode that elsewhere delivers on many impressionist expectations.[61] Indeed, Conrad deploys that most emblematic of modernist tropes – the moment of being – in a manner that precisely allows him to pose an 'existential problem' while creating a level of narrative stasis, if not paralysis, that enables him in turn to evoke its 'essence'.

'Only the young have such moments. I don't mean the very young. No. The very young have, properly speaking, no moments. It is the privilege of early youth to live in advance of its days in all the beautiful continuity of hope which knows no pauses and no introspection'.[62] Here Conrad opens *The Shadow-Line* with the apparently abstract notion of the memorialised 'moment' that those in their 'early youth' can enjoy with crippling self-absorption, for 'hope' overwhelms incipient regret. As much an idea as it is an experience of palpable time, the 'moment' serves like a structural motif punctuating *The Shadow-Line*'s episodic progression, as the novel's spatial navigation of the ocean becomes analogically connected to its narrator's temporal journey from youth to maturity on his debut voyage in command. The moment thus provides a compositional resource in itself, one that Conrad draws on to evoke the ominous effects of passing time and, more ominously still, later in the novel, the effect of time that seemingly refuses to pass, when the ship is stricken in dead calm. Here, with the young captain immobilised, his journey of maturation stalled, our attention is directed away from the immediate action towards the novel's existential subplot. Conrad offers the trope of the disabling moment to the reader as a lens on his narrator's self-inspection, freeze-framing a situation whose perils are as much ontological as physical. A becalmed sea intensifies the atmosphere of an environment in which time has become unquantifiable, the only measurable phenomena being the accumulation of one paranoiac anxiety on another:

For myself, neither my soul was highly tempered, nor my imagination properly under control. There were moments when I felt, not only that I would go mad, but that I had gone mad already; so that I dared not open my lips for fear of betraying myself by some insane shriek. Luckily I had only orders to give, and an order has a steadying influence upon him who has to give it.... Luckily, again, there was no necessity to raise one's voice. The brooding stillness of the world seemed sensitive to the slightest sound, like a whispering gallery.[63]

The language of the closing observation sounds, with its audible sibilance, like a taunting counterpoint to relative silence that is only exacerbating the narrator's inwardness. This final sentence not only onomatopoeically complements the image of the 'whispering gallery' with which it ends; its hissing inflections also reinforce the sense of the animate, 'brooding stillness' of this environment. Capable of making noises of its own accord, the scene merely reminds the young captain of how little chance he has of keeping anything exterior to his own inner existence 'under control'.

This counterpoint between what diction itself suggests and how the perceiving character feels highlights the correlations of tonality and implication that Kundera has applied to his own narration. I have lingered here on the details of Conrad's register in order to spotlight their kinship, in spite of Kundera's reticence towards impressionism's supposed tendency to psychological introversion. In a narrative that dramatises existential and historical paralysis without compromising its own lucidity, Conrad anticipates the protocols of what Kundera calls 'a new art' for the novel, involving a 'radical honing that allows the inclusion of the vertiginous complexity of the world without the loss of architectonic clarity'.[64] This affiliation, though never quite amounting to a substantive influence, corroborates in turn Kundera's belief that 'each work is an answer to preceding ones, each work contains all the anterior experience of the novel'.[65] According to this notion, that combination of 'complexity' and 'clarity' is better understood as traditionally rather than radically 'new'. It is a combination that reinforces Conrad's imperatives, honouring James and Hardy before him: to have the novel attend to that momentary realm of impressions but with architectural precision, to engage with the sophistications of sensory perception with diction that is connotative yet exact. Demonstrating none other than that 'skill in selection' that Ford admired in his sometime collaborator Conrad but also in the work of less overt experimenters like John Galsworthy,[66] Kundera's fiction exercises its own 'anterior experience' rather than seeking outright novelty. When Hana Píchavá notes that Kundera 'does not burden the literary critic with stylistic innovations, puzzles, or games', but instead 'works his style into an art of elegant simplicity and stark precision',[67] she highlights how we can legitimately observe Kundera extending the very task inaugurated by an early modernist figure with whom he has rarely been identified: to find a language that makes the reader 'see', to recall Conrad's phrase, the significance of how characters respond to impressions, especially as the most everyday impressions often harbour the largest existential implications.

If Kundera's technical aspirations for the novel, therefore, place him closer than he might admit to modernism's novel-of-consciousness, then it is more revealing still to consider how those aspirations correspond with Roth as someone whose work *does* take up modernist lessons in interiority, and who practices what he praises in Saul Bellow as the effort 'not only to infuse fiction with mind but to make mentalness itself central to the hero's dilemma'.[68] As we have noted, Kundera sees that the novelist's most subtle demonstration of craft is 'to set different emotional spaces side by side'. In formal terms, this explains his promotion of '[v]ariation form', going so far as to vaunt it in *The Book of Laughter and Forgetting* (1978) as 'a sovereign form'.[69] According to this model, the reader is involved in, rather than a mere spectator of, the novel's formal process of alternation, a 'voyage of variations' which 'leads into that *other* infinitude, into the infinite diversity of the interior world lying hidden in all things'.[70] Interiority features only intermittently in Kundera's writing, more concerned as he is with the kind of 'existential mathematics' with which *Slowness* (1995), for instance, theorises the experience of 'speed and forgetting' by charting that experience from *outside* the minds of those characters involved.[71] His advocacy of formal variation as a vehicle for the novelist 'to go straight to the core of the matter', however, speaks directly to Roth's manner of evoking subjectivity from various points of view. In this way, both writers make deliberate use of juxtaposition: a poetics of contrast in which discrete emotional states are organised side by side, and in some cases refracted by different focalising consciousnesses.

Kundera's 'synthetic' view of 'the novelist's desire to grasp his subject from all sides and in the fullest possible completeness',[72] thus closely corresponds with Roth's own 'ideas about style and consciousness' that have been central to his practice from as early as *Portnoy's Complaint* (1969).[73] In that early novel, Roth experimented with '"blocks of consciousness", chunks of material of varying shapes and sizes piled atop one another and held together by association rather than chronology'.[74] Although he admits to discovering this structural pattern only 'while writing', it stands in a predictive sense as an affinity with Kundera's work to which Roth, at this point in the 1960s, had yet to be acquainted. Which is to say that 'blocks of consciousness' resemble Kundera's way of orchestrating successive, yet self-contained, movements – small chapters that he analogically compares, as we've discovered, with symphonic forms of progression and recapitulation. Roth too reaches for musical comparisons, but this time for literary 'tone' rather than structure: 'Beginning with *Goodbye, Columbus* [1959], I've been attracted to prose that has the turns, vibrations, intonations, and cadences, the spontaneity and ease, of spoken language, at the same time that is solidly grounded on the page, weighted with the irony, precision, and ambiguity associated with a more traditional literary rhetoric'.[75] Holding 'traditional' modes of articulation and rhetorical control in balance with the effort to evoke the unpredictability and tempo of characters' everyday reflections, Roth epitomises the level of self-identification with the past I have been associating with Kundera. What they both understand, what they hold in common, is the idea that a novelist's technique, however much he or she wishes for 'spontaneity and ease', occurs in dialogue with tradition, a dialogue in which novelty and heritage, linguistic heterodoxy and 'solidly grounded' devices, coincide to produce approaches that are formally new.

PRACTICING ANTI-MODERN MODERNISM

'It is an inviolable right of a novelist to rework his novel', writes Kundera in *The Book of Laughter and Forgetting* (1978).[76] In Roth's world, that right has been given most liberally to the novelist Nathan Zuckerman. With a propensity to self-analyse his own renderings of mental attention and apprehension, Zuckerman renders in a knowing and often confessional mode what Max Saunders has described as modernism's intensive 'interest in phenomenology', an interest spurred by literary impressionism's 'awareness of how language or form *mediates* between the subject and the object'.[77] We shall return in Chapter 4 to the implications of this stylistic mediation in Ian McEwan's fiction, even though he has seemed increasingly to hold modernism at arm's length, becoming less interested in phenomenology than with the so-called hard problem of consciousness – dramatising neurological explanations for why his characters cognitively process sensations in the fashion they do. In Roth's case, however, the 'interest' Saunders isolates at the heart of modernism's concern with the relation of novelistic language to perception continues unabated. Perceptual mediation is for Zuckerman (as, of course, for his creator) all part of the drama of ventriloquising another person's past experiences; it is also what spotlights Roth's fascination with the consequences of having 'forever to remember', as Marcus Messner wonders in *Indignation* (2008), 'each moment of life down to its tiniest component'.[78] A similar fascination, we notice, propels Kundera's quest for an appropriate form, or series of forms, for narrating how one's 'past contracts, disintegrates, dissolves', just as Tamina, the heroine of *The Book of Laughter and Forgetting*, is perceived as 'shrinking and losing her contours'.[79] For both Roth and Kundera, therefore, it is the impossibility of fully retrieving and managing versions of historical reality that produces the most stylistically inventive results. Just as Tamina futilely 'tried initially to recover memories that could serve as reference points in time's flow and become the underlying framework of a reconstructed past',[80] so Nathan proclaims as a kind of modesty *topos* or prefatory disclaimer, early on in *American Pastoral*, that as the observer (and narrator) you have to 'fight your superficiality, your shallowness, so as to try to come at people without unreal expectations', though it may often be the case that you'll fail. 'It's getting them wrong that is living', declares Nathan, 'getting them wrong and wrong and wrong and then, on careful reconsideration, getting them wrong again. That's how we know we're alive: we're wrong'.[81]

Getting it wrong in comprehending oneself, or one's past, let alone when trying to re-imagine (as Nathan so often does) someone else's conception of his or her own remembered actions, recalls many of modernism's monumental experiments in retrospective narration. When Ford wrote *The Good Soldier* (1915), for instance, he created in John Dowell a domestic counterpart to Conrad's seafaring Marlow. Contrasts in occupation, though, are superficial in comparison to what both characters stylistically enabled their authors to do. In the same way that 'Joyce set a microphone in Bloom's head', as Kundera pictures it, so Ford and Conrad took that microphone and held it up to catch the inflections and implications of self-decoding recollection.[82] It is '[t]hanks to the fantastic espionage of interior monologue [that] we have learned an enormous amount about what we are'. For 'myself', admits Kundera, 'I cannot use that microphone'.[83] In its place, as we have seen, he advocates the novel of existential rather than phenomenological inquiry, an idiom that allows him to ward off psychologism and to refuse the mimetic rendering of his characters' mental lives. As he maintains in *The Unbearable Lightness of Being*, '[i]t would be senseless for the author to try to convince the reader that his characters once actually lived'.[84] Yet at the same time, my analysis has tried to show that it would be wrong to suggest that only existential scenarios can safeguard the novelty of the novel for Kundera and facilitate its 'own unrealized possibilities', as *Unbearable Lightness* calls them.[85] Despite his professed heritage, and despite his leanings towards externalist rather than impressionist modes of narration, he continues to advance along an inherited path whose coordinates are not always in keeping with his own map of filial predecessors.

Reframed comparatively alongside Roth's stylistic ambitions, Kundera's contradictory affinities with different modernist phases of innovation start to make sense. Indeed, what Roth said of his own brand of modernist satire in the late 1980s evinces a curious intersection between psychological and existential modernisms that is germane to Kundera's impulse, exemplified in *The Book of Laughter*, to take us on 'a voyage leading into the interior of a theme, the interior of a thought, the interior of a single, unique situation'.[86] As Roth admitted, 'it's self-serving to bring in Kafka', because for 'any comedy of humiliation there's an inevitable likeness to what Kafka wrote about'. Nonetheless, he adds that 'if you do shake up Kafka and Bellow together, you get some kind of concoction that is inspiring'.[87] To 'shake up' such very different traditions in order to yield something new might not appear to satisfy the precept of artistic autonomy that early modernists inherited from Flaubert, for whom the ideal novel would be 'dependent on nothing' and 'held together by the internal strength of its style' alone.[88] But the fortunes of traditionalism have changed, and so have writers' attitudes towards the fact that originality might be 'dependent' less on their break with the past than on how inventively they choose to inherit and remake it.

Without implying that they share the same stance, let alone the same imaginative response to immediate or historical conditions of experience, such an attitude may be attributed to the remaining four writers considered in this book. As we shall see in the chapters to come, the 'inherited path' often turns out to be the most radical one, because the route it sets for the novel's development is always open to fresh mappings. What the contemporary innovator might discover on that route is the difference between treating modernism as a tradition and treating it as an ongoing resource – an original use of the past that Michael Ondaatje epitomises, as I argue in the next chapter, by responding to the unfinished lessons of Cubism – without subjecting it to impersonation. Retaining modernism's recalcitrance rather than wresting its commitments into a monument to their own later twentieth-century conventionality, both Kundera and Roth uncover the means for regarding the *idea* of modernist fiction in such a way that refuses to pacify, normalise or contain it. With their example in mind, we can see how being an original traditionalist is not so paradoxical after all: it is the role contemporary writers assume in the business of moving fiction forward without listening too reverently to the ghost of modernisms past. To Kundera, as for Roth, irreverence and inheritance need first to coincide, before novelists can get close to extending a genuinely modernist understanding of how literary heritage relates to what their craft has yet to achieve. To be irreverent – as McEwan has recently been towards the early-twentieth-century impressionists he so admires, and as Morrison periodically is towards the Faulknerian prose with which she has often been affiliated – means to unsettle many of the premises that modernists held dear in the early twentieth century, though precisely in order to ensure that modernism remains salient for the twenty-first. On these terms, Kundera implies that writers can do more to reinvigorate modernist aesthetics by hosting their re-initiation while repudiating their imitation, so that the 'farther we advance into the future, the greater becomes the legacy of "antimodern modernism"'.[89] It seems particularly apt that this brand of opposition should remain part and parcel of safeguarding modernism's futures, because it presupposes the writer's alertness to that balance of artistic debt and dissent which in itself is nothing less than a thoroughly modernist ethic.

CHAPTER 2

'The perfect state for a novel': Michael Ondaatje's Cubist imagination

Looking back in 1923 on Cubism's achievements from a decade when its successor, arguably in the shape of Futurism, held sway, Fernand Léger noted that 'being inventive can come very close to being imitative'.[1] Léger's painterly concern could very well be a novelist's one too, resonating as it does with a writer whose fiction has often been affiliated with cubist ideals. Nearly sixty years later, Léger's conviction – carried forward from his earliest essays on pictorial form – that the 'value of a work of art is completely independent of any imitative character',[2] finds common sentiments in Michael Ondaatje's duty 'to start each book with a new vocabulary, a new set of clothes', and to 'burn the previous devices which have got us here but which now are only rhetoric'.[3] First and last, Ondaatje's duty here is to no one but himself, of course. And we should be careful to distinguish between Léger's larger claims about the representational challenges facing 'the modern picture', and Ondaatje's personal pledge to embark on new drafts in fresh linguistic 'clothes'. Nonetheless, standing here at opposite ends of the century, painter and writer speak to one another in a fashion we cannot afford to ignore. More than a matter of loose resemblances, it is also – for our purposes – more than anecdotal. To treat their commensurate impulses as such would be to dismiss as mere discursive echoes what is in fact an instance of profound artistic complementarity.

This transhistorical affinity between temperaments thus seems to imply more than the very idea of 'affinity' can name or contain. The terminological difficulties of classifying Ondaatje's Cubist inheritance – if indeed he sees it as something he inherits in the first place – are less important to solve than the question of why he puts Cubism *to use* in the manner he does. In this chapter, I consider what Cubism's utility for a famously (some would say, notoriously) poetic novelist like Ondaatje can tell us about the creative afterlives of modernist movements as they are transposed from one artistic medium to another. Ondaatje has himself said that '[a] true literary tradition' is 'not a line', nor should it be plotted by 'categories'.[4]

As my analyses of his major fiction will reveal, his compatibilities with Cubism exist not as examples of straightforward adaptation, or influences that we can categorise once and for all. More modestly, they offer a starting-point for telling a story of inter-artistic kinship that can acknowledge where conflicts arise when text and image coincide, even if such an account *does* indeed end up showing how pertinently artistic aims chime across time.[5] Carrying forward the impulse across this book, I consider how modernism's persistence can be discerned in Ondaatje's imaginative intervention in cultural and historical narratives, tracing what it is about Cubism that enables him to offer forms of critique in his transnational fictions of memory and migration. How, in other words, might his association with the structural principles of Cubism help us to understand what Milena Marinkova has called Ondaatje's 'sustained interest in a particular kind of materialist aesthetic, which has, albeit implicitly, political and ethical underpinnings'?[6] Additionally, if Cubism does indeed facilitate this kind of oblique or implicit critique, how might we evaluate the urgency of such an act of recuperation for a novelist so interested in nation-state conflict and traumas of exile? In his words, he is 'a mongrel of place. Of race. Of cultures. Of many genres'.[7] How far, though, does this militant border crossing translate into craft? For a writer who doesn't 'want to become the representative of a county', what kind of political or ethical commentary does Cubism facilitate that other modernist innovations do not?[8]

Such questions resonate with those I pose to other examples spotlighted in this book of the political recalibration of modernist aesthetics. Just as we shall see later in Coetzee's case, where minimalism becomes the vehicle for evoking, in arid and uncompromising ways, the realities of colonial violence; so, in this chapter, Ondaatje's correspondence with Cubism enables us 'to rethink', in Laura Doyle's words, 'the relationships not only among earlier works typically called modernist but also between these and later works mainly designated as postcolonial, relations which are too often still described in terms of borrowing'.[9] What follows will contend that Ondaatje does more than simply borrow Cubist traits in an imitative fashion, just as Toni Morrison – as I will argue in the closing chapter – exceeds those condescending claims of critics who have sought to measure her virtuosity against Faulkner's or Woolf's. Like Morrison's progressive relationship to modernist strategies that she reconfigures as her own, Ondaatje's active relation to tradition as a resource rather than a relic points to the salience of Doyle's warning that '[e]ven among critics specialising in postcolonial literature, modernism is often taken as a historical and autonomous given, and postcolonial writers are then characterised as either resisting its forms and choosing realist techniques or adopting them', thereby garnering the artistic capital of being associated with a 'modernist mainstream'.[10] As a novelist whose resistance in this respect has also been to the very label of 'postcolonial' writer, Ondaatje's dialogue with Cubism sets the scene for my discussion later of Coetzee and Morrison, who offer further examples of how modernist procedures have become enabling rather than anachronistic for writers concerned with the consequences of colonialism and the contexts of racial disenfranchisement.

RECONJURING CUBISM

Cubism was famous for its geometrical treatment of features whose apparent disparity could nonetheless be subject to dynamic assimilation. Modernism itself 'owes much to this brilliant conjuring trick', as Yves Alain-Bois has remarked, whereby the Post-impressionist shift from the sensuous merging of images to the recovery of line may be tracked in the transitional career of Cézanne, as he moves from diffusing the edge of objects to expressing their volume through deliberate faceting. It was this 'cubist semiology', as Alain-Bois calls it, that 'allowed one to turn the Cézannesque cave-in to the profit of form (no longer a matter of figures or perspectival space, but of structure)'.[11] When viewing this prioritisation of structure and volume at work, it is not that we need to stand back to make sense of the pictorial whole, because the end result is less important than that process of assimilating shape, perspective and colour to a picture-plane where individual optical elements are synthesised without being dissolved.

A close cousin to this process can be witnessed at work in the built environment: in viewing the trusses of a cantilever bridge alternatively from afar, then in close-up. We may notice the symmetrical spacing between arches, the way its purpose in connecting land over water takes the bridge beyond functionalism – rendering sublime that basic engineering solution of which it remains something of an aesthetic spectacle. If we're so inclined, we might even feel the awe that Heidegger reported, seeing as he did the bridge as a form that 'designedly' transfigures space into location, as it *gathers* the earth as landscape around the stream', while simultaneously 'escort[ing] the lingering and hastening ways of men to and fro', to produce a location that 'comes into existence only by virtue of the bridge'.[12] That kind of solemn reverie, however, is premised on distance, on our capacity to observe from some remove how a bridge imposes on its background. Another story altogether emerges when we draw up close: where the steel latticework of a single arch reveals in miniature that geometrical management of force and scale which bridges emblematise in their entirety, where the curving trusses appear like microfilaments that soon merge into indistinctness when we withdraw again to view the arch at range.

This attention to discrete elements that play an integral part in the success of a larger whole has as much to do with Cubism's effect on the novel as it might with comparing modern steel bridges to, for instance, Georges Braque's *Viaduct at L'Estaque* (1908). It's surely no coincidence, then, that Ondaatje has been drawn to such feats of architectural design, choosing to focalise sections of his first widely acclaimed novel, *In the Skin of a Lion* (1987), through the experiences of an esteemed Macedonian bridge-builder. Working on Toronto's Bloor Street Viaduct, Nicholas Temelcoff is, much like his creator, a structural risk-taker. We meet him in the present tense, as Ondaatje adopts the tone of a reporter in thrall to a man who gladly takes on the most perilous tasks. It appears as though Ondaatje is retrieving Nicholas from the viaduct's emerging spectacle, putting a trace of human accomplishment back into what looks like a triumph of truss-arch engineering:

Nicholas Temelcoff is famous on the bridge, a daredevil. His is given all the difficult jobs and he takes them. He descends into the air with no fear. He is a solitary.... Even in archive photographs it is difficult to find him. Again and again you see vista before you and the eye must search along the wall of sky to the speck of burned paper across the valley that is him, an exclamation mark, somewhere in the distance between bridge and river. He floats at the three hinges of the crescent-shaped steel arches. These knit the bridge together. The moment of cubism.[13]

We move from a register of objective reportage to a more collusive second-person account, one that conveys the experience of what it is like for 'you' to scan 'archive photographs' that seem to have absorbed their own subject, rendering him 'difficult to find'. Gradually contracting the length of those last four sentences, Ondaatje replicates on a phrasal level the action of the searching 'eye' as it zeroes-in on Nicholas at work. Allowing the subclause to drop away over the course of two descriptive sentences, before closing with a verbless declarative observation, Ondaatje correlates these shortening syntactical structures with the picture emerging of architectural structures. Increasingly condensed phrases thus harmonise with the image of geometrical convergence formed by the 'steel arches'. This sense of rhetorical truncation also equates with the implied viewer's action of homing-in to Nicholas's 'speck'. Suspended 'between bridge and river', he becomes the fugitive subject of a photo which itself seems happenstance, unplanned – a photo which, like a Cubist painting, has no self-evident vanishing point, only a 'knit' of focus set against the interaction of figure and ground, bridge and environment. Ondaatje's narration embodies rhetorically, then, characteristics of Cubism's principle of allowing contrasting elements to converge, a principle that's appreciable in that vertiginous, underside view of the bridge which reader and character finally share.

This passage encapsulates how Cubism can enter Ondaatje's practice formally and figuratively, at macro and micro levels – structuring the way whole scenes are framed while also inflecting individual phrases. The episode serves as a guide for reading how Cubism's aesthetic influence on Ondaatje's work is manifested in particular *processes* rather than through more explicit moments of ekphrasis or allusion that pay tribute to particular painters. Not that all of Ondaatje's influences are so oblique. One of these more direct allusions is indeed worth exploring for what it tells us about his commitment to setting new frontiers for form germane to the Cubists themselves. In the last sentence from the previous passage, he references a seminal essay from John Berger, whose art criticism Ondaatje found influential many years before he began fiction writing full-time. In that 1969 piece, Berger reminds us that it is 'impossible to *confront* the objects or forms in a Cubist work. Not only because of the multiplicity of viewpoints ... but also because the forms portrayed never present themselves as a totality. The totality is the surface of the picture, *which is now the origin and sum of all that one sees*'.[14] Berger seems to be gesturing towards the paradoxical state of engagement that Cubist paintings presuppose in the viewer. Internal dissonances between picture-planes nevertheless constitute a 'totality' of sorts, because that is 'all that one sees'; or to put it the other way around, as Léger did, '[f]rom now on', with the coming of Cubism, artists are showing how 'everything is brought together, in order to attain essential variety along with maximum realism'.[15] What this means for the audience is that a convergence of contrasting planes and interlocking facets occupies our frame of attention even though, reciprocally, the proliferating perspectives by which objects are depicted can distract us, fragmenting the viewing experience. Theorising these visual and compositional paradoxes for themselves, Salon Cubists like Robert Delauney, Jean Metzinger and Albert Gleizes would soon begin to demonstrate what, in 1913, Léger called 'an art of dynamic divisionism'.[16] Such ideas of variance and division – as Léger displayed in his own series executed from 1913–14, 'Contrasts of Form' – had constellated into the defining signature of modern painting, and that deliberate 'breaking up of forms', together with the artist's conscious 'break with time-honored habits', would provide 'a basis for a new pictorial harmony'.[17]

That one of Cubism's hallmark innovations was its 'break' with Renaissance conventions of single-point perspective is crucial for what Ondaatje has consistently tried to do structurally with narrative focalisation. Here we get to the gist of why he is continually 'drawn to a form that can have a more cubist or mural voice to capture the variousness of things', rather than the 'one demonic stare' akin to first-person narration.[18] What Henry James famously denounced as 'the terrible fluidity of self-revelation' that would have characterised *The Ambassadors* (1903) had he written it as Strether's monologue,[19] the first-person mode is for Ondaatje too 'a terrible oppression', and this compulsion to have a single character speak for every event encapsulates how, for him, novelists still 'tend to be so strict about narrative voice'.[20] Ondaatje's solution to that constriction would be to pluralise how a given scene's action is relayed: refracting it, rather than adopting one centre of consciousness. From the beginning, he wanted to evolve a narratological equivalent enriched by his having 'been allowed the migrant's double perspective' – a 'gift of displacement', as Caryl Phillips has called it, that we could again equate with the way James's own transnational thematics are played out in the shifting perspectives of his late work.[21] In what follows, I want to chart the implications of this multi-perspectivism in terms of the extent to which it enables alternative modes of seeing to carry out certain kinds of politico-ethical work, revealing Ondaatje to be doing more than aestheticising the act of observation. Cubist manipulations of perspective don't simply complicate the politics of point of view, but become his way of placing 'emphasis', as Marinkova puts it, 'on the materiality of language as an opaque experience rather than as a transparent vehicle'.[22] It also allows him to pose the ethical question as to whether this opacity which is the guise of the other – the very opacity that accompanies our experience of encountering rather than dominating otherness for what it is – ought ultimately to be sustained rather than explained.

In dramatising such encounters, Ondaatje's fiction often creates an atmosphere that's equivalent to what the political philosopher Jane Bennett has recently called a 'mood of enchantment or that strange combination of delight and disturbance'.[23] By using the multiperspectivism that is the hallmark of Cubist painting 'to capture the variousness of things',[24] to 'catch everything that's happening around me or around the story', Ondaatje produces, as we will see, fictional scenarios that substantiate Bennett's speculation that 'moments of sensuous enchantment with the everyday world – with nature but also with commodities and other cultural products – might augment the motivational energies needed to move selves from the endorsement of ethical principles to the actual practice of ethical behaviours'.[25] Entering that realm of everyday enchantment and its ethical ramifications, Ondaatje sees 'an opportunity' in 'getting lots of cross-references' from his characters' experiences – multiplying narrative perspectives accordingly.[26] In so doing, Ondaatje relinquishes the job of simply evoking the sensuous plenitude of perception, that trademark of literary impressionism; instead, he turns plenitude into a principle of relaying different moments of feeling at once, moments observed from proliferating angles. Being drawn to the way 'perceptions and ironies double and triple and quadruple', he thus aligns himself with one of impressionism's successors for whom analogies with Cubist art have loomed larger than any other twentieth-century writer: Gertrude Stein. For Ondaatje, the aesthetic rewards of having had a migrant's 'double perspective' identifies him with the way Stein herself 'was "re-focused" by Paris' just as he was by moving to Canada in his late teens.[27] Uniting life-changing events he experienced personally with his ambitions for how the novel might develop formally, this art of multiplying narrative foci became his chosen medium, a medium for 'getting everyone's point of view at the same time, which, for me, is the perfect state for a novel: a cubist state, the cubist novel'.[28]

What is at stake for Ondaatje in making this claim? What might it tell us in turn about Cubism's futurity in contemporary fiction? While these two interrelated questions will circulate throughout this chapter, to begin to answer them we should explore whether Ondaatje is consciously appropriating Cubism's creative, intellectual and philosophical aspirations, or else drawing our attention to looser affinities with the visual *effects* (rather than specific motivations) that make Cubist painting so iconic. What I'm going to suggest is that Ondaatje is doing both, not consistently, but always significantly, by taking forward the formal possibilities that Cubism opened up, in order to refract the ethical implications of that 'combination of delight and disturbance' with which he frames his characters' experiences of displacement.

Though Ondaatje isn't trying to replicate in words what individual artists were achieving on canvas, one concern of his is particularly recognisable as belonging to the 'synthetic' brand of the movement, promoted by Picasso and Braque. In tune with their collagist approach to assimilating contrary colours, Ondaatje has, across his fiction, ventured to accumulate disparate elements through the numerous and often incompatible perceptions of his characters, thereby assembling episodes that have their own structural and semantic coherence, even as they are filtered through different mindsets. 'I didn't want the reader to feel locked into one character', he recalled, shortly after *The English Patient* appeared in 1992: 'I prefer a complicated history where an event is seen through many eyes or emotions, and the writer doesn't try to control the viewpoint'.[29] In spotlighting how this impulse can be traced back to Cubism, I don't mean to suggest that Cubism is the sole source from which all multiperspectivism flows. Woolf's nimble movement between observers and voices in *To the Lighthouse* (1927) and *The Waves* (1931) shows the principle of varied focalisation was very much part of the way impressionist fiction rendered the profusion and multiplicity of urban experience. My point, however, is that Ondaatje's idea about the novel's 'cubist state' corresponds in substantive ways with principles debated by such founding figures as Gleizes, Metzinger and Léger himself. Their commentaries allow us not simply to verify the nature and depth of Cubism's legacies for contemporary fiction, but to be more specific about reading their technical ambitions through Ondaatje's own – enabling us also to take the next analytic step of asking what the efficacy of those ambitions might be.

COLLAGE AS CRAFT AND CRITICISM

It should be clear by now that our interest in attaching a Cubist heritage to Ondaatje's work is unlikely to be sustained simply by matching words with pictures, but rather by focusing instead on his capacity to extract the essence of what Berger called the Cubist *moment* – a moment that marked a climate in which, as Léger reported, formal 'contrasts used in their purest sense' became 'the structural basis of modern pictures'.[30] It is this chapter's objective, in tune with my argument running across this book, not only to note the occurrences but to analyse the consequences of compatibilities between modernist methods and contemporary fictional strategies, in order to consider *why* the former are being reimagined by the latter in facilitating particular ethical or political interventions.

In addressing this question, we might draw useful methodological lessons from the very notions of contrast and juxtaposition that were the premise of so much Cubist art. The approach I have in mind resembles one of the transnational critical strategies recently endorsed by Susan Stanford Friedman, based on 'collage'. Within this framework, the critic 'makes an archive of radical juxtaposition, through the paratactic cutting and pasting of narratives that are not typically read together'.[31] Ondaatje's response to Cubism at the level of form, and his use in turn of Cubist perspectivism to refract his dramatic content, drawing our attention to the demands he places on his characters' perceptual judgments, appeals directly to this kind of 'juxtapositional comparative methodology', as Friedman outlines it, one that 'negotiates between sameness and difference by setting up a relational structure in which neither is privileged over the other'.[32] In understanding Ondaatje's sensibility as novelist by juxtaposing his work with the structural ambitions of Cubism, we need to bear in mind that he has never been interested in simply mimicking techniques pioneered in modernist painting. As we have already heard, his emphasis lies on beginning afresh, still discovering in his later career that '[i]t's exciting to start anew', if at the same time 'terrifying: you're in a new land, with new language, new rules'.[33] Yet it's precisely his ability to find new opportunities through inherited means that points to a more valuable account of influence and innovation, such as the one that this book attempts to provide as a whole: an account, in Ondaatje's context, that can delineate his kinship with Cubism's creative processes rather than with its finished products; one that takes seriously his claim that writers 'are interested in' the 'architecture' and 'undercurrents of shape and tone as opposed to just meaning';[34] one that takes equally seriously his concern that a novel in both register and organisation should '*reflect* as fully as possible how we think and imagine';[35] an account, finally, that is willing to pursue the hypothesis that if Ondaatje is 'not really interested in inventing a form', he might be out to revive one.[36]

In sum, by offering a collage reading of Ondaatje that juxtaposes him with this particular moment in modernism's art-historical archive, we need at least to reflect on the goal – even if we don't abandon it – of creating analogies across time as they occur between painterly and fictional innovations. There is no doubt we can hear in the kind of sentiments voiced by Léger in 1914 that '[c]omposition takes precedence over all else' a trace of Ondaatje's own sense that being inventive 'all comes down to nuts and bolts and tone'.[37] Audible though such affinities in artistic purpose seem, what's important about them, critically speaking, is that they lead us on a path from the materiality of the work itself back to the moment of its making, from end results back to creative procedures. Along the way, we can move from the text alone to what its workmanship can tell us about the anterior instincts that shape it. Those instincts, in Ondaatje's case, reveal that same paradox, or seeming paradox, that we first encountered in Chapter 1. Just as we posed it to Roth and Kundera in order to discover their original uses of tradition, so too we need to ask the question of Ondaatje: why should a novelist working under the personal decree '[t]o take the writing further than you have before' look ahead at what he has yet to achieve by utilising a phase from modernism's past?[38]

In responding to this question, I want to distinguish Ondaatje's rapport with Cubism's structural aspirations – as well as the impact it makes on the putative viewer – from the more contradictory relation of his *compositional* aims to those Cubist working methods he admires. This distinction is neatly summed up by a productive tension in his procedures, a tension that sees him oscillating between design and chance. It would appear that Ondaatje has assumed the guise of a conscious artist who often reverts to shooting in the dark. Although his care in 'repeating and building images and so making them more potent' is self-evident,[39] as is the meticulousness it takes to 'get one image from a small gesture and ... build a whole book from that',[40] Ondaatje is equally open about the disorganised, happenstance nature of the whole activity. If 'at first I write in a kind of loose, random, sort of accidental way',[41] then even as the plot develops his planning doesn't increase. On the contrary, making plans 'beforehand would bore the hell out of me', such that crucial 'things are discovered in the actual writing' and its overall 'structure happens as the story unravels, with each discovery, at each plateau'.[42] What we have, then, is a writer who professes not to be 'concerned with art or aesthetic issues'[43] – at least while he's *consumed in* the act of writing – yet who at the same time, '[w]ith each book', is purposefully 'try[ing] to do something I think I can't do',[44] posing technical questions to himself about whether 'this is the right shape' or 'the right pacing'.[45] It would be wrong to regard these contrary habits as the mark of discrepancies between Ondaatje's aims; nor should all his talk of the chanciness with which 'small' narrative components 'are knitted together' lead us to view his commitments as anything less than experimental – even if his decision, 'with all books', to 'begin them tentatively' belies a cautiousness that sounds unbecoming for any would-be innovator.[46] His attitude towards the importance of *balancing* spontaneity and technique is instead firmer than his self-assigned image of creative randomness implies. A writer, he asserts, 'has to be on the border where ... craft meets the accidental and the unconscious'.[47] More than a decade before beginning his mature fiction-writing phase, Ondaatje corrects the view that authorial self-discipline is antagonistic to the procedures of unforeseen discovery – combining as he does the value of both, cultivating that 'rare ... artistic moment' when 'everything kind of coalesces'.[48]

What these two ways of working reveal is ultimately more significant than the insider's view they afford of Ondaatje's (un)conscious artistry.

It was that same negotiation between intuition and design that threaded throughout the Cubists' own early writings. Confronted with the challenge of integrating the inspired and the planned, they sought to tell the difference between two manifestations of the new. On the one hand, newness could be something that has, so to speak, *already arrived* – something endemic to culture, wrought by the experience of modernity itself for which art is obliged to find ever more original forms of expression. On the other hand, however, newness could assume the guise of what Eliot famously called the 'supervention of novelty'. As we saw in Chapter 1, the legacy of Eliot's model is a three-tiered understanding of originality, whereby newness can only be *arrived at* against the backdrop of 'existing monuments', where 'the introduction of the new' itself is facilitated only with 'great labour', and where, finally, the artist must develop an acute 'historical sense' of tradition.[49] These separate conceptions of how originality is consciously brought about informed some of the earliest discussions about whether or not Cubism should possess a set of predetermined aims. While in 1912 Gleizes and Metzinger, for instance, saw that the new will 'to compose, to construct, to design, reduces itself' to a purely intuitive task of 'determin[ing] by our own activity the dynamism of form',[50] four years earlier, Henri Le Fauconnier foresaw a rather different path ahead by anticipating the progressively mathematical character of Cubist art after the Great War. In contrast to letting the spontaneous potentialities of form guide the way, Le Fauconnier observed that '[a]t the present, our pictorial research is leading us to an aesthetics that is less changeable, more stable, and more theoretical, seeking to find synthetic expression through cerebral concepts based on argument and a preordained, rigorously espoused logic'.[51] These are the priorities, branching into what Apollinaire would categorise as the opposite poles of *Scientific* and *Instinctive* Cubism,[52] which bear comparison with Ondaatje's way of integrating discipline and intuition, the calculated and the processual.

Combining these seemingly antithetical doctrines of creativity, Ondaatje can be seen to undertake consciously localised work – refining the sonority of individual phrases, asking himself 'how a scene works: should I cut it back?'[53] – while satisfying a different impulse altogether, the impulse, as his memoir *Running in the Family* describes it, to '[w]atch the hand move. Waiting for it to say something, to stumble casually on perception, the shape of an unknown thing'.[54] Given this way of working, we might justifiably place Ondaatje somewhere between two of Apollinaire's less programmatic subspecies: where the 'Instinctual' artist meets 'Orphism'. By coining this particular phase after the Greek poet Orpheus, Apollinaire allied it with a lyric rather than narrative or depictive impetus. This would seem aptly consistent with Ondaatje's own path towards fiction, having first established himself as a poet, and it's not surprising that he has lent many of his novels' focalising characters the intensity of a lyric speaker. Often 'each scene' is compositely conceived, being 'pieced together with little bits of mosaic', as Ondaatje remembered it from writing *The English Patient* (1992), yet also 'written from the point of view of that private, poetic voice – not so much in terms of language but in how one sees things'.[55] Here, as Gleizes himself might have noted, '[b]asic principles take up all the artist's attention', as they 'take on an importance in the external appearance of the work going beyond the essential but *internal* role which they must place in what will finally be achieved'.[56] Gleizes's relevance for Ondaatje is not simply coincidental, pointing as it does to their common emphasis on the visibility or tangibility of a work's construction and the aesthetic integrity thereby attained, as that work's 'finally ... achieved' outward shape makes no attempt to disguise the internal procedures from which it is formed.

If such Cubist affinities run deep for Ondaatje in the compositional stages of his work, they also play a dramatic part in a preoccupation that recurs throughout his *oeuvre*, despite its different contexts: his attraction to forms of labour that unite creativity and professional expertise, spontaneity and learned technique. We might remember the Sikh sapper in *The English Patient*, whose 'craft' would be to 'create a space around himself and concentrate';[57] the 'obsessive tunneling toward discovery' that drives forensic archaeologists against the Sri Lankan backdrop of atrocity in *Anil's Ghost* (2000);[58] or the 'visionary craftsmanship' of a belfry in *Divisadero* (2007), whose spirals the central observer Anna compares to 'a villanelle', since its 'form refuses to move forward in linear development, circling instead at those familiar moments of emotion'.[59] We could simply take such moments as evidence of Ondaatje's 'aestheticization of work', as Louis Menand has called it.[60] But this tendency to dramatise craftsmanship for its own sake might be better understood in light of Ondaatje's conviction that '[f]iction tends to be staid in the way it tells a story', that novelists have been 'handcuffed to realism' in a way that painters at least since impressionism's revolution in colour-form have not, and that as a writer faced with the limitations of narrative he has become 'interested in forms of art which have a different structure'.[61] This is not to apologise for Ondaatje's romanticised depictions of the skill of perilous professions, where the elegance of hands-on work (and the rhetorical grace of its focalisation) tends to finesse the dangers involved. It is to suggest instead that his concern with testing the formal limits of fiction is indissolubly linked to his concern with the ethical dimensions of moments of everyday enchantment that accompany observations of skill. As Robert J. C. Young has pointed out, 'things that are learnt rather than mere gifts ... fascinate Ondaatje, and he clearly identifies such skills with the exact observations of the writer who, as if by magic, conjures an unknown scene or peoples imaginatively before our eyes with such precision'.[62] That capacity to conjure unknown places or selves is enabled, as this chapter argues, by his re-conjuring of Cubist perspectivism in order to see the material world aslant. Through this combination of narrative indirection and optical dispersion, Ondaatje realises the idea, as critics have noted, that 'it is only in oblique moments of revelation' that we may 'glimpse the implicit connections of things'.[63]

Apollinaire's portrait, then, of the Orphic artist who 'must offer simultaneously pure aesthetic pleasure, a clearly perceptible construction, and a meaning, the subject, which is sublime',[64] corresponds not only with the 'pleasure' Ondaatje finds 'in the physical beauty of a book'.[65] What's also rendered 'perceptible' is the link between design and diegesis, between authorial choices and skilled protagonists, when 'a difficult and recondite occupation' around which events are often plotted matches the ethical commitments underpinning Ondaatje's own 'art of writing'.[66] We will return to the implications of this correlation of the aesthetic and the artisanal later, with its implied 'celebration of humble labour over arrogant capital'.[67] For now, however, the important thing to recognise is the way Ondaatje's affiliations with Cubist tendencies ramify on formal *and* politico-ethical levels, such that we can identify them narratologically but also within the world of his texts, incorporated in the careful arrangement of scenes 'taken not from reality as it is seen', in Apollinaire's phrase, 'but as it is suggested to the artist by instinct and intuition'.[68]

Arrangement and instinct: whatever else they do in Ondaatje's prose, it is the paradoxical integration of these imperatives that sees him extending Cubism's investment in the equally paradoxical synthesis of figuration and abstraction, plasticity and rhythm, through an approach to organising contrasting motifs. Ondaatje's alertness to the palpability of contrasts in his narration is commensurate with the Cubists' priority, as Léger saw it in 1913, to exploit the tactility of differing 'Lines, Forms, and Colours'.[69] As Ondaatje has asserted: 'Plot comes out of language as much as it comes out of the described event'.[70] So much of his plots are indeed borne out by the innovative *way* scenes are perceived, regardless of what physically takes place. As we will see elsewhere in his more recent fiction, where readers are often drawn to 'engage in a reciprocated act of affectionate witnessing',[71] Ondaatje's assertion holds true: that it's often the alternations in the perception of an event that are more ethically arresting than the action 'described' therein.

AN UNFINISHED MOMENT?

Ondaatje, as we have noted, found John Berger's art criticism influential well before his 'turn' from poetry to fiction. In turn, Berger himself has developed a friendship with Ondaatje through their shared sense of what the modernist novel, more than visual art, can do. Echoing Jonathan Franzen's notion with which this book began – that 'the novel is the greatest art form when it comes to forging a connection between the intensely interior' life of the individual 'and the larger social reality' – Berger has recently recalled that after studying art history he was drawn 'to the novel form because I was attracted to the mystery of a person's subjectivity and behaviour, their destinies and choices. The things that can't be schematised. The challenge is to try not just to explain the mystery, but to ensure the mystery is shared and doesn't remain isolated'.[72] Cubist multi-perspectivism provides Ondaatje with a means of avoiding 'isolated' or ideologically confined depictions of selfhood, while also ensuring that other viewpoints share and distribute the perception of behaviours, actions and their ethical consequences.

As I will continue to suggest throughout this book, however, for kinships of this kind it's often critically appropriate to grasp counterpoints as well as compatibilities. One such point of contention arises in a reminder Berger offers in that essay to which *In the Skin of a Lion* alludes: 'To the Cubists, Cubism was spontaneous. To us it is part of history. But a curiously unfinished part'.[73] While Berger, in tune with the broader argument of this study, is certainly keen to widen the ambit of modernism's postwar afterlife, his remark about Cubists' supposed spontaneity seems odd. It implies they revealed a certain naivety towards why they should continue to achieve the advances they were making. His assertion sounds especially odd, that is, when we remember how purposively Gleizes and Léger spoke about why they were doing what they were doing – how adamant they sounded about innovation as something to be worked out rather than conjured impromptu. As Metzinger had noted after Cubism's early 'Analytic' stage, his peers had already showed an 'exemplary discipline' that was hardly *sui generis*. Quick to caution those who assumed their movement was founded on aesthetic rebellion, in 1911 he asked in the

Paris-Journal: 'How could they break with tradition, an uninterrupted sequence of innovations in itself, those who, through their innovations, actually perpetuate it?'[74] In light of Berger's remark, however, Metzinger's correction is as interesting for the tone it assumes as for the appraisal it offers of Cubism's capacity for conserving its heritage. In other words, Metzinger emblematises precisely the kind of self-conscious tenacity that characterised Salon Cubists' engagement with their own signal aims, whether celebrating possibilities or acknowledging restrictions. All of which seems a far cry indeed from that romantic aura of inspiration implied by the view of Cubism as a purely 'spontaneous' movement.

Léger, for one, would concur. Nowhere more candidly than in his early writings does he exemplify that degree of persistent intellectual debate that such questions of originality and traditionalism required. So much so, in fact, that he courts self-contradiction when attempting conceptual self-qualification. While declaring in 1913 that '[a]ll great movements in painting, whatever their direction, have always proceeded by revolution, by reaction, and not by evolution', a page later he cuts across this model of newness-as-departure by noting 'that the modern concept is not a reaction against the impressionists' ideas but is, on the contrary, a further development and expansion of their aims through the use of methods they have neglected'.[75] Shifting from that language of rupture, soon to become such a familiar clarion call for high-modernist esteem, to a proposal for the progressive 'development' of impressionism's lessons, Léger sheds light on what I take to be Berger's urge to trace Cubism's possible futures. Although he is the subject of Berger's analysis, it is Léger, in fact, who speaks forward in time to Berger. And it's Léger's sense of the dialectical (and developmental) relation of 'the modern concept' to the past that offers us, in turn, a rationale for asking why these two figures at opposite ends of the twentieth century are important for framing Ondaatje's modernist aesthetics.

To swap the direction of commentary, that is, by reading Berger through Léger, is to discover how compatible their respective prophesies are for what Cubism has yet to do. What is 'unfinished' about Cubism – or rather, what has enabled it to resist any subsequent artistic movement with pretensions to finishing it off – is its capacity (as Léger predicted) to expand on the techniques it inherits while intimating (as Berger himself does) how that process of expansion initiates new enterprises in form. Certainly this is one corollary of Berger's praise for how Léger capitalises on what the 'very concept of the avant-garde suggests': showcasing 'the art of tomorrow as opposed to the conservative tastes of today'.[76] If that praise is levelled in an individuating way, setting Léger apart as a 'painter of the future', it resonates on an epochal scale too.[77] What Berger was also doing in this series of essays through the 1950s and 1960s was encouraging his readers – Ondaatje, the emerging poet, among them – to look back at Cubism as an *event* that brought together the inherited and the new; an event that recuperated what impressionism had neglected but not completed, precisely in order to forecast emergent procedures; an event that we can only fully grasp retrospectively, therefore, by understanding how it was 'defining desires which are still unmet'.[78]

Meeting those desires has meant questioning the very adequacy of the novel form; at least, this is the impression Ondaatje gives us. He does so by holding to two related convictions. Firstly, his feeling is that modernist poets achieved what 'most novels have not yet picked up on', and he isolates Pound and Niedecker as examples of how 'the scope, the simultaneity, the sharpness of language' all evince the kind of 'exploration', as Ondaatje terms it, which 'still hasn't reached the novel'.[79] His second type of interrogation reveals the way fiction itself defines equivalent desires, in Ondaatje's view, to those 'which are still unmet' after Cubism. This stems from his belief that '[t]here is such a variety of form and devices in the other arts'.[80] Belief shades into envy here; and his underlying frustration with the novel is audible enough. What is equally notable, though, is his attraction not simply to the 'variety' of innovations that painters have pioneered, but also to *how* such advancements are classified:

Technically, what's happening in the other arts is much wilder than in the novel. If something unusual happens in a novel, it still gets labelled experimental. Somehow the novel demands a comfort level of realism that is quite high. The equivalent of Cubism ... still hasn't been allowed into the novel except on the periphery – whereas we accept it, even complacently, in the other popular art forms.[81]

While Ondaatje isn't shying away from being pigeon-holed as an experimentalist, he *does* imply that this vague category is as inadequate for particularising what inventiveness involves from a writer's compositional point of view, as it is for distinguishing between one virtuosic novel and another from a critic's evaluative point of view. More explicitly, he suggests that fiction has been foiled by its own status quo, where novelists feel obliged to achieve 'a comfort level of realism' – to some extent, because readers expect them to – a comfort-zone that delays the novel's reach for 'wilder' horizons.

Ondaatje's forecast is ultimately not as bleak as his picture suggests here of the supremacy of visual art and the marginalisation of innovative writing. To his mind, while fiction has been waylaid in comparison to other twentieth-century aesthetic formations, it's the novel, nevertheless, which 'is more advanced in terms of possibility'.[82] As we have heard, his claim to that sense of potentiality is far from systematic, moving as he does from creative serendipity in the early stages on to a more deliberate process of redrafting and self-editing. It is, however, precisely his alternation between the spontaneous and conscious artist that typifies what has become an appropriately flexible way of looking for the novel's states of 'possibility' – Cubism providing one such recuperative state, and in his words a particularly 'perfect' one at that.

If Ondaatje's attitudes to composition may often seem polarised, little of that reaches his published work. Discrepancies of this kind confronted 'many cubist writers' of high modernism, as Wendy Steiner has noted, to the extent that they 'were rather ambivalent about whether theirs was a perceptual or a conceptual art'. Indeed, it's 'not so much the side a writer chooses that makes him a cubist, as the fact that he sees this opposition *as* a choice, as an issue for him to confront in his stylistic experimentation'.[83] The choice Ondaatje makes, again, is to leave the designed and unwilled aspects of his creative vision profitably unresolved. As proof of that profit, it can be hard for us to detect his contrary ways of *making* in his published texts, their crystalline prose readily smoothing any ripple of authorial uncertainty. Prose with such finish, however, is also prone to occasional sumptuousness; and 'Ondaatje's metaphor-laden aesthetic', as Stephen Henigan calls it,[84] has predictably been made the object of some criticism. Perceived to be in danger of acquiring a signature style that's all too uniquely his, 'Ondaatje's voice', in Gail Caldwell's estimation, with its 'prismatic perspective on time and memory', has become 'so particular and distinctive that you can spot it at 20 yards'.[85] Unmistakable though Ondaatje's timbre may be nowadays, George Bowering's 'praise' is at best ill-pitched, at worst sarcastic, when he couches it in the claim 'that there is a genre called the Ondaatje'.[86] On closer inspection, Ondaatje's elegiac register appears not so easily reducible to type. This is because, for each novel, he has favoured a discursive mode whose obliquity often resists critical attempts to decipher intentions (or tensions) in his craft, either by speculating on the stylistic self-indulgence that Henigan hints at, or by recourse to events where Ondaatje's characters yield their own 'prismatic' perspectives, emulating their creator's Cubistic concern with diversified viewpoints.

Certainly, there are times in Ondaatje's plots when, for the critic, the most natural, if not inevitable, thing to do is spotlight aesthetically concentrated moments and connect them by analogy to writerly acts of deliberate or unintentional will. We should be mindful, though, of the limits of doing so. In practice, what this caution means is that even when Lucien Segura – the writer in *Divisadero* whose biography consumes much of Anna's time because his familial separations mirror her own, and much of the novel's final third as she 'piece[s] together the landscapes he had written about' (*D*, p. 144) – declares that 'I love the performance of a craft, whether it is modest or mean-spirited, yet I walk away when discussions of it begin' (*D*, p. 192), it would be all too convenient for us to detect here the ventriloquised sentiments of Ondaatje himself. If he's tempting us to do so, however, why *not* allegorise such resonant instances? He strongly invites us to pursue such readings: as someone who seems reticent about pinning down his methods under interview, Ondaatje's privacy about work-in-progress complements Segura's belief that 'any trade or talent could be shaped discreetly without the sparks of exaggerated drama' (*D*, p. 193). Furthermore, Ondaatje would probably agree with his novelist-protagonist that the 'skill of writing offers little to a viewer' (*D*, p. 193). His attraction, likewise, to the 'magpie work' of making 'small discoveries' and 'circl[ing] around them' to 'piece them together in some kind of mural' is echoed in the way Segura finds technique interesting only in terms of 'the care taken, and those secret rehearsals behind it' (*D*, p. 192).[87] Although Ondaatje offers us all these opportunities to strike analogies between character and creator, between dramatic events and their underlying design, he is also instructing us to do otherwise.

This instruction may be as paradoxical as any. Which is to say that the challenge of reading Ondaatje's fiction *closely* requires us to gain a critical *distance* on what remains a most distinctive, some would say patent, style. Knowing when to stand back and contemplate the ethical import of our own findings would thus be an apt approach for tracing tradition in a writer whose modernist inheritance is frequently subsumed in the lushness of his own narration. More specifically for our present concerns, such an approach might also help us to distinguish what Cubism means to Ondaatje – as a conscious practice, for him, and as a series of critical analogies between art and fiction, for us – from the way he foregrounds artisan characters in episodes of specialised work. Such episodes, as we have seen, are those involving *Divisadero*'s Lucien or *In the Skin of a Lion*'s 'daredevil' Nicholas, and they connect Ondaatje with that broader tendency, recently identified by Mark McGurl, for postwar writers to respond to modernism in a hall of mirrors: writing novels that could actively dramatise the 'value of painstaking craft' upheld by their author.[88] We can observe Ondaatje working occasionally in this fashion, as I've mentioned, as he uses protagonists' occupations to cipher the very technical commitments his writing sustains. I want to suggest, however, that we pursue the less convenient route-in to reading his modernist lineage, one that can navigate between, on the one hand, what Ondaatje says about his art and, on the other, what we can *make* his narratives say (allegorically or metafictionally) about how his art is put to use. As we'll see in the following examples, Ondaatje elicits from both his characters and his readers 'that strange combination of delight and disturbance', to recall Bennett, a combination that's derived from instances of enchantment with apparently mundane, everyday things, yet that mobilises the 'endorsement of ethical principles' into an 'actual practice of ethical behviours'. Facilitating this drama of responsible enchantment via his formal ambitions, Ondaatje signals an engagement with the ethics of innovation that we shall see again when turning to Toni Morrison in the closing chapter. For now, though, in Ondaatje's case, it also highlights the ethos of integration that corresponds with one of the basic imperatives of synthetic Cubism: the 'simultaneous ordering' of 'components' that was so crucial to the case Léger and others made for achieving a sense of 'pictorial harmony' from, and through, perspectival diversity.[89] It is an imperative that Ondaatje fulfils more rigorously – and with greater ethical purpose – than we might think, given the picture he so often paints of his chancy, 'magpie' way of working.

CLAUSAL CUBISM

How pervasive that integration can be in Ondaatje's fiction is something we have already seen in *In the Skin of a Lion*, where the procedures of Cubist art are literalised in the viaduct just as they govern the composite perspectives that refract that very setting. Where formal and scenic elements compete like this for our attention, questions arise to do with the *scale* on which we read.[90] In a sense, Cubism features in Ondaatje's writing not only in the larger, structural ways we would expect (such as his manner of segmenting chapters into short sections, often with typographic breaks between single paragraphs that represent no caesural gaps in narrative time), but also at the level of individual sentences, where he replicates the effect of Léger's 'dynamic divisionism' in syntactical organisation. Clausal progressions can themselves reproduce what Cubism *does* and how it thereby affects the viewer or reader.

Nowhere are these compound phrases more delicately employed by Ondaatje than in those episodes framed by characters' intensive reflections.

Like her books that shape those periods spent as a nurse at the burnt officer's bedside, Hana's own attention throughout *The English Patient* has 'gaps of plot like sections of a road washed out by storms, missing incidents as if locusts had consumed a section of tapestry, as if plaster loosened by the bombing had fallen away from a mural at night' (*EP*, p. 7). Those 'gaps' are repaired in the course of their unfolding, insofar as Hana's interior thought patterns are all the more credibly evoked when phases of distraction punctuate their textual representation, culminating in the realisation that '[h]er inwardness was a sadness of nature' (*EP*, p. 272). With its analogy of broken 'plaster', the scene speaks directly to Ondaatje's attraction, as we've heard, to a 'form that can have a more cubist or mural voice to capture the variousness of things'. Yet the coincidence of these mural motifs is less important than the transposition of artistic media they both imply, a transposition in which he puts a pictorial structure to rhetorical use. Finding it so useful in *The English Patient*, in fact, Ondaatje extends through that essentially oxymoronic phenomenon (the 'mural voice') the iconic modernist plight – one that will become the focal point of my discussion of McEwan in Chapter 4 – to evoke the interplay of feeling and understanding, sensation and intellection. By expressing the 'variousness of things' in a voice whose composite nature echoes the Cubist ideal of simultaneity, Ondaatje thus carries forward a task equivalent to the one famously undertaken by Woolf in her own free indirect style – relating the sensible to the intelligible in order to grasp a 'sense of personality vibrating with perceptions'.[91]

Cubism thus informs the fibre of Ondaatje's syntax, including, we might say, the very *aims* of that syntax – to encode and express, in the case of *The English Patient*, the patterns of Hana's introspection. As he reintegrates Cubist principles at this particular syntactic level, however, we might also argue that Ondaatje is doing nothing so radically different from other contemporary writers who are extending a more general modernist aim: 'to present', as Ian McEwan puts it, 'obviously in a very stylized way, what it's like to be thinking'.[92] What makes this trademark concern with mentation distinctive for Ondaatje, though, is the way he has *required* Cubism in order to fulfil it. 'Stylized' it may be; yet it has remained fundamental even to those novels that don't use Cubist principles, in the way *In the Skin of a Lion* does, as explicit points of literal or motivic reference. Indeed, where McEwan would seek 'to present' thoughts in motion but without necessarily making the modality of presentation explicit, Ondaatje's prose is deliberately less transparent, incorporating Cubism's characteristics from the figurative turn of phrase to a page's typographical segmentation. A more accurate term for describing this embodiment of thought processes in the very materiality of the text (instead of rendering mental reflections as transparently and mimetically as possible) is coined by *The English Patient* itself. 'The word should be *thinkering*', ponders Caravaggio, as his 'mind slips into this consideration, another syllable to suggest collecting a thought as one tinkers with a half-completed bicycle. Words are tricky things' (*EP*, p. 37). In a brief, capsule moment of pause in the action, we're provided with a keyword for Ondaatje's practice as a whole. 'Thinkering' stands as a synecdoche for a process of accretion that is familiar to synthetic Cubism; yet it's also a fitting adjective for the gathering of 'half-completed' collections that comprise the piecemeal movement of Ondaatje's plots.

While we can certainly speak of this graduated sense of progression on a plot level, it would, as we've seen, neglect the precision of Ondaatje's language were we to speak of motion or structure purely with respect to events. In more intricate ways, the accretive motion implied by 'thinkering' affects Ondaatje's more localised decisions about syntactical arrangement and diction. In *The English Patient*, Ondaatje often gives Hana pause, taking her retrospection away and beyond the Villa San Girolamo, beyond Florence even, to return us to the Toronto childhood first sketched in In *The Skin of a Lion* by her adopted father, Patrick. While the patient undetected as Count Ladislaus de Almásy remains the derelict home's most static presence, exerting his gravity nonetheless, Hana ranges widely across the emotional geography of her past. A modest request, rarely granted, motionless peace generates predictably if paradoxically her most active recollections:

She finds rest as opposed to sleep the truly pleasurable state. If she were a writer she would collect her pencils and notebooks and favourite cat and write in bed. Strangers and lovers would never get past the locked door.

To rest was to receive all aspects of the world without judgement. A bath in the sea, a fuck with a soldier who never knew your name. Tenderness towards the unknown and anonymous, which was a tenderness to the self.

Her legs move under the burden of military blankets. She swims in their wool as the English patient moved in his cloth placenta.

What she misses here is slow twilight, the sound of familiar trees. All through her youth in Toronto she learned to read the summer night. It was where she could be herself, lying in a bed, stepping onto a fire escape half asleep with a cat in her arms. (*EP*, pp. 48–9)

Beginning in the subjunctive mood, Hana sees in the idealisation of writing a profession that counterpoints her own. Ritualising the simple technology of the work, lingering on the anticipation of seclusion that 'collect[ing] pencils and notebooks' would ignite, she imagines a form of domestic and intellectual liberation from her current routine consumed by the ethical act of care. But the episode's very typography and articulation enact something more of their own accord: performing the Cubist activity of framing contrasting tonalities, while reminding us, through the scene's stillness, of the way 'the freeze-frame of Cubism', as Ian Davidson calls it, can 'simultaneously represent despair at a lack of unity and coherence, while suggesting that coherence might result from a process of rearrangement, as well as demonstrate the increasingly individualized nature of experience'.[93] Segmented into four short paragraphs, each quadrant of the passage develops its own distinctive register, each standing for a different sensation. From the hypothetical tenor of that opening vision, we shift to a declarative catalogue of the benefits of 'rest'. Here the second paragraph's depersonalisation (accentuated by the modulation into the second-person 'your name') has the effect of turning Hana's most intimate experiences (swimming, lovemaking) into the basis of an epigrammatic statement of fact: that the best kinds of 'tenderness' are also the most 'anonymous'. With its impersonality, then, this verbless final sentence encodes discursively the very sentiment 'towards the unknown' that it endorses. In direct contrast to this verbal and sentimental anonymity, the third paragraph interjects with present scenic details about Hana's current state. To compound this perspectival variation again, Ondaatje devotes the final paragraph to a kind of summative memory, a memory that encapsulates all the different facets of 'rest' that the episode explores through writing, bathing, lusting and here, finally, reading. Again the rhetorical texture of what is recalled mirrors the sensation of the situation being described. A trace of those rustling 'trees', for instance, is phonetically replicated in the sibilance that resounds throughout the first sentence, beginning, no less, with the verb that denotes the paragraph's sentiment as a whole: 'misses'. Likewise, the assonantal relation of 'slow' to 'sound' decelerates the parataxis in keeping with the subsiding 'twilight' that Hana wishes to savour. Where the episode thus began in a speculation about living the life of a writer, it ends with Hana finding solace in something more substantial: in a memory whose *genius loci* is made as tangible to us as it is to her mind's eye, by virtue of the way Ondaatje's narration not only rhythmically, lexically and tonally simulates the ambience of that evening scene but also, in doing so, conveys to us something of *why* that scene 'was where she could be herself'.

Ondaatje's Cubist imagination

All this may certainly confirm Ondaatje's sense of *The English Patient* as a novel that 'primarily concerns *situation*, as opposed to theme'.[94] The way he refracts that situation, however, tells us something more. For while his use of focalisation may be fragmentary, shifting provenance from one statement to the next, each contrasting focus has a fractal relationship to the scene as a whole. What Grail Jones says of *In the Skin of a Lion* could equally apply to the scene we've just read: 'Although the trajectory of the text is apparently redemptive – cast as retrospective, from the space of freedom – the epistemological ambiguity of narration is crucial to its fractured telling'.[95] Indeed, despite the strikingly different idioms that Ondaatje assumes – from a depersonalised assertion about 'tenderness' to Hana's deeply personal memories of home – their differences reveal the way he is drawn instinctively to evoke a 'situation' in multiple facets, no slave to descriptive consistency. One result of this contrastive faceting is the proliferation of perspectives that shuttle the reader along from one paragraph to the next. On a second reading – and if we 'rescale' our attention from isolated clauses to detect unities within the episode as a whole – we can begin to see how these viewpoints, disparate though they may seem, do in fact coalesce within, and contribute to, the emotional arena of Hana's inner thoughts, an arena that seems so obliquely addressed as to appear almost inaccessible to the reader. Here the ethical dimension of the scene comes to light, as we get an insight into the extent to which Ondaatje preserves the intractable otherness of the individual who remains, at the same time, the novel's sympathetic centre. The Cubist multi-perspectivism of this sequence thus allows Ondaatje to elicit pathos and solicit sympathy by showing how 'history leaves traces on bodies' at the most personal level, and yet also 'to exemplify both irreducible *presence* and the opacity' of human character itself.[96]

As an analogy for *The English Patient*'s synthesis of perspectival intensity and characterological opacity, Gleizes's analysis of picture-planes premised on the 'harmonious coming together of the measures and the cadences in their infinite combinations' offers a suggestive way of accounting for the composite construction of that scene we witnessed previously.[97] Gleizes was speaking here about the 'organic' role of *rhythm*,[98] a role that we would expect Ondaatje to have mastered more than most, as a writer bringing to the novel a poet's attention to phrasal momentum and metrical stress. Searching for 'beauty ... in the rhythm', though, is a quest not without moral or political consequences,[99] especially when it's the case that exquisitely paced events in Ondaatje's fiction often turn out to be the most ethically propelled.

CONFLICT-ZONE CUBISM: COMPASSIONATE IMPERSONALITY

How well Ondaatje has squared that highly poetic sense of design with the traumatic circumstances he depicts has provided another occasion for critics to disagree over his style – and the pitfalls his style faces in aestheticising violence. No novel has exacerbated these divided opinions more than his first of the new millennium: *Anil's Ghost*. In *In the Skin of a Lion*, we see Patrick as serving Ondaatje's portrait of the modernist émigré consumed with impressions of new material and psychic territory, when in fact he brings to the narrative a less romantically mobile story of an immigrant undertaking manual work for his host nation's development. Likewise, in *Anil's Ghost*, Anil Tissera enters as the emigrated perfectionist returning 'home' to Sri Lanka after her initial training in the UK, followed by time spent in North and Central America. Rather than replanting her professional esteem in native soil, Anil finds herself in a sectarian war zone. A specialist in human rights violations, she undertakes forensic work overseen by a government-appointed archaeologist, Sarath Diyasena. Initially restricting, emotionally cold, he later becomes a colleague with a shared cause but also with a political perspective that counterbalances her own, as Anil confronts and tries to comprehend the country's decline into civil war. After a body they subsequently name 'Sailor' is unearthed from the government-patrolled Bandarawela Caves, Anil comes to suspect that he may be one of the countless victims of government torture. The corpse is later discovered to be Ruwan Kumara, kidnapped by the government for unknown motives, leading Sarath to Colombo to trawl state target lists. In his apparent absence, Anil attempts to defend the incriminating outcomes of her forensic work on the skeleton before a threatening congregation at the state Armoury Auditorium. Reappearing to distract attention from her there, Sarath preserves Anil's research evidence at the expense of his life, as we learn that his mutilated corpse is discovered by his younger brother, the ward doctor Gamini, while leafing through snapshots taken by civil rights campaigners of the latest atrocities.

Such is the unrelieved atmosphere of impending violence in *Anil's Ghost* that the novel might not appear to be an appropriate home for Ondaatje's more abstract painterly strategies. A military-political climate of this kind surely invites a responsibly realist mode to do it justice, just as McEwan and Coetzee could be charged with the tendency to evoke traumatic content in oblique forms. In Ondaatje's case, critics have sometimes struggled to gauge the extent to which his internalist mode of narration – fascinated as he is with tracking meandering emotions – can be reconciled with an unflinching, outward-looking vision of brute historical events. If some have taken issue with Ondaatje's propensity to interiorise what is a national crisis, or to provide only a partial perspective on a factional conflict, others have come to his defence. Questions of style's ambivalent purpose again loom large, even for these sympathetic critics. Chelva Kanaganayakam, however, circumvents that stock response in which Ondaatje is blamed for indolent lyricism, arguing instead that *Anil's Ghost* marks a departure that should be distinguished from *The English Patient* – a novel that is 'in stylistic and formal terms, more typical of the Ondaatje aesthetic mode that appeals to some and irritates others'.[100] Where Kanaganayakam implies that Ondaatje has achieved a level of historical particularism that *The English Patient* compromised by prioritising its own elegance over empirical details, so Margaret Scalan goes further to suggest that in *Anil's Ghost* one of the 'most remarkable accomplishments is that its faithfulness to a time and place of seemingly intractable violence does not produce a cynical account of human nature', because Ondaatje makes 'no attempt to project fictional solutions to terrorism and guerrilla war'.[101]

While it is true that Ondaatje may have been more watchful than ever of his style's aestheticising tendencies, in other respects *Anil's Ghost* is nonetheless fulfilling ambitions of an unmistakably aesthetic kind. For one, the novel demonstrates Ondaatje's admission, from a decade before, to 'prefer[ing] a complicated history where an event is seen through many eyes or emotions'; and in doing this, he surely vindicates his multiperspectival narration as an ethically accountable mode, by using it to evoke perceptions of the same context of terror but from alternative angles. Secondly, with frequent paragraphic breaks indicating the slightest shift forward in time (with even divides marked by an asterisk implying only minutes have passed), Ondaatje takes to an extreme the principle he applied to *The English Patient* where scenes, as we've seen, are 'pieced together' like a mosaic. And finally, in spite of its prismatic construction – carefully preventing any one perspective from dominating its moral economy – *Anil's Ghost* also quite audibly belongs to 'that private, poetic voice' with which Ondaatje wants to show us how the world might be sensed and understood, not only 'in terms of language but in how one sees things'. Often that voice is noticeably impersonal; but paradoxically, it is one that he assumes to convey some of his most affecting scenes.

One should pause before assuming there is any ethical discrepancy between intimacy and impersonality. We have already noted the way Ondaatje can move from self-effacing, externalised narration to focalised introspection in *The English Patient*, reproducing for his reader the sensation of observing Hana as she observes herself in both imaginary and remembered situations. The seemingly contradictory harmony of distance and interiority is precisely what the Cubists confronted, reaching for increasingly geometrical arrangements to evoke the dynamic perceptions that typify modern life. As Paul Crowther notes, '[i]t may seem odd to associate Cubism with expression, since it is frequently remarked how "austere" or "dispassionate" it is as a style'. The Cubists, however, were in fact 'moving towards closer and more total contact with the subject matter through the medium', by emphasising 'formal elements and tonal relationship'.[102] In *Anil's Ghost*, not only is Ondaatje moving closer to the medium by manipulating narrative mode; he is also alerting us as readers to the processes through which that proximity is achieved. In the figure of Gamini, that alternation between touch and detachment is dramatised in the surgery he performs. A man who feels 'more comfortable and intimate with strangers' (*AG*, p. 224), his distance belies his despair. This doctrine of impersonality (matching the narratorial self-effacement that Ondaatje sustains through episodes following Gamini at work) soon becomes a way of transcending the fear of abduction by the Tamil faction, upholding in the face of his own peril the supremacy of medicine at war. Thus we are told how he 'talk[ed] intimately and with humour to strangers', and how, although he 'knew all this was a sickness', as a means of self-protection 'he did not dislike it, this distance and anonymity' (*AG*, p. 224). Likewise, while in 'surgery he asked for just one assistant. Others could watch and learn at a distance' (*AG*, p. 224). Ondaatje's staccato notation of Gamini's desensitisation actually brings us closer to this 'obsessive' doctor's mindset, just as a painting born of 'rigorously espoused logic', in Henri Le Fauconnier's phrase, may still elicit sensuous responses from viewers even as it subjects the object or person it frames to mathematical arrangement. In this manner, Ondaatje uses the rhetorical resource of perspectival focalisation to evoke a portrait of Gamini's sense of his own complicity before the wounds he tries to repair, a portrait whose intimacy directly counterpoints the affective trauma that he is routinely experiencing: 'Eventually he felt himself on a boat of demons and himself to be the only clearheaded and sane person there. He was a perfect participant in the war' (*AG*, p. 224). By focalising Gamini's austere summary of his implication in events, it's as though Ondaatje allows style itself to counteract the emotional reality it so sparely colours and conveys. Far from aestheticising violence, these moments reveal the way he actively adopts the Cubist ethos of getting closer in touch with subject-matter through what appears, at first, to be a dispassionately spare or impersonal mode of depiction.

Ironically, then, stylistic depersonalisation here has the effect of consuming the reader more intensely in a character's personal plight – creating a medium that enchants and unsettles us with equal measure. Through episodes of this kind, which may unexpectedly affect us in spite of their tonal coldness, Ondaatje stages what Mark Roskill calls Cubism's 'concern with creative procedures as they may or may not prove relevant to the understanding', and in turn 'what may or may not count as an appropriate response on the part of the viewer'.[103] This can occur in less obviously dramatic sections of the novel, where the reader is offered a momentary reprieve from brutality. In these instances, Ondaatje invites us to consider that moments of stasis or bleak introversion stage ethical implications through their very inactivity. One such occasion is our encounter with the disused property where Anil and Sarath have stationed their temporary laboratory. Ondaatje moves his characters aside to allow the *walawwa* house to take centre stage. Again, as a detached commentator, Ondaatje is able to draw us in, describing factually, flatly even, how '[t]here is a long stone path from the village road up to the *walawwa*' (*AG*, p. 201). Assuming a tour guide's voice, he gives logistical information about what will become a focal setting for much of the novel. In practice, this distanced commentary intensifies our sense of that place's tangible ambience:

> It is a classic building, two hundred years old, handed down through five generations. From no viewing point does the house look excessive or pretentious. The site and location, the careful use of distance – how far back you can stand from the building to look at it, the lack of great views of another person's land – make you turn inward rather than dominate the world around you. It has always seemed a hidden, accidentally discovered place, a *grand meulne*. (*AG*, p. 201)

The measured present-tense description may distract us from what is really being framed here: something resembling the very experience of viewing a Cubist painting. We are compelled to take in a scene that can be encompassed by 'no viewing point' in particular, but whose impressive subtlety, its lack of pretence, emerges from the combination of contrasting prospects, 'far back' and close up. Having established this kind of visual logic to the scene we read, facet by facet, Ondaatje addresses us in the second-person not so much to conscript us to a particular opinion or preferred stance as to include us in the spectatorial motion of synthesising different lines of appreciation. It's as though he offers programme notes for how we might appropriately observe the way this building refuses grandeur, thanks to the effect that its visual positioning has on the onlooker. This very refusal becomes the novel's synecdoche for political quietude, based on a Buddhistic ethos of spiritual control that Ondaatje pits against military dominance and the moral anarchy of state-sanctioned aggression.

Where *In the Skin of a Lion* gave us a builder's view of how a viaduct's arches come into being in a convergence of force and steel, here, for an equally 'classic' feat of design, Ondaatje orients our attention to the resonance of architectural form and its capacity to exceed the perceived functionalism of its everyday purpose. He leads our eye beyond exterior properties of shape and scale to observe the way structure relates to location, and the reciprocal impact of this for the viewer (here also the *walawwa*'s potential inhabitant) when the building ultimately 'make[s] you turn inward'. This scene continues thus, unfolding through what Douglas Cooper calls 'the cubification of space and form'.[104] Ondaatje striates it into planes of offset colours (between 'two locations of shade'), of area (contrasting the home's 'shadowed porch and the shadow under the great red tree'), and finally of height, as our eye is drawn up the tree's canopy only then to follow the sunlight its leaves refract down to ground-level again, where it 'throws a hundred variations of shadow textures onto the sandy earth' (*AG*, p. 201). What begins with a generalised division of shade in 'two locations', ends with splintered light revivifying blank ground. It is a progression from simple to multiplied colours akin to the phenomenon that Christopher Green identifies in Picasso's portraiture, where the seemingly 'flattened geometry most often associated with Cubist painting' disperses, giving way to another, more dynamic 'vocabulary of forms' that 'compellingly conveys the possibility of mutation, metamorphosis'.[105] By virtue of this process of perspectival mutation, we as readers are positioned – or are obliged to reflect on our hypothetical standpoint – as witnesses. Just as Ondaatje, at a scenic level, refuses to consign the *walawwa* to a function that might give it a practical reason to be preserved, so *Anil's Ghost*, at a politico-ethical level, 'neither envisages a solution to the crisis in Sri Lanka', notes Marinkova, 'nor does it sublimate the crisis into a cathartic artistic creation'. Instead, the narrative 'carries out an act of witnessing', like the one staged in the previously described episode, 'which maps the violent encounter between the public and the intimate and which testifies to the irreparable corporeal inscriptions of this encounter, without adjudicating through a final verdict or offering a lasting cure'.[106] Thus, for Ondaatje, the most static locale can still be set in motion by alternating the perspectives from which it is surveyed, just as he alerts us, in the most violent and traumatic instances, to the ramifications of adopting any one perspective and leaving it unquestioned for too long.

BEYOND MIRROR IMAGES

Finding such drama in stasis, such an integral interest in location (rather than action) for its own sake is Ondaatje's niche. This says much about his compositional aims, as we have seen; but it is also about what he savours in the finished work: 'The scenes in books of mine that I like the most are often scenes where nothing happens'.[107] In a rather different look ahead at what she had yet to accomplish (rather than sharing Ondaatje's delight in memorable moments), Stein also pondered in 'Portraits and Repetition' (1935) whether what happens is necessarily what matters:

> I wonder now if it is necessary to stand still to live if it is not necessary to stand still to live, and if it is if that is not perhaps to be a new way to write a novel. I wonder if you know what I mean. I do not quite know whether I do myself. I will not know until I have written that novel.[108]

Stein's attraction to stillness as a new creative framework hypothesises an alternative authorial sensibility as much as it foresees any reward in conjuring a style for stillness as such. By providing this picture of 'a new way to write', she of course complements her ongoing interrogation of representationalism at large. Later in the same essay, Stein tells us how she became 'more and more excited about how words' that could make an object 'look like itself' were not the words that had in them any quality of description'.[109] Stillness, and its relation to the functions we expect novelistic description to carry out, has been a touchstone for this chapter: from Nicolas's suspension, as he 'floats' beneath the knitting point of a steel arch, to Hana's longing for the kind of twilight 'rest' she can only achieve in memory, to 'the aesthetics of the *walawwa*' that Anil misses at the time, consumed in her own static forensics, but recalls '[y]ears later' as 'a location of refuge and fear, in spite of calm, consistent shadows' (*AG*, p. 202). If stillness brings Ondaatje close to Stein, her excitement in releasing words from their referents allies her to a 'Cubist attitude' of the kind summarised by Amédée Ozenfant in 1928: that 'effort to evoke emotion without resorting to representational forms'.[110] Holding much in common with that attitude, Ondaatje's 'effort' is in rescuing the novel from being 'handcuffed to realism', to recall his terms, by incorporating 'forms of art which have a different structure'.

These lines of affinity, just to be clear, ought to be treated with caution by the literary historian tracing the legacies of modernism. It is a caution that I exercise in the forthcoming chapters, not least for a writer like Morrison whose singularity has been critically mediated by comparative approaches that occasionally give an impression (inadvertent or otherwise) of her as a practitioner more in debt to than productively inspired by modernist predecessors. Equally, however, a key aim of this chapter has been to show that we *can* account for modernist impulses in a contemporary writer like Ondaatje without resorting to an argument rooted entirely in analogies, while also acknowledging where such analogies can be historically and aesthetically useful. 'We must keep in mind', warns Wendy Steiner, 'the fact that Cubist painting is a generalisation, a construct perhaps as questionable as its purported literary echo'.[111] If analogical connections are hard to avoid, too much can be made of the benefits of avoiding them: the epithet *Cubist* will always be to some extent prone to woolliness when applied to the very literary techniques that are fashioned in its honour. Precisely because of this propensity, Ondaatje's work urges us to explore further ways of analysing the painterly *in* the novelistic, but without reducing the particularity of either.

In order to track Ondaatje's appropriation of Cubism through its aesthetic and ethical consequences, I have entertained a way of reading that 'establishes a montage of differences', to recall Friedman's terms, 'where setting texts side by side illuminates those differences at the same time that it spotlights commonalities'.[112] I have also tried to show how, irrespective of his affinity with Cubism, contrasting compositional imperatives keep each other company, as he may conscientiously 'collect' 'small discoveries' as 'first principles' only then to give the script over to chance – all guided, if guided at all, by his overarching avoidance of planning.[113] It ultimately seems less important, then, to reconcile those self-portraits of a novelist alternately disciplined and free, than to consider how they work as two sides of the same creative coin – and what, in turn, that combination reveals about his concordance with Cubism's own disparities over the issue of creativity. For Léger, to be inventive you have to run the risk of being imitative, a sentiment echoed by Berger in the essay that so fascinated Ondaatje, where '[i]nspiration', he claims, 'is the mirror image of history: by means of it we can see our past, while turning our back on it'.[114] Despite his own contradictory ways of composing, Ondaatje combines these related notions of innovation for which the inspired and the inherited coincide in productive friction, a friction that indeed exists for each of the novelists considered throughout this book. Cubism is one mediator among others considered later in this study – as impressionism is for McEwan and, as we will see next, as minimalism has been for Coetzee – that demonstrate how writers coordinate invention with a deep engagement with the modernist tradition in order to perform ethical or political interventions.

'To discern a form', declared Gleizes and Metzinger, 'is to verify a pre-existing idea'.[115] Ondaatje has had no qualms about discerning in his own practice the realisation of formal possibilities that Cubism first initiated and with which, to him at least, the novel has yet to keep pace. This shouldn't be an excuse to canonise Ondaatje's work as the paragon of *authentic* Cubist fiction. If anything, this chapter has shown that there is no true state in which a novel may work Cubistically, which is itself a recognition of 'the angled nature of Modernism's intervention', as Malcolm Bradbury once put it, exemplifying that 'oblique, divergent relation it proposed between the historical and the aesthetic, the world of modernization and the works of Modernism itself'.[116] This recognition, however, still doesn't alter the fact that it is worth asking why Ondaatje should uphold Cubist perspectivism as a 'perfect state' for fiction. In turn, to develop a vocabulary of the kind I've employed here for describing that affiliation, is to take on board Wayne Booth's suggestion that critics themselves 'must innovate by revolutionising the very medium of innovation', extending the critical 'language in which it is carried out'.[117] Never quite comprehensible via a set of hard-and-fast generic rules, Cubism's fulfilment in contemporary writing is better understood through the compatibilities between those practices it stimulates. Not only does this reveal how modernism's literary-painterly heritage has re-emerged as a late-twentieth-century lineage, and a dynamic one at that – where technical goals are reactivated rather than merely emulated. It also allows us to see how writers today can reckon with the artistic past without merely reciting it, transmuting styles without aping them, and inhabiting the resources of modernism in ways that are coeval with building the novel anew.

CHAPTER 3

'Spare prose and a spare, thrifty world': J. M. Coetzee's politics of minimalism

Just as Ondaatje has regarded Cubism as more than just an episode in art history, refusing as he does to treat it simply as part of modernism's imitable past rather than an aspect of its futurity, so too for J. M. Coetzee, various phases of the modernist project have compelled his re-engagement, however ambivalent to him their message has seemed. 'I have never known', he admits, 'how seriously to take Joyce's – or Stephen Dedalus' – "History is a nightmare from which I am trying to awake."'[1] The very fact that Coetzee has done this double take – looking again, as here, at his own position as modernism's legatee by questioning how seriously one should regard its most emblematic slogans – suggests that he hasn't altogether been willing to think of modernism as finished. Adamant that 'an unquestioning attitude toward forms or conventions is as little radical as any other kind of obedience',[2] Coetzee has responded dynamically to modernism in ways that resemble disobedience more than reverence, stringently avoiding pastiche. Never passive in the face of his modernist heritage, his work could well be aligned with what Kundera called that 'anti-modern modernism', whose legacy, as we discovered in Chapter 1, becomes ever more apparent the further the novel advances. In what follows, though, the recuperative aspects of Coetzee's relationship to modernism will play as prominent a role as those that seem more rebellious. Returning to a phase some years before he became a leading figure in world literature, this chapter retraces Coetzee's crucial first encounter with Ford Madox Ford, an encounter that prepared the way to his more widely recognised affinity with Samuel Beckett. My purpose in doing so, however, is not simply to paint a portrait of Coetzee at a stage when he was most influenced by early (instead of late) modernism; rather it is to explore how, from the outset of his writing career, he has engaged actively with the political implications of reviving modernist aesthetics in ways that might further our understanding of modernism's futures.

Understandably enough, the self-consciousness of this engagement with the politics of modernism has invited critics to position Coetzee among a generation of supreme metafictionists, who in the 1970s and 1980s were more likely to parody rather than perpetuate literary heritage. Or else, he invites interpretations that set out to show how his affinities with modernism become an unwanted privilege, a reason to turn the moral tables on a European lineage of artistic production to which he has been both connected by his scholarship and indebted by his craftsmanship. Within this kind of framework, Coetzee's representations of imperial violence knowingly reveal their susceptibility to the modernist ethic of artistic supremacy, thereby exposing the 'shame', in Timothy Bewes's recent account, that postcolonial novelists are compelled to confront in their effort 'to write conscientiously while also acknowledging the complicity of one's writing in the conditions one hopes to bring to an end'.[3] Coetzee's utilisation of the technical accomplishments of what could still have been perceived – at the time of his first novel's release – as a Eurocentric movement, drawing on its resources to narrate interracial violence in colonial South Africa, is undeniably tendentious.[4] Implications linger for the critic too, of course, as two interrelated questions arise. To what extent are we ignoring matters of difference, tyranny or inequities of power when reading *for* modernist strategies in postcolonial fiction? By virtue of this very focus, are we compromising our exposition of cultural and racial politics by invoking a discourse of formal attentiveness that one could trace back to the Enlightenment's theories of appreciation and the tacitly universalising tendencies they entail? These questions are valid; but they depend for their validity on the assumption that the predilections behind certain modes of reading modernism – namely, and most notoriously, the cultivation of expertise in ahistorical interpretation associated with New Criticism – are somehow reproduced by new modes of writing modernism, in ways that ideologically undermine contemporary novelists' efforts to represent the atrocities of imperialism.

It is undoubtedly crucial to highlight the ethical ramifications of charting modernism's discursive and cultural authority via Coetzee's creative conversation with that authority, not only at the level of his craft but also at the level of content, as modernist tactics enable his often oblique and perspectival manner of narrating the horrors of colonial domination. Yet this contentious relation between the formal inventiveness Coetzee exhibits and the colonial legacies that he relentlessly examines could itself be seen as part of the 'double paradox', as Simon Gikandi terms it, which lies at the heart of Anglo-American modernism's confrontation with social customs and artistic formations beyond its domains. As Gikandi contends, 'modernism represents perhaps the most intense and unprecedented site of encounter between the institutions of European cultural production and the cultural practices of colonized peoples'. Despite the impulse of postcolonial critics to situate 'modernism as the site of Eurocentric danger', Gikandi shrewdly suggests that in fact 'without modernism, postcolonial literature as we know it would perhaps not exist'.[5] To suggest, therefore, that Coetzee's formally adventurous fiction is somehow compromised by its own kinship with modernist innovation – reproducing through its style the very structures of power that he seeks to expose in the events he plots – would be to dismiss the potential for understanding modernism's contribution to enhance that very capacity for critique that we associate with, and indeed expect from, postcolonial fiction.

In what follows, I extend some of the imperatives of the previous commentary on Ondaatje while anticipating the forthcoming consideration of McEwan's impressionism, approaching Coetzee's modernist inheritance not as an object of narratological investigation but as an imaginative process – a process in which, as I argue throughout this book, the reader is intimately and ethically involved. To ensure that his readers 'work *with* the author in the construction of the book', to recall Morrison's phrase, remains Coetzee's motivation for revitalising modernist strategies, thus eliciting our emotional as well as analytical responses to his fiction's political consequences. As Derek Attridge has remarked, Coetzee's 'reliance on the resources of modernism' should not simply be regarded 'as a technical feature to be assessed and interpreted ... but as a moment in the reader's experience of the work'.[6] This implies that questions to do with *how* Coetzee's novels unfold, how they are textured, how they impact affectively on us – whether it's across the discrete space of an arresting paragraph or more gradually over the course of a series of episodes – are as crucial as what they literally show. Arguing against the prospect of 'instrumentalizing' Coetzee's narratives as allegories of colonialism and its late-twentieth-century afterlives, Attridge implies that what's most arresting about his narratives is less their ostensible 'critique of colonialism and its various avatars'. While colonial violence could be read as the foundation and ultimate horizon for critique in two early novels I consider here – *Dusklands* (1974) and *Life & Times of Michael K* (1983) – at the same time, these texts 'provide no new and illuminating details of the painful history of Western domination'. What makes them so 'singular', in Attridge's phrase, is precisely *how* they operate when 'otherness is engaged, staged, distanced, embraced', when the formal and figurative effects of which are 'manifested in the rupturing of narrative discourse'.[7]

By paying close attention to Coetzee's reprise of modernist aesthetics, then, I want to demonstrate not only how he orchestrates these affective and ethical dynamics at the level of form. I also want to extend the larger argument of this book, which concerns the reason *why* certain contemporary novelists are creatively reemploying modernist methods precisely in order to reinvigorate the novel's capacity to engage with changing socio-political environments after an era of self-interiorising metafiction. Like the other five very different writers considered in this study, Coetzee has always maintained a more effective alliance with modernism than with the age of postmodern writing on whose cusp Coetzee published his debut novel, yet with which he would subsequently never remain in tune. Coetzee's early diffidence towards 'self-referentiality' is a testament to how acutely he foresaw that the attractions of postmodern play would 'soon pall', because in terms of the novel's political and aesthetic future 'writing-about-writing hasn't much to offer'.[8]

Coetzee's recalcitrance in the face of postmodern fiction's rise through the 1970s is for our purposes more than an excuse simply to debate literary-historical labels. Earlier still in his career, Coetzee was more alert to the pitfalls of postmodernity than to its artistic or political potential. We might expect this reticence from someone who favoured the prospect of learning from the modernist project even at a time when that project seemed to have entered a phase of postmodern dismemberment. This much is evident from his synoptic master's dissertation covering the majority of Ford's *oeuvre*, which he undertook in the early 1960s before proceeding to doctoral work on Beckett. Beyond his scholarly engagement with these early and late figures from the modernist period, however, Coetzee was also thinking in terms of his own writing practice when predicting the declining appeal and eventual exhaustion of postmodern strategies. To claim that postmodernist fiction could, from its inception, never really abandon or surpass the modernist ideals it sought to lampoon is, of course, something of an old chestnut for criticism of the postwar era. Coetzee was not simply concerned with extending such debates for their own sake or with classifying trends, but also with what postmodernism's move against the 'subjective method' exemplified by those modernists he studied might eventually mean for his own craft. In this practical sense, he intimated that 'in the end there is only so much mileage to be got out of the ploy. Anti-illusionism is, I suspect, only a marking of time, a phase of recuperation, in the history of the novel'.[9] Perhaps it's no coincidence that Coetzee echoes the forecast of another then-emerging writer, who was limbering-up for his first novel: Ian McEwan. In the year after Coetzee's *Heart of the Country* (1976) appeared, McEwan announced that '[e]xperimentation in its broadest and most viable sense should have less to do with [...] busting up your syntax', than with what is effectively a matter of 'content' – what he called 'the representation of states of mind and the society that forms them'.[10]

How an individual's mental states become so horrifically shaped either by society or as a result of the actions carried out in the name of cultural supremacy is the dramatic focus of *Dusklands*. Those shaping forces in turn affect not only the novel's 'content' but also its manner of address, as each of its two sections employs a first-person register that disturbingly blends cruelty and confession. This register initiates some of Coetzee's most audacious – and most recognisably modernist – simulations of interiority, simulations that give us perceptions of the world refracted by monomania and derangement. Divided into two sections, *Dusklands*'s first part, 'The Vietnam Project', tracks the production of a report on psychological warfare written by Eugene Dawn, whose reach for a rational analysis of military conflict is matched by his own increasing irrationality and the eventual insanity which leads him physically to harm his own son. The second part of the novel, 'The Narrative of Jacobus Coetzee', is an explorer's account of imperial domination and revenge. For this, Coetzee drew material from researching the colonial history of South Africa as a graduate student in Texas in the mid-60s, reaching 'further back in time', as he recalls, to trace 'the fortunes of the Hottentots in a history written not by them but for them, from above, by travelers and missionaries, not excluding my remote ancestor Jacobus Coetzee, *floruit* 1760'.[11] Intersecting circumstances therefore inspired a novel that enters, in part two, the historical moment of Afrikaner brutality in a way that invites the reader to reconnect events there with the contemporary moment of U.S. military warfare. Thus, the world-historical events of an accelerating bombing campaign against the North Vietnamese and Coetzee's archival work on 'the earliest linguistic records of the old languages of the Cape' coincided to inspire the depiction of – and unnerving comparisons between – alternate contexts of colonial power in the novel's two halves.[12]

If these circumstances give us an insight into the genesis of the novel's geopolitical interrogations, then Coetzee also qualifies assumptions about its formal inspirations. He insisted that *Dusklands* 'didn't emerge from a reading of Beckett', a disclaimer that reflects his broader scepticism about 'questions of influence' (Beckett's or otherwise) which 'entail a variety of self-awareness that does me no good as a storyteller'.[13] His reticence about self-revelation has turned into a hallmark of his persona, such that it's tempting to see Coetzee's famous reserve as synonymous with his fiction's rhetorical economy. Where the job of the literary historian is concerned, though, there is a more pertinent upshot of his antipathy towards influence. It suggests that we would be doing better justice to the style of his psychologically forbidding work, as well as to the sensibilities that inform its response (or not) to Coetzee's more obvious precursors, by approaching *Dusklands* as a modernist enterprise in itself, rather than as one of modernism's heirs. By this I mean that we should treat it as a narrative that refuses to rehearse past modes – as though modernism were a period-style – precisely in order to counteract the 'rejection', as Angus Wilson once described the early postwar response to modernism's technical legacy, of 'overexploited devices still rich in promise'.[14] As I indicated previously, that Coetzee sets out to realise modernism's surviving promises in this way is hardly unproblematic, in view of the journey he undertakes into the colonialist psyche. Yet once we start to appreciate how Coetzee's extensions of earlier twentieth-century strategies advertise 'his ability', as Attridge sees it, 'to test' his own 'absorption in European traditions in the ethically and politically fraught area of South Africa',[15] then we can begin to analyse how modernist devices are precisely what facilitate his scrutiny of the interior, psychological dimensions of imperialist violence.

Such a self-reflexive process of testing the politico-ethical ramifications of absorbing literary heritage might not sound conducive to the project of retaining modernist aesthetics for a postcolonial age, as I am suggesting Coetzee does, if that level of reflexivity is understood as merely metafiction. Certainly *Dusklands* has been read as a text that exploits the unreliability of its narrators to rehearse what is a distinctively postmodern conceit of undermining the viability of historiography. As I have argued, however, we would only get so far in reading Coetzee's work as a self-conscious meditation on, or admission of, its own 'absorption in European traditions', for he is well aware that 'there is no hope', in his phrase, 'of successfully arguing the political relevance of what, in the present South African context, must seem Eurocentric avant-gardism of an old-fashioned kind'.[16] What he achieves instead is what my following reading of *Dusklands* – and, beyond that, of Coetzee's interaction with Ford and Beckett – will aim to show: that formal innovation at its most responsible, its most ethically attuned, reaches beyond 'mere prose reverie', proving in contrast to any indulgence in style-for-style's-stake that 'every element of the novel must be extremely "justified"'.[17] These remarks come from Coetzee in 1963, drawn from a dissertation in which he made a convincing case for the way Conrad and Ford revealed that modernism was not all about technical mastery because '[t]he ultimate demands were those of the artistic conscience' (FMF 2.27). These early observations would lead him to value modernist writers who were able 'to disengage technique from intuition sufficiently to make statements of principle about narrative procedures' (FMF 2.63), concerned as they were (and as Coetzee continues to be) with the ethical ramifications of employing such 'procedures' in the interests purposive – and in Coetzee's case, postcolonial – critique.

In the novel Coetzee completed some ten years after his dissertation on Ford, these lessons in making 'statements of principle' about technique came to fruition. *Dusklands* negotiates the distinction between craftsmanship and political commitment in order not merely to enlist features of modernist style that are appropriate to interrogating colonialism. It may also be read as a novel about its creator striving to show that he knows the difference between passively depending on modernist conventions – however seductive and influential they may be – and understanding how conventions can instead be remade 'new in their *relation* to a past', in Peter Brooker's phrase, exemplifying that '[w]hat is "new now" emerges from an active, contestatory remembering of the defeated or forgotten'.[18] Thanks to his similarly 'active' engagement with Ford, Coetzee had the chance to discover various blueprints and pointers. It was *The Good Soldier* (1915), though, that drew his attention, particularly Ford's brilliantly handled conceit of ensuring the novel's 'scheme' remains 'depend[ent] solely upon the mental tactics of the narrator' (FMF 5.23). Much the same could be said of *Dusklands*, for a similar kind of device is in play from the opening page. 'I deserve better', complains Dawn, reflecting on the fact that his mentor 'Coetzee' has instructed him to 'revise' his draft report of psychological warfare.[19] In this mixture of plangent defensiveness and resignation, we hear echoes of the man whose surname is Dawn's phonetic neighbour, John Dowell who, in the unforgettable opening stages of Ford's 'Tale of Passion', poses to readers the question of 'why I write'. While his 'reasons', we learn, 'are quite many', they are united by the belief that recollection will at least memorialise – even if it doesn't entirely make sense of – relations that have become 'unthinkable'. As Dowell attests, 'it is not unusual in human beings who have witnessed the sack of a city or the falling to pieces of a people, to desire to set down what they have witnessed for the benefit of unknown heirs or of generations infinitely remote; or, if you please, just to get the sight out of their heads'.[20] Although Dawn shares his introspective tone as well as his propensity for occasional divagation, the first part of *Dusklands* hardly endorses Dowell's logic of getting destruction out of sight and out of mind. In place of Dowell's hesitation and doubt, Coetzee introduces us to a narrator who seems to have taken quite literally Ford's famous advice from 'On Impressionism' (issued a year before *The Good Soldier* appeared) that to write in this mode is to articulate 'a frank expression of personality':[21]

> Here I am under the thumb of a manager, a type before whom my first instinct is to crawl. I have always obeyed my superiors and been glad to do so. I would not have embarked on the Vietnam Project if I had guessed it was going to bring me into conflict with a superior. Conflict brings unhappiness, unhappiness poisons existence. I cannot stand unhappiness, I need peace and love and order for my work. I need coddling. I am an egg that must lie in the downiest of nests under the most coaxing of nurses before my bald, unpromising shell cracks and my shy secret life emerges. Allowances must be made for me. I brood, I am a thinker, a creative person, one not without value to the world. I would have expected more understanding from Coetzee, who should be used to handling creative people. (*D*, p. 1)

What sounds at first like an indulgent exercise in self-pathologisation turns out to be a commentary on the need for such an exercise to be carried out in the first place. It is as though Dawn is standing at some distance from the subject of his own self-dissemination. This same distance invites or indeed coerces us to pay more attention to *how* he recounts that 'conflict' with the supervisor from whom he 'would have expected more understanding', than to what it is, professionally, that this clash involves. Consequently, in place of a measured recollection of the causes of dispute, we get a performance of rhetorical prowess, a performance that unfolds at some remove from the stuttering confessions and frustrations we might expect from a genuinely unsettled mind. What *does* potentially unsettle the reader, however, is the insinuation that the intimacy of candid reflection here is fabricated, and that the emotional economy from which Dawn's complaints stem has already been exhausted. That is, his words sound like they have been rehearsed, which gives the impression that he's merely offering an emotive reprise rather than an emotional response – replaying a sense of indignation that's already evacuated of its original sentiment. This notion of an affective state being recycled finds verbal expression in Dawn's repetitions, 'unhappiness' being a case in point as he repeats the word in order to theorise its consequences rather than feel its repercussions. Despite the dehumanising side effects of having worked on 'The Vietnam Project', Dawn speaks in creamy prose that objectifies 'unhappiness' as something less to be experienced than to be observed as a link in a causal chain leading from 'conflict' to 'poison[ed] existence'. Similarly, Dawn's identification with 'an egg' has the effect of replacing his own ontology with an abstract analogy, so that he starts to reveal less about his disappointment with his 'superior' than about his agility as a rhetorician in the face of those hideous images of U.S. imperialism he has dissected. At the level of idiom, then, Coetzee draws our attention at this early stage to the pseudo-rational language that later in the novel will characterise Dawn's responses to photographs of brutality inflicted on the Vietnamese. As we will see later in this chapter, Coetzee's minimal, pared-down description of such images, reveals Dawn all the more disturbingly to us. Through his facility with spare language, Dawn tries to screen any kind of scrutiny of his own culpability as a mythographer of military tactics – tactics that reproduce, and are indeed dependent on, the self-legitimating logic of Western domination.

From his first steps into fiction writing, Coetzee thus never gave up on the possibility of using the early modernist resources he drew from Ford to refract imperialism's insidious re-emergence, enabling him to recreate the kind of quasi-rational mindset in *Dusklands* that would be content to legitimise late-twentieth-century forms of colonial authority. In this chapter, I go back to those formative (and sometimes forgotten) years, when Coetzee was reassessing the legacies of modernism even as he was breaking new ground. Retracing his path of development further back still than this debut novel, I want to recreate something like a genealogy for Coetzee's hallmark style – namely, his minimalism. My motivation for doing so is to historicise some of the reasons why he has continued to find this idiom of brevity especially useful for engaging either directly or allegorically with the formations and ramifications of Apartheid. By providing this backstory, I mean not simply to show from which writers, and when, Coetzee chose to remodel a minimalist medium of his own. It is an effort, instead, to understand why he has deliberately chosen to advance along this 'inherited path', to recall Kundera's phrase, as he aligns himself with a particular modernist credo of economy to dramatise imperialism's remnants along with the tensions and contradictions of an age of decolonisation.

BY THRIFTY DESIGN

With his austere yet crystalline idiom, Coetzee is often seen as the leading descendent of Beckett or Kafka. It was his exhaustive study of Ford's corpus, however, that paved the way for his subsequent adoption of the severer minimalism epitomised by Beckett. Written while he was working in London and awarded in 1963, Coetzee's University of Cape Town MA dissertation invites us to measure degrees of Ford's influence, but also to entertain the possibility that his impact on Coetzee was disparate, even dispiriting. From its opening preface, 'The Works of Ford Madox Ford with Particular Reference to the Novels' takes as its starting point Ford's transitional, even culturally exilic status, less in respect of what he wrote than of his precarious relation to the patterns and exclusions of postwar canonisation in Britain. 'Almost forgotten in England', begins Coetzee, 'Ford has fittingly been restored to his proper place by Americans' (FMF viii). It is worth noting the surprise and admiration with which Coetzee first encountered Ford, the tone of which is preserved in his novelistic memoir *Youth* (2002). Writing in the third-person present tense, he enfolds us in his burgeoning admiration: 'He is dazzled by the complicated, staggered chronology of Ford's plots, by the cunning with which a note, casually struck and artlessly repeated, will stand revealed, chapters later, as a major motif'.[22] What *Youth* doesn't quite make plain is just how severe Coetzee's dissertation turned out to be. He states his 'conclusion' barely ten pages in, commending *The Good Soldier* as 'probably the finest example of literary pure mathematics in English' (FMF x). This conviction, alongside the reminder that Ford saw it as 'his finest achievement' (FMF x), almost undermines the need to move on and survey the rest of the *oeuvre*. Coetzee evidently worked out a rationale, though, for writing a panoramic dissertation that so boldly marked the superiority of this one text above all others. His justification lay in offering a survey that doesn't revolve around the singularity of *The Good Soldier* but recovers the transitions that facilitated Ford's path to this 'technical triumph' (FMF 5.23), by discovering 'in earlier novels experiments without which *The Good Soldier* would have been impossible' (x). Indeed, Coetzee's chronological reading of Ford's *oeuvre* is relentlessly inclusive: for each text in turn, analyses of style and diction emerge after extensive plot summaries. This often makes it hard for us to pinpoint firm opinions or even the rationale for Coetzee's brisk evaluations, let alone the lessons he retains from Ford's craft.

With its ambivalent stance, Coetzee's dissertation invites us to accept him at his word, yet also to distrust the very status of his remarks as a master key to his own fictional work. In the end, we are left with a suspicion that Coetzee had made up his mind about Ford in advance, insofar as *The Good Soldier* and *Parade's End* both assume a kind of talismanic brilliance that outshines their predecessors, lending his remarks on *The Rash Act* (1933) and *Henry for Hugh* (1934) an audible pity for what these later works could never live up to. Coetzee is perhaps most instructive on the very question of *how* we read Ford's continuing presence today. He reckons that if the 'essence of Ford's influence is indirectness and pervasiveness', then 'one cannot venture further than more or less enlightened critical guesses' (FMF Appendix B.27–28). Stylistically and thematically, mutual distinctions between these writers seem at times more pronounced than anything held in common. As we shall see, though, by virtue of this uneasy alliance, Coetzee's homage to Ford doesn't lead him into the creative cul-de-sac of mimicking devices but towards working and re-workable models of craftsmanship – models that lead to a rejuvenation of the kind of minimalism that Ford himself may never have practiced, yet which Coetzee employs for a new age of political and ethical demands.

Given the complexity of this politico-ethical terrain, however, what does it mean for Coetzee to use minimalism as a stylistic guide? Minimalism could be perceived as synonymous with simplicity, and simplicity doesn't immediately sound like a fitting aim for any would-be modernist, whether in Ford's time or ours. To restrain, to underplay, to resist elegant variation, might not seem compatible with literary experiment – a reservation shared by writers working in the very era bookended by Ford and Beckett. For instance, in response to F. Scott Fitzgerald's endorsement for the idea of writing fiction from carefully 'selected incidents', Thomas Wolfe offered a prickly counterblast to the ethos of restraint, insisting 'that a great writer is not only a leaver-outer but also a putter-inner, and that Shakespeare and Cervantes and Dostoyevsky were ... greater putter-inners, in fact, than taker-outers'.[23] Prudent selectivity, as Wolfe interpreted it, would shackle virtuosity and leave barren the prospects for individual ambition.[24] Sixty years later, Fitzgerald's advice about expressive self-discipline would strike a different chord entirely with Toni Morrison. Wholly positive about prudence, Morrison suggests that the 'sense of knowing when to stop is a learned thing', implicitly part of the writer's 'experience' of what 'it mean[s] to be thrifty with images and language'. As we shall see in this book's closing chapter, however, for Morrison (as for Coetzee) economy becomes the basis for a purposively responsible kind of innovation. Rhetorical underplay is commensurate with ethical accountability, restraint being the litmus test for whether the writer is doing justice to her subject over and above the wizardry of technique. Like Coetzee, Morrison associates a peculiar grace with compositional minimalism, prioritising discrimination over verbal amplification: 'You must practice thrift in order to achieve that luxurious quality of wastefulness – that sense that you have enough to waste, that you are holding back – without actually wasting anything. You shouldn't overgratify'.[25] Personal sentiment and professional esteem fuse in Morrison's preference for 'thrift', echoing Joyce's famous aim to maintain 'a style of scrupulous meanness' in *Dubliners* (1914), lean yet limpid enough to evoke the city's ambient spaces.[26]

This commitment to cutting back, shared by Coetzee and Morrison, is itself nothing new; arguably it predates modernism as well, returning us to the peak of Aestheticism and Pater's call for authors to write 'in the simplest, the most direct and exact manner possible, with no surplasage'. Pater insisted that '[s]elf-restraint, skilful economy of means, *ascêsis* [...] has a beauty of its own' and that there is 'an aesthetic satisfaction in that frugal closeness of style which makes the most of a word'.[27] As the affiliation Coetzee and Morrison both display to this 'constant practice' makes clear, formal frugality is not simply about setting benchmarks, practical limits or adopting tricks of the trade; it reveals something deeper about these writers' personal, aesthetic and intellectual commitments. Yet we can only understand the implication of such commitments by historicising them, reconstructing their genealogies. We need to acknowledge, for example, that Morrison's imperative that novelists 'should never satiate' gestures at a range of neighbouring analogies between writerly appetite and verbal exactitude, analogies which glance back to fin-de-siècle aesthetics, and particularly to debates surrounding the way compositional precision in a given work should be evaluated. From a novelist's perspective, we might recall Henry James's self-scrutinising preface to *The Princess Casamassima* (1886), where he cautions against the idealisation of economy as a 'sovereign principle'.[28] From a psychologist's perspective, G. H. Lewes invoked the 'law of economy', as he called it, in a penetrating exploration of the psychophysical bases of literary creativity. Joyce might well have agreed with Lewes's assurance that being scrupulous shouldn't be confused with writing overly austere prose, because '[e]conomy is a rejection of whatever is superfluous; it is not miserliness'.[29]

All these reflections on economy, though, could have been referring to lessons that Coetzee took from his early acquaintance with the work of Ford, turning, as he eventually did, into an ethical imperative Ford's assertion that '[i]f you are not simple you are not observant'.[30] Even James could scarcely have disputed Ford's assurance in *The English Novel* (1929) that '[s]cenes [...] presented with even a minimum of artistry will remain in the mind as long as life lasts'.[31] That 'skill in selection' which Ford so appreciated in Galsworthy, for one, adequately satisfies James's advice when reflecting on *Casamassima* that any attempt at the 'refinement of economy' must be made in the interests of detailed observation.[32] Formal thrift affects both sides of the writing process, from structural rules to habits and intuitions. A perfectible, objectively discerned part of narrative design, thriftiness also taps into a writer's personal attitude to available materials. It is 'personal' because the mandates of prudence and composure recalibrate what it means to experiment with form, marrying the novelist's ambitions for invention to a more stringent process of self-adjudication.

Ford saw himself as a guardian of these compositional aims, holding that 'the first province of style is to be unnoticeable'.[33] Purposeful pruning of this kind offered an antidote to indulgent lyricism and ornamentation. Cutting back in the face of late-nineteenth-century Aestheticism, 'the crisp sparks of immensely artificed prose', as Ford noted, became the hallmark of early modernist writers who refused luxurious sonorities in laying claim to a more straightforward style.[34] Such advances from the 1890s onward were typified, in Ford's account, by 'all pervading [...] precisions': a scrupulousness that not only influenced fiction in formal respects but also reoriented its affective reception. Stricter methods intensified the relationship between the reader and narrative texture. Predisposed to a model of self-effacing authorship, Ford's emphasis on accuracy over finesse could become 'an integral part of the story', evinced by fictional settings described with bare inventories alone, or by dialogue reduced to skeletal exchanges. Thrift itself, however, also had interpretive consequences, matching that 'increasing task in you and your readers for exactitudes in psychologizing, in projected incidents, even in narrating'.[35] Although Coetzee and Morrison might seem unlikely heirs to this dispensation, Ford's aesthetic of 'self-forgetfulness' has endured for contemporary fiction in revealing ways, inviting us to explore how a range of recent novelists — beyond my scope in this book — have revived his 'quite modest task of getting down to one's least rhetorical form of mind, and expressing that'.[36] Tempting as it is to build an argument from analogies or to pinpoint speculative affiliations, my aim in this chapter is basic yet bold: to situate Ford as a theorist (though not a practitioner) of minimalism, who is substantially responsible — more so than the majority of critics have hitherto recognised — for the fact that Coetzee has become one of the most ethically demanding novelists today precisely because he is also one of the most economical.

WRITING FOR A SPARE WORLD

As *Youth* documents them, Coetzee's own first attempts at fiction aimed to transcribe lyric poetry's affecting 'compression' into narrative but without 'spilling mere emotion on the page'. Coetzee's graphic simile for prose – 'a flat, tranquil sheet of water on which one can track about at one's leisure, making patterns on the surface' – aptly corresponds with Ford's vision of a register so exact and disciplined as to achieve a high sheen.[37] 'What we need', wrote Ford in 1914, 'what we should strive to produce, is a novel uniform in key, in tone, in progression, as hard in texture as a mosaic, as flawless in surface as a polished steel helmet of the fifteenth century'.[38] I want to suggest that this attitude of refinement is what attracted Coetzee, for it epitomised the way Ford could retain his 'singular openness to experiment' (FMF 7.22) while writing in such a self-effacing register. A brilliant harmony of imperatives becomes Ford's bequest to Coetzee, whose paean in turn can be heard in the disciplined 'compression' of his own earliest prose. Stylistic homage, for Coetzee, is neither copyism nor a salute to a precursor's prestige; it is rather more instrumental in process and effect, transcribing common convictions rather than obeying iconic prototypes. As concerned with extending compositional beliefs as he is with redeploying admired techniques, Coetzee's homage actively takes up Ford's example of how to balance a devotion to innovation with a style that 'gains its effects without impressing itself on the reader' (FMF Appendix B.12).

More nuanced patterns of kinship emerge, then, when we read Coetzee's own experiments not simply as solutions for the tics and exaggerations he criticised in Ford. Certainly in his dissertation, disappointment often forestalls Coetzee's opinion of Ford's fiction, in spite of the praise given to Ford's rigour as a critic – a rigour that has hardly been inconsequential for Coetzee's craft, with his 'unwavering commitment', in David Atwell's terms, 'to the exigencies of his artistic practice'.[39] Admiration thus resides with disenchantment, and Coetzee frequently holds Ford at arm's length, describing him in *Youth*, for example, as that 'half-German celebrator of English laconism'.[40] The 'celebrator' here, though, might equally be Coetzee himself. For among the Fordian lessons that resonate most audibly in his style, that distinctive 'laconism' certainly informs his cool manner of address. Recalling at the close of the 1980s how he was drawn to Ford in the 1960s, Coetzee matches Morrison's imperative to 'practice thrift' when he points to the continuing appeal of Ford's art of restraint: 'The kind of aestheticism Ford stood for struck a chord in me: good prose was a matter of cutting away, of paring down (though Ford actually wrote voluminously); novel-writing was a craft as well as a profession; and so forth'.[41] Yet his admiration goes further still as he finds rewarding in Ford the correlation of stylistic priorities and the demands of moral or psychological enquiry. Beyond the local aims of stylistic experimentation,

Coetzee writes: 'I now suspect that there was more to that. Ford gives the impression of writing from inside the English governing class, but in fact he wrote as an outsider, and as a somewhat yearning outsider at that. [...] I now suspect that what attracted me to Ford was as much the ethics of Tietjens as the aesthetics of *le mot juste*'. For Coetzee, Ford's 'gruff stoicism' manifested itself as a register and as an ethical stance.[42] Equally, the standpoint of an expatriate insider presented Coetzee with both philosophical and formal opportunities. If Henry James, as Morris Dickstein notes, felt that 'the life of the outsider heightened the intensity of consciousness, the acute perspectivism, that was part of his legacy to modernism', then Ford set a similar example for writers with 'late modernist' inclinations, and thereafter for Coetzee.[43] While James embellished his late fictions, Ford demonstrated how novelists could innovate with perspectival modes and yet aspire to a new order of frugality – staking their 'claim', as he called it in 1915, 'to the epithets restrained or exact'.[44]

Just as Ford recalls how Flaubert taught him that 'aloofness' epitomised what it is 'to render and not to tell',[45] so Coetzee honoured Ford's own stance as a 'yearning outsider', fashioning throughout the 1980s an impassive and exacting narrative voice that revealed him 'laboriously search[ing] out the right word': 'I do believe in spareness – more spareness than Ford practiced. Spare prose and a spare, thrifty world: it's an unattractive part of my makeup that has exasperated people who have had to share their lives with me'.[46] Far from being merely an aesthetic preference for Coetzee, literary modes of concision complement the lived experience of spareness. While mirroring Morrison's use of *thrift* as her watchword for handling symbolism and syntax, Coetzee's 'makeup' embodies that 'frugal, temperate and infinitely industrious strain of mind' which in *Provence* (1938) Ford equates with the kind of 'accuracy' and 'erudition' so 'necessary to the imaginative writer'.[47] That Coetzee can be revealed here in dialogue with such different chroniclers of discrimination and exile in this book, spotlights the awareness he shares with them of the ramifications of turning modernism into a repertoire of political and ethical means. Like Morrison and Ondaatje, Coetzee has faced head-on the consequences of assimilating a modernist heritage that includes figures, tendencies or artistic movements that aren't straightforwardly radical or oriented to the process of envisioning social and racial justice. In his work both early and late, Coetzee strives to answer the question he posed in a commentary about Alex La Guma as far back as 1972, where he wonders 'if a literature based on African traditions and a literature employing Western "techniques" are equally valid choices for the African writer, are we not entitled to ask ... whether there might not be a whole spectrum of valid literatures open to Africa, and to suggest that the writer should not, so to speak, choose his tradition at random, but rather choose it with some sense of the social implications of his choice?'[48]

ON FRUGALITY AND FORM

One positive answer to this question becomes clear when we examine that dialectic in Coetzee's work between social principles and stylistic aims which emerges in conjunction with his personal affinity with 'thrift' – in itself 'a complex, value-laden word', he notes, 'with a long history'.[49] This affinity crosses literary sensibility with lived reality, fusing artistry with attitude. With that integration in mind, Coetzee defers to the cultural historian and wheelwright George Sturt as an early spokesman for the evolution of thrift.[50] We are not told which of Sturt's commentaries on English rural customs Coetzee is invoking; but it's likely that the popular *Change in the Village* (1912) is his reference point for linking the transformation of subsistence farming in late-Victorian Britain to his own emigrant past: 'the culture of the western European peasantry was a culture of thrift. My family roots lie in that peasant culture, transplanted from Europe to Africa. So I am quite deeply ambivalent about disparaging thrift.'[51] Coetzee's inner conflict here can be heard in Sturt's own account of the 'genial, steadfast, self-respecting' nature of 'the village character'.[52] Sturt's primary concern is with how profit-driven agriculture has the potential to exhaust a 'great fund of strength' in rural communities, a fund invested by centuries of self-management.[53] This conversion in modes of exchange from mutual beneficence to mercantile competition threatened the 'survival of a venerable thrift'.[54] Rapid trade characterised by acquisitive self-promotion brought with it the 'unnecessary expenditure' that Ford bemoans in *The Heart of the Country* (1906). For communities in late-nineteenth-century England, this level of surplus spending would have been inconceivable only a generation before; and in its wake, complains Ford, it has left 'a picture of improvidence' whose prospects are 'eminently disturbing'.[55]

What is so compelling about Sturt's memoir is that it demonstrates a way of writing in the aftermath of threatened, even vanishing, forms of life, while appealing beyond local case studies. Complementing Ford's later symbolism of 'spiritual regeneration', as Coetzee praised it in *The Rash Act* and *Henry for Hugh* (FMF 7.07), Sturt's intentions were reparative; yet he nonetheless exceeded an account of provincial civility slowly ebbing away.

Projecting ahead rather than simply mourning a lost vision of England fossilised in pastoral terms, he translated the legacies of vanishing agricultural customs onto a wider plane of significance.[56] Too urgent to be elegiac, Sturt complained that 'the modern thrift' simply 'is not elastic enough; or, rather, the people's means are not elastic enough, and will not stretch to its demands'.[57] In making these charges, *Change in the Village* looks outward, speaking beyond its epochal moment, demonstrating what David Gervais calls Sturt's 'art of letting a fact grow in suggestiveness without squeezing it for meanings'.[58] This art of suggestion plays into our reading of Ford's influence on Coetzee. Charting thrift's gradual reconstitution, Sturt's local examples touched on universal themes that so clearly 'struck a chord' with Coetzee. By allying his remarks on Ford's influence with the personal affinities he holds with thrift, Coetzee allows us to appreciate the powerful transhistorical import of Sturt's cultural commentary.

Undertones of nostalgia might well be heard in these endorsements, via thrift, of durability and persistence, whether they are about narrative aesthetics or communal acts of resisting agrarian change. That correspondence between rural endurance and rhetorical minimalism can seem all the more contentious when provincial histories are retold in uncritically bucolic terms, giving the quaint impression that feudal systems were inherently benign. We're immediately reminded of Ford's commemorative vision of Groby in *Parade's End*, an estate that virtually advertises its own antiquity. Coetzee has the disconsolate close of that tetralogy in mind, when he compares Ford's progressive vision for experimental fiction against 'his failure to recognize that he was writing of paradigms and myths rather than of convincing plans or the reconstruction of civilization' (FMF 7.25). In a similar vein, charges of privilege and nostalgia have, of course, become familiar to readers of Ford's own roving documentaries of provincial life. In *The Heart of the Country*, Ford claims to have 'undertaken this projection of the rustic cosmogony as it presents itself to me',[59] but despite this emphasis on the subjective viewpoint he warns that the writer 'must be careful not to sentimentalise over the picturesque. His business is to render the actual'.[60] Ford's effort to distance himself from nostalgic retrospection, however, didn't prevent the young Coetzee from rehearsing a now-predictable critique, derogating *Parade's End* as a 'swan-song' for conservative pastoralism. In tone, the tetralogy proved too resigned for Coetzee, as it chronicled the waning spirit of English self-sufficiency. Economically phrased but lengthily plotted, the volumes together could never be as incisive or 'pure' as *The Good Soldier*, with the ceremony of Tietjens's decline 'in the end' becoming 'a little romantic', in Coetzee's view, 'a little soft, backward-looking in spite of its technical modernism' (FMF 6.38).

Reductive though he sounds here, Coetzee reveals an important dialogue in Ford's work between societal models from the past and artistic creativity, a dialogue that allowed Ford to encompass contradictory persuasions in his own work, as he simultaneously promoted aesthetic innovation and cultural traditionalism. What Coetzee's uncompromising remarks indicate is that Ford addressed matters of literary and social evolution alike by treading a fine line between recuperation and anticipation, restoration and newness. Such are the ideological tensions between nostalgia and advancement, cutting back and moving on, which not only surround the interface of tradition and innovation in Ford's style but also lie at the very heart of *thrift* itself. In common parlance, we tend to equate thrift with purposeful and personal restraint, a trait expressed by an exceptionally careful or watchful use of available resources. At its root, however, thriftiness implies the opposite. As the *OED* reminds us, its Middle English sense of 'prosperity, acquired wealth, success' arises from a more dynamic, *verb*al form of the word derived from the Old Norse meaning of *thrífa*: the act of grasping or getting hold of some valued possession, if not of human values themselves. In everyday discourse, thriftiness is so customarily linked to the adjectival use of leanness (and to less appealing notions of efficiency and orderliness) as to exclude the more active side of thrift – that is, its association with prosperity. Insofar as thriftiness entails self-denial, it also involves growth, steady increase. Reflexive of *thrífa*, *thrífask* conjoins the etymology of *thrift* with the derivative essence of *thriving*, thereby correlating rigour and prudence with vigour and abundance.

These semantic correspondences help us to make sense of formal and ideological paradoxes in Ford's craft while tracing the legacies of that craft for a frugal stylist like Coetzee; they also offer us a prelude to Coetzee's subsequent attraction (as a linguistic as well as a novelist) to the altogether different kind of minimalism that Beckett emblematised. Before reaching his turn to Beckett, though, I want to read Coetzee's early engagement with *A Call* (1910) alongside a novel that more explicitly than most embodies the thriftiness that, in his view, enabled Ford's mature prose to become 'subdued enough for nuances of tone to sound in' (FMF 2.25): *Life & Times of Michael K* (1983). Although it's also a relatively early novel, I have chosen it less because of its chronological proximity with *Dusklands*, than for the way it unfolds a story of thrifty self-subsistence that in turn embodies structurally the 'slow and inevitable process, like growth' which, for the young Coetzee, captured Ford's economically controlled device of *progression d'effet* (FMF 7.17). One of the novel's provocations is characterological, centring as it does on a self-insulating protagonist who is gradually isolated from recognisable social processes and immediate political events. K relinquishes his job as a Cape Town city gardener and begins a voyage with his dying mother in a rickshaw to the Prince Albert farmstead where she was raised. After a spell of hard labour on the construction of a railroad after his mother dies, K travels on to the district his mother longed to return to and establishes his own miniature reservation on land once owned by a white farmer. Thereafter, the novel tracks a series of repeated evictions and returns, as K alternately eludes and is recaptured by authorities, finally to be impounded in Kenilworth camp where his attending doctor tries to communicate, if not commune, with K as though he were an oracle rather than the subject of medical care. Despite this mobility across key events as they follow K's vagrancy, *Michael K* is frugally and tightly crafted. More than simply an object lesson in minimalism, however, the novel is exemplary for our discussion here because it allows us to observe how Coetzee registered Ford's influence in that dialectical relation between thrift as an ontological ideal – or, in K's case, the ideal of resisting a post-Soweto political environment through individuated agriculture – and the very texture of literary form.

Certainly, *Michael K* demonstrates the ways in which Coetzee's homage to Ford may be partial and selective. It also, however, resolves those antinomies between restraint and innovation, verbal strictures and the will-to-experiment – antinomies that were among the factors that drew him to Ford's solutions in the first place. Coetzee has observed that while Ford's conscious artistry set an example for fellow modernists and future generations by promoting a process of 'paring down', this deliberate investment in 'cutting away' seemed incongruous with his own productivity: formal self-restraint conflicted with the brute fact that he 'actually wrote voluminously'. Coetzee's emphasis on Ford's prolific output points to a fissure between aesthetic ideals and published results that seems unjustified, once we view Ford's parsimonious approach to diction and phraseology as itself a catalyst for creativity – a means of thriving by thrifty designs.

Punctilious expression and the ideal of self-regulation: opposite sides of the same coin that Ford and Coetzee share as their adopted currency. If any aspect appealed to the young Coetzee more consistently than others, it was Ford's emphasis on syntactic and verbal exactitude. 'Selection was to be the keynote everywhere', Coetzee tells us, 'selection of impressions, selection of instances, and, in the province of style, selection of *le mot juste*, as long as the word was not too surprising' (FMF 2.30). With *The*

English Novel (1930) in mind, Coetzee notes that although Ford honoured a tradition of conscious artists bent on obliquity over self-advertisement, he could equally sound detached from other innovators of his time when promoting the kind of economy that could be misconstrued as retrogressive. It was W. H. Hudson who provided an admirable precedent for Ford's claim 'that the exact use of words seems to me to be the most important thing in the world'.[61] Hudson's narration, in Ford's view, emanated a sense of 'engrossment': scenes are evoked apparently without contrivance, limned without decoration, watched in a manner 'so enamoured and so rapt that the watcher disappears becoming merely part of the surrounding atmosphere'.[62] Likewise, Ford commended Conrad in similar terms, noting that '[h]is leavings-out are as matchless as are his inclusions'.[63] In his own take on their collaboration, Coetzee gives us a slightly different comparison. 'Conrad's tendency was toward toning up,' he reckons, 'Ford's toward toning down' (FMF 221).[64] In his view, Ford did not need Conrad to show him the formal benefits of such thrift. After *The Benefactor* (1905), the threshold between inheritance and self-advancement had blurred to the point at which Ford needed to write himself out of 'a phase', as Coetzee calls it, 'in which he took over James's narrative tone comparatively uncritically' (FMF 3.10). Paths away from Jamesian prolixity led to a hybrid 'genre': writing a novel that combined psychological and historical perspectives enabled Ford to 'disguise himself in an approximation to the language of the period' (FMF 3.10). Significantly, Coetzee's roadmap of this route to economy is revealing for the way it plots Ford's legacy. In a visible 'stripping down of language' after *The English Girl* (1907), Ford averted new 'ventures into further Jamesian elaboration'; and in Coetzee's chronology, '[b]y the time of *A Call* he had a style so subdued as never to be obtrusive' (FMF 3.10, 3.11).

'Subdued' is perhaps misleading, implying as it does that Ford suspended all flair. For the avoidance of obtrusion in *A Call* hardly inhibits Ford as he moves dexterously between inner and exterior spheres, offering close inspections of bodily postures and shifting moods. Physiognomic descriptions, for instance, are outlined with the simplest of adjectives; but they compel us, as in the following instance, by relaying a queasy view of Grimshaw through a lens that blends intimacy and impersonality. Ford works in close-up, but in a voice that can be at once cold and discreet:

What was at all times most noticeable about him, to those who observed such things, was the pallor of his complexion. When he was in health, this extreme and delicate whiteness had a subcutaneous flush like the tangible colouring of a China rose. But upon his return from Athens it had, and it retained for some time, the peculiar and chalky opacity. [...] But little by little the normal flush had returned to Robert Grimshaw's face; only whilst lounging through life he appeared to become more occupied in his mind, more reserved, more benevolent and more gentle.[65]

The dehumanising image of 'chalky opacity' seems to have been coined by an austere narrator, whose voiceover operates at considerable remove. But Ford is then careful to incorporate it into the action itself, displacing the image's provenance by refracting it through his character's perceptions, rather than those of some exteriorised commentator. No longer under the sole ownership of the shadowing narrator, the simile is braided into the thread of events. Framed by Ellida's glance, it takes her by surprise, before piquing her concern: 'It was on observing a return of the excessive and chalk-like opacity in Robert Grimshaw's cheeks that Ellida, when that afternoon he called upon her, exclaimed: "What's the matter? You know you aren't looking well"' (*AC*, p. 19). Recurring throughout the novel, this device of transposing imagery showcases Ford's abstemiousness with regard to lexical variation. Such was his preference for duplication: either by repeating epithets deliberately and unequivocally, or by allowing discrete phonemes to reverberate across episodes, shaping networks of alliteration that acoustically connect the language of narratorial commentary and the description of physical events.

To Coetzee, *A Call* represents a minor contribution to Ford's corpus because it is formally so slight. Literary minimalism, however, is precisely what Ford applauds in his defensive 'Epistolary Epilogue'. Pulling in contrary directions, yet somehow unfazed by his disingenuous posturing, Ford's marriage of assertion and self-demotion typifies the way he skirts around labels like impressionism. It is a conceit with a heritage, though: gesturing back to Hardy's pithy assurance that '[a] writer's style is according to his temperament', such 'that if he has anything to say which is of value, and words to say it with, the style will come of itself';[66] and gesturing forward to Elizabeth Bowen's deliberate surrender of authorial control when admitting that *The Demon Lover* volume contains stories that 'have an authority nothing to do with me'.[67] Ford's version of a kind of modesty *topos* results in something more than self-abnegation. In fact, it is pointedly critical of stock classifications. Assuming a tone of ignorance, his claim not even to 'know what an Impressionist is' (*AC*, p. 162) provides a ruse for reasserting his counterclaim to self-restraint. It also allows Ford to elude commonplace labels as a way of announcing his faith in clarity, which in turn offers a request to fellow writers. Thus, his own preference for 'us[ing] as few words as I may to get any given effect, to render any given conversation' (*AC*, p. 162) resounds like a new dictum, calling for a more commonsensical way of categorising innovation.

A Call is a minimalist narrative predisposed, in Coetzee's estimation, to the 'ironic toning down of the action of tragedy' (FMF 4.16). It 'develops the low-voice narrative tone to near-perfection' (FMF 4.22), setting an example for Coetzee's own stylistically subduing performance in *Life & Times of Michael K*. Entering 'innumerable places of small magnitude', writes Ford in *The Heart of the Country*, the townsman 'will have gone through a sort of purification'.[68] So it is for K, whose narrative recounts 'the beginning of his life as a cultivator', inviting us to posit Coetzee's novel between a self-interrogative form of pastoral and the *Plaasroman*, the latter typified by the centrality of a homestead where ancestral attachments are tested and reformed.[69] It's often the case in this genre, as Coetzee has observed, that 'aspects' of natural and built environments 'merely coexist', yet together 'form no synthesis'.[70] This lack of synthesis is something K in isolation seeks to overcome, once '[t]he impulse to plant had been reawoken in him' (*MK*, p. 81). This reach for harmony in an organic world is also complemented by the novel's formal diminution. It seems as though Coetzee is paring down to essentials, in the same way as K gradually hunkers down to agricultural self-subsistence. Just as we're told that when '[d]ucking through fences, he could feel a craftsman's pleasure in wire spanned so taut that it hummed when it was plucked' (*MK*, p. 133), so Coetzee intensifies his own attention to simple diction, 'looking at the matter', as Ford might advise, 'with the eyes of a craftsman surveying his own particular job'.[71] Divested of flashbacks, prolepsis and authorial interjections, the novel tracks K from one location to the next, in a way that can feel deceptively serene. Coetzee's language is held in this relative poise, oriented so intently towards picturing scenes of natural persistence as to resist all decoration. Coetzee shadows K's increasing awareness that 'there seemed no limit to his endurance' (*MK*, p. 48), and this trope of illimitable opportunity recurs through the novel as we shift between immediate routines and existential reflections. K balances necessity and self-management in ways that allow him to idealise temperance while coordinating his idleness with his imperative to be frugal.

So uterine is that zone where idleness and thrift intersect that civil conflict intrudes only peripherally for K. Coetzee offers only fleeting access to K's contemplations, especially in moments of stoical resolution: 'All that remains is to live here quietly for the rest of my life, eating the food that my own labour has made the earth to yield' (*MK*, p. 156). Forever in attendance as a silent witness, Coetzee's strategy in these instances is often to intrude on K's thoughts by reiterating their phraseology and sentiment in third-person mode. Such apparent intrusions, however, don't provide any sure-fire interpretive guidelines for ideology critique. What Jim Hansen notes of Beckett, could legitimately apply to Coetzee's strategy here, whose 'writing – in all its pallid ambiguity, its minimalist abstraction, and its stripping down of … "the human condition" – remains impervious to even the most basic techniques of political criticism'.[72] Transcribing Sturt's criteria into a postcolonial context, Coetzee allows spare, quotidian reflections to become euphonic in a way that broadens their scope for suggestion but without yielding any critically definitive conclusion.

In *Michael K*'s latter half, the penitentiary doctor reflects in a confessional mode that works at a level of abstraction that enables him to compare the hostility of detainment to the inhospitable prospect of rural self-subsistence. Awe-struck with seeing K's bodily and mental resistance, the physician wonders what K 'must have looked like in the days before he turned into a skeleton' (*MK*, p. 220). In the absence of personal records, he imagines this pre-emaciated figure with reference to painterly archetypes, aligning K with the 'genuine little man of earth' caught in freeze-frame as an emblem of an organic community. From portraiture, he is conjured as

> the kind of little man one sees in peasant art emerging into the world from between the squat thighs of its mother-host with fingers ready hooked and back ready bent for a life of burrowing, a creature that spends its waking life stooped over the soil, that when at last its time comes digs its own grave and slips quietly in and draws the heavy earth over its head like a blanket and cracks a last smile and turns over and descends into sleep, home at last, while unnoticed as ever somewhere far away the grinding of the wheels of history continues. What organ of state would play with the idea of recruiting creatures like that as its agents, and what use would they serve except to carry things and die in large numbers? The state rides on the backs of earth-grubbers like Michaels; it devours the products of their toil and shits on them in return. (*MK*, pp. 220–1)

Here, the run-on sentence has the effect of eliding all human or historical specificity, an elision compounded by the depersonalised pronoun 'it'. Accumulating snapshots of seclusion reflect the doctor's knowing recourse to a bucolic vision of agricultural isolation. He accelerates from simple sentences into this periodic catalogue of peasant life, from cradle to grave, delineating a romanticised narrative of agrarian struggle over which 'the wheels of history' impersonally roll. If the idyll of pastoral subsistence has become a sentimental fiction, the persecution of such communities through 'the products of their toil' remains a sanctioned reality. Coetzee implies that such accounts of a 'life stooped over the soil', based on the wishful picturing of remote peoples immune from systemic abuse, are no less exploitable for being chimerical.

The arc of K's fate traces the dissolution of this chimera, torn as he is from a 'landscape [that] was so empty that it was not hard to believe at times that his was the first foot ever to tread a particular inch of earth or disturb a particular pebble' (*MK*, p. 133). In the doctor's transcription of K into 'peasant art', Coetzee offers a multivalent meditation on agrarian resilience, glancing to Ford's own reflexive manner of celebrating feudalism's social and economic precedence. For, if the kind of 'industry and determination' that Tietjens 'had quite advisedly and of set purpose adopted [as] a habit of behaviour' appoints him as a spokesperson celebrating an irrevocable feudal order, then Tietjens is also Ford's case study for testing the point at which that celebration tips into idealisation – thereby making redundant, or at least anachronistic, the very temperament Tietjens seeks to revive.[73] Like *Parade's End*, *Michael K* does not merely parody the escapist longing for a feudal and frugal past. Instead, both novels stage temporary episodes of communion with an unrecoverable pastoral age of refuge, in order to mark the dissolution of organic societies and the subsequent abuse of peasant labour. This memorialisation of what Coetzee calls the 'culturally homogenous' constitution of 'pre-capitalist' communities allows us to appreciate the parallels between Tietjens and *Michael K*'s self-conscious physician.[74] Both are keenly aware of the temptation to eulogise the growth of civilisation out of smallholdings, aware too, it seems, that 'every return to the farm', as Coetzee claims, 'tends to be a version of pastoral, sharing in the anxiety of (high) pastoralism about the moral justification of such a return'.[75] K's own withdrawal appears never to leave him open to these moral anxieties. Instead, he savours the fact that 'it is not hard to live a life that consists merely of passing time' (*MK*, p. 143). Thriving on inertia just as he feasts in the face of meagreness, K's version of indolence without luxury exemplifies, in Coetzee's words, how the purposeful 'relapse into sloth is a betrayal of the high pastoral impulse'.[76] By valorising the recalcitrant force of isolated self-governance, *Michael K* offers us a new 'way of reading idleness', of seeing it, as Coetzee recommends, 'as an authentically native response to a foreign way of life, a response that has rarely been defended in writing'.[77] Indeed, by the time we reach the novel's quietist denouement, K's self-imposed thriftiness will 'have driven in upon him', to use Ford's own phrase, 'that fact of the extraordinary solidity and solidarity, the extraordinarily close grain of life in the heart of the country'.[78]

Coetzee thus evokes thrift's complex figurative and physiological associations, albeit in solitary terms – privatising that very system of agrarian values fragmented, for Sturt, by successive enclosures. Policies of containment of a more vicious kind, of course, punctuate Coetzee's parable of subsistence. His double-vision of rural integrity, in which idleness and thrift coexist in a time of conflict, bears comparison with that interaction of opposing sensibilities which Ford isolates in *The Last Post*. Just as civil upheaval sets the backdrop for K's hermitage, so Valentine retrospectively admits that '[i]f the war had done nothing else for them – for those two of them – it had induced them at last to instal Frugality as a deity. They desired to live hard even if it deprived them of the leisure in which to think high!' (*PE*, p. 818). Where K's solitary introspection focalises Coetzee's parable of thrift as a honed form of resistance, Valentine is one of several characters who cipher Ford's ontological conjunction of thrift and indolence. Stoically resolving to suppress all appetite, there's also a sense in which these figures are 'learning to love idleness' (*MK*, p. 158) as a conduit for more virtuous forms of self-denial. As K, indifferent to manual work, takes pleasure in 'a yielding up of himself to time' (*MK*, p. 158), so after the long opening exchange with Mark in *The Last Post* we find Marie Léonie 'repeat[ing] to herself that she did not demand a better life than this'. Again, like K, she recoils from further self-antagonism, assuming an air of serene resignation when conceding '[t]here appeared nothing for it but to wait, and that side of her nature being indolent, perhaps being alone indolent, she was aware that she was contented to wait' (*PE*, p. 697).

We might indeed align *Michael K* with Ford's tetralogy as offering similarly ambivalent parables of thrift – an inherited virtue in some contexts, an imposition in others. In so doing, both novels contribute to what Coetzee calls that 'wider historical perspective', by which 'we can appreciate what a massive cultural revolution must occur when a people move from a subsistence economy to economy of providence and from pastoralism to agriculture, a move, indeed, in which the notion of *work* may be said to make its appearance in history'.[79] What this 'revolution' also reveals, though, is just how intimately and personally thrift is redefined, even as it is symptomatic of broader socioeconomic changes. Nurtured individually, thriftiness may be passed on discretely, inculcated as a unique and unifying principle of kinship; yet at the same time, it applies to group concerns where thrift functions as a collective noun. As Coetzee and Ford furthermore imply, thrift, as a sensibility, bridges life and art. Frugality, in all its facets, remains an impetus shared between generations, an impetus that finds its lexical and syntactical correlatives in Ford's search for a 'form that will produce the effect of a quiet voice [...] without the employment of any verbal strangeness – just quietly saying things'.[80] It's intriguing to note that *homage* itself denotes the public acknowledgement of feudal allegiance. And as Coetzee's own homage to Ford's 'quiet voice' exemplifies, just as thrift had once offered survival strategies, 'delicately balanced' in rural communities, so as a creative ethos it unites economy and experimentalism, while pointing to the influence of surviving traditions on the latest transitions in novelistic craft.

Rather than salvaging forms of social or literary heritage as an antiquarian exercise, both writers reactivate former tactics in the light of new and pressing concerns. We sense this impulse of revival in Coetzee's refusal to disparage thrift, making it the starting point for his style. Likewise, we sense it in *The Heart of the Country*, expressed by Ford's affection for the 'peasant imagination', for its capacity to endure, for its 'philosophy of keeping on going'.[81] In each case, sociocultural and novelistic visions endorse one another, enabling these writers to consider their purist refinement of learned techniques as a task analogous to industrious self-subsistence. In Ford's words, 'there are only two schools of Art of any authenticity: that of the conscious artist who is ground as fine as a needle by the necessities of conscious self-expression, and that of the peasant who is ground down into a knowledge of how life works by the hard necessities of the wind, the soil, and by hunger and death that accompany all weathers'.[82] Hardly one to restrain his appetite to the point of self-denial, Ford was never as 'ground down' in life as the temperance he celebrates in art would imply. Neither did Ford entertain the idea of structuring fiction with the durational swiftness that epitomises Coetzee's earliest work. Even if Ford would never practice the kind of eviscerated prose that subsequently drew Coetzee, as we will see next, to the later and darker minimalism of Beckett, those 'necessities of conscious self-expression' nonetheless reinforce Ford's and Coetzee's complementary insistence on giving primacy to conveying the 'knowledge of how life works' over the surface attractions of stylistic flamboyance.

Meshing alternative schemes for survival, Ford links artistic and feudalistic conceptions of self-cultivation to associate writerly diligence with an ancient yet vanishing way of life, one attuned to the idea of thriving in all elements. Acts of literary innovation, in this model, need not encourage authorial self-promotion or pyrotechnic display but rather emphasise the novelist's obligation to the artistry of precision. Coetzee increases the ethical voltage of that obligation by allowing his own formal economy to coexist with narrative events – in essence, depicting the lived experience of frugality in a manner that echoes Toni Morrison's dictum that '[l]ess is always better'.[83] Thrift, in its economic, ontological and syntactical manifestations, is thus one instance of the connections that modernist and contemporary writers can make between the politics and aesthetics of minimalism.

'A SENSUOUS DELIGHT': ABSORBING BECKETT

Youth draws to a close with Coetzee switching precursors. Hastily forged allegiances have caused him to misdirect his energies and have elicited false hope: 'How could he have imagined he wanted to write in the manner of Ford when Beckett was around all the time? In Ford there has always been an element of the stuffed shirt that he has disliked but has been hesitant to acknowledge ... whereas Beckett is classless, or outside class, as he himself would prefer to be'.[84] The rejection is adamant; and yet, as we have seen, Coetzee's own fiction has never quite dissociated itself from Ford's aesthetic. Indeed, despite his initial attraction to Beckett's way of standing 'outside class', it was Ford's capacity to write as that 'yearning outsider' which seems to have alerted Coetzee to a range of ex-centric innovators, from Defoe to Faulkner, regardless of their eventual influence on his creative work. This tempts us to conclude that even if Coetzee has allowed Beckett to stand as his pre-eminent precursor, it was nevertheless his earlier attraction to and disappointment with Ford that prepared him to inherit Beckett's own iconic brevity. It's not simply that Coetzee needed Ford in order to appreciate Beckett's minimalism; rather, the time he spent scrutinising Ford's *oeuvre* allowed him to witness the way literary techniques could be modelled and remodelled on certain personal and social principles. Ford's advocacy of frugality, in attitude as in style, offered a primer that conditioned Coetzee's attention to what was so essential about Beckett's own sparseness.

In contrast to the austerities of thrift, it was the pleasure of 'sensuous response' that characterised Coetzee's encounter with Beckett. Subsequently, his critical and linguistic work on Beckett was sustained by how the early novels – especially *Murphy* (1938), *Watt* (1945; publ. 1953) and *Molloy* (1951) – gave 'a sensuous delight that hasn't dimmed over the years', such that even Coetzee's most rigorous and pragmatic analyses of Beckett's syntax were 'grasping after ways in which to talk about' that unusual pleasure of reading this late-modernist minimalist, finding a vocabulary 'to talk about delight'.[85] For Coetzee, while Beckett's prose 'is highly rhetorical in its own way', remaining amenable to the 'formal analysis' of statistical stylistics, it is his early work, rather than those later 'post-mortem voices' of *How It Is* (1961) and *Worstward Ho* (1983), that first piqued Coetzee's interest in 'how the voice moves the body, moves in the body'.[86] That this tracking of a moving voice within the human physique can be a source of 'delight' for the reader might seem obscure, because it still implies the forensic separation of anatomy and articulation, of physiological operations and linguistic rapture, that Coetzee sees as less severe in Beckett's early prose. What's important here, however, is not so much Coetzee's ability to convince us of the compassionate aspects underlying Beckett's minimalism, as his ability to face Beckett's influence through a pleasurable rather than antagonistic dialogue. Instead of writing himself out of Beckett's legacy, Coetzee sees his debt as an 'obvious' one: an inheritance that he does not even attempt to conceal.

In addition, then, to his semiotic work on Beckett as a scholar in the heydays of structuralism, 'there has also been a more conscious process of absorption' at play for Coetzee as a novelist aligning with modernism in that era of what he called postmodern 'anti-illusionism'.[87] If, after his first encounters with Beckett, Coetzee quickly knew what he liked, knowing too where it lay in his predecessor's *oeuvre*, he continues to know that his affinities have much to do with the generic ambivalence of his own work. Just as Beckett is often seen as the ambassador of modernism's exhaustion, so Coetzee's most recent philosophically ruminative work has so eluded classification that he is perceived to have exhausted his own fidelity to fiction. If Coetzee can be accused of giving up on the novel in favour of cerebral pseudo-autobiography, then he has been equally careful to distance himself from the 'common ploy[s] of postmodernism'. Writerly self-consciousness comes in a rather different form – not in the shape of metafictional self-scrutiny but in the acknowledgment of the difficulties and seductions of rearticulating influence. Coetzee recognises the 'temptations', as he calls them, of recuperating Beckett's style.[88] How, and with what consequences, he has taken pleasure in absorbing the techniques that have most tempted him are what this final section intends to explore. And to demonstrate the long arc of his engagement with Beckett, I will return first to *Dusklands* once more before then linking it with Coetzee's post-millennial work.

Beckett's 'stories', says Coetzee, often 'become the fictional properties of their narrators'.[89] In *Dusklands*, Dawn's solipsistic disorientation emerges as both his property as well as his experience when he attests that '[i]t is only recently that I have begun to falter. It has been a bewildering experience, though, being possessed of a high degree of consciousness, I have never been unprepared for it' (*D*, p. 5). Like the subject of 'unhappiness' in the novel's opening, bewilderment here is posited as a theme for rumination, one that Dawn can mull over theoretically as much as he endures it viscerally – providing him with yet another lens through which to observe and applaud his own susceptible 'consciousness'. We might detect something here of the perpetual and self-perpetuating cycle of knowledge and uncertainty that besets the eponymous character of Beckett's 1945 novel, *Watt*, a cycle which implies that insofar as 'there seemed no measure between what Watt could understand, and what he could not, so there seemed none between what he deemed certain, and what he deemed doubtful'.[90] Certainly, hesitation and unease are present enough for Dawn to affiliate him with the eternal doubt that afflicts Watt. The difference, though, is that we watch Watt at a distance, with a pseudo-comic third-person commentator as our guide, whereas in *Dusklands* the first-person narration creates a more collusive and unstable mood, giving us the suspicion that Dawn is entirely in charge of his own demise, both literally and rhetorically, in a way that few of Beckett's displaced characters can ever hope to be.

Objectifying one's own grievances is one thing; doing the same to the grief of others is quite another. Coetzee highlights this unsettling transition when Dawn imaginatively projects himself into a '"12x12" blow-up' of a caged Vietnamese prisoner taken on Hon Tre Island:

I close my eyes and pass my fingertips over the cool, odorless surface of the print. Evenings are quiet here in the suburbs. I concentrate myself. Everywhere its surface is the same. The glint in the eye, which in a moment luckily never to arrive will through the camera look into my eyes, is bland and opaque under my fingers, yielding no passage into the interior of this obscure but indubitable man. I keep exploring. Under the persistent pressure of my imagination, acute and morbid in the night, it may yet yield. (*D*, pp. 16–17)

The moment is not only an account of the imperious desensitisation of images of war-victims, an account that Dawn gives as a kind of testimony whose confessional idiom nonetheless bears no trace of compunction. It is also a demonstration by Coetzee – facilitated by the coolly handled, sibilant inflections with which he renders Dawn's self-observations – of the maintenance of discursive power over the imagined victim, when that victim becomes the fantasised possession of 'morbid' Western pleasure. Spare yet somehow unnervingly elegant, the present-tense narration facilitates a palpable degree of closeness, of immediacy (expressive of the extent to which atrocity is pornographic for Dawn) an immediacy which is directly at odds with the separation that comes with Dawn's incomprehension: the separation that indicates his failure to identify with, in the very process of festishising, this 'obscure but indubitable man'.

Instead of attempting to bridge that void, Dawn orients his empathy towards the aggressor, ventriloquising the self-legislating policy of invasion but in a manner that gestures ahead to the brutalities of part two, as he adopts the anachronistic language of wonderment akin to early colonial explorers:

> Our nightmare was that since whatever we reached for slipped like smoke through our fingers, we did not exist; that since whatever we embraced wilted, we were all that existed. We landed on the shores of Vietnam clutching our arms and pleading for someone to stand up without flinching to these probes of reality: if you will prove yourself, we shouted, you will prove us too, and we will love you endlessly and shower you with gifts. (*D*, p. 17)

With its grandiloquence, Dawn's condescension anticipates the self-mythologising discourse of Jacobus Coetzee in part two, who pontificates about 'the effective meaning of savagery' as a condition defined by 'enslavement to space, as one speaks obversely of the explorer's mastery of space' (*D*, p. 80). In each case, the righteous process of categorising populations to be encountered, penetrated and idealised, if only thereafter to be fought and suppressed, is conducted in self-congratulatory terms. For both Dawn and Jacobus have conversations with themselves, despite their outward gesture to the communities or individuals subjected to imperial domination who they expect – hypothetically in Dawn's case, literally in Jacobus's – to contain within the imaginative retelling of events, which is nonetheless conducted (in another tonal affinity between their perspectives) in tangibly paranoiac terms. In the interests, then, of accentuating the manner and ethical consequences of both characters' tendency towards introverted self-justification, Coetzee enlists the modernist device of interior monologue, tracking from the inside-out the perpetuation of imperial worldviews that gestate and flourish in states of moral and epistemological insularity. More perversely, such states breed a sentimentality that coexists with violence. Coetzee's minimalism persists, but less in terms of verbal sparseness than at the level of syntax, where the scarcity of subordinate clauses allows the cumulative effect of shortened phrases to correspond with the mercilessness of Dawn's righteous projections of conquest:[91]

> From tears we grew exasperated. Having proved to our sad selves that these were not the dark-eyed gods who walk our dreams, we wished only that they would

retire and leave us in peace. They would not. For a while we were prepared to pity them, though we pitied more our tragic reach for transcendence. Then we ran out of pity. (*D*, p. 18)

This warped logic of 'pity' emerging from military ferocity is one that readers will see again in Jacobus's nostalgic view of the Hottentots in the second half of *Dusklands*, a people he desires at once to preserve as a living monument to his explorer's authority and to destroy in a demonstration *of* that authority's endurance. In this episode, though, the important point to recognise is not simply that the scene of annihilation is vicariously imagined rather than historically located, or that Dawn is empathising with the lost consciences of combat soldiers who will go to commit those atrocities against civilians who he romanticises more avidly than he researches. Instead, what's key is also the form in which this violence is anticipated. Coetzee's narration 'cannot satisfactorily be contained in interpretation', as David Attwell maintains, 'for the aggressiveness [of his prose] remains a *social* fact that readers have and will continue to give witness to'.[92] As the exhaustion of pity is aptly registered in dispassionately staccato syntax, we become that kind of witness – a stance that's very much in keeping with the position that Coetzee, via the testimonial idioms of his two narrators, wants his readers to assume throughout.

This invitation to, or conscription of, the reader also disproves the assumption that the modernist difficulty of Coetzee's early fiction serves to estrange his audience more so than to immerse them. For, if anything, this prose – written though it was after he had absorbed so formidable a precursor as Beckett – complements the way recent literary historians have come to regard modernism as an intensification, rather than repudiation, of the emotionally involving and ethically demanding strategies of the realist fiction from which it followed. As Stephen Mulhall points out, 'one cannot intelligibly reject realistic novels as necessarily failures simply on the grounds that they rely on representational conventions of some kind'. In this model, Coetzee's work exemplifies how a 'faithfulness to the realist impulse that is so deeply embedded in the genre of the novel may be precisely what pushes a writer into the condition of modernism'.[93] Conventions of depiction, of course, enter the very action of *Dusklands*, as Coetzee thematises questions of knowing and showing, perception and articulation, in the most climatically disturbing of scenes, where Dawn is holding hostage his son whom he uses as a human shield as police descend on his hideout:

something which I usually think of as my consciousness is shooting backwards, at a geometrically accelerating pace, according to a certain formula, out of the back of my head, and I am not sure I will be able to stay with it. The people in front of me are growing smaller and therefore less and less dangerous. They are also tilting. A convention allows me to record these details.

I have missed certain words.

But if I am given a moment I will track them back in my memory and find them there still echoing.

'... put it down ...' Put it down. This man wants me to put it down.

This man is still walking towards me. I have lost all heart and left the room and gone to sleep even and missed certain words and come back and here the man is still walking across the carpet towards me. How fortunate. They are indeed right about the word *flash*.

Holding it like a pencil, I push the knife in. (*D*, p. 42)

A twin register that Coetzee has identified in Beckett as 'the impulse toward conjuration, the impulse toward silence' directly informs this episode,[94] especially in the way it hovers between what Dawn is able to 'track' down in words and those seconds that his rearward 'shooting' 'consciousness' fails to capture. Most explicitly, Beckett's dual emphasis on conjuring and silencing is also played out in Dawn's admissions about omission that sit alongside his desire to 'record these details', despite his difficulty in apprehending them. A further pair of twinned yet seemingly opposed devices are revealed in aspects of tone: Dawn's heinously impersonal displacement of accountability towards the injuring of his son is nonetheless accompanied by a distinctly personal series of concessions about what he can and cannot recall 'echoing' from his 'memory'. Like much of the novel's dissonance between its modes of telling and what is told, Coetzee deliberately contrasts the inhumanity of Dawn's actions with the apparent candour and collusiveness of his testimony.[95] In such cases as these, '[t]onal undecidability', notes Molly Hite, 'defamiliarizes, not only for aesthetic purposes ... but to open up spaces for ethical questioning without necessarily guiding readers to a definitive conclusion'.[96] Hence this episode could legitimately be read as the expression of encroaching psychosis; but we could also see it as part of Coetzee's effort to simulate, with the aid of minimalism, a desensitised vision of imperial violence that will reappear in part two, sanctioned by colonial expansion, in the monomaniacal adventures of Jacobus Coetzee. What is evidence, for Dawn, of insanity will be for Jacobus a statutory 'convention', as he exercises white authority in ways that are nothing *other than* conventional, just as the severity of imperial control is predictably decided according to racial ascriptions.

I began this chapter by suggesting Coetzee was quick to prevent his early fiction – in much the same way as the other writers in this book did in their formative years – from jumping on the postmodern bandwagon of metafictional self-reflexivity through the late 1970s. In winding the clock forward and turning now to the most Beckettian of his post-millennial narratives, *Slow Man* (2005), that defence of Coetzee's distance from the postmodern might appear to buckle somewhat. Two thirds of the way into *Slow Man*, the return of Coetzee's fictionalised novelist and celebrated Australian intellectual, Elizabeth Costello, ruptures the psychological realism prevailing up to this point – largely devoted as the novel's first half is to the inertia and building despair of Paul Rayment, who is left crippled by the cycling accident with which the text opens. Costello's entrance turns what had been a novel of one man's recovery into something more like a fable of the evacuation of existential purpose and moral agency. Ultimately, though, this rupture is only superficially metafictional, and it serves to reveal more about Coetzee's inheritance than about his temporary recourse to postmodern games. *Slow Man* provides its creator with a ripe opportunity for historicising his own technique, as the novel begins to acknowledge, ponder and even diegetically incorporate Beckett's influence. Momentarily, at least, this genealogy is announced in the most literal sense. As relentless as ever in comments on the cast of the fiction she inhabits, Costello highlights everyone's 'unhappiness', her own included, diagnosing it as a result of 'nothing happening'.[97] She gives us a bird's eye view of their own scene of collective stasis – a stillness thematised by the novel, of course, and closely registered by its focalisation of Paul Rayment's reflections on his own crippled body – turning that scene into a stage set: '"Four people in four corners, moping, like tramps in Beckett, and myself in the middle, wasting time, being wasted by time"' (*SM*, p. 141). Despite the lure of such explicit references, what concerns me here is not Coetzee's literal restagings of Beckett's famous preoccupations with immobility, however appropriate they may seem for a novel about forms of incapacitation, both psychic and physical. Instead, more pertinent is the question of how Coetzee has re-invoked what Beckett saw as the compromise that narrative style itself faced after high modernism. Our attention is drawn to Beckett's oscillation between, on the one hand, repudiating 'style as consolation', as Coetzee describes it, 'style as redemption, the grace of language', and, on the other, the risk of falling for style, as *Watt* does, falling for its seductions in 'narcissistic reverie'.[98] This path between alternate compulsions is precisely the one that *Slow Man* treads. With its tone pitched on that dividing line between recuperation and disconsolation, the novel offsets a graceful documentary of Rayment's post-traumatic recovery of his life's sense of direction – showing how '[t]ime is gnawing away at him, devouring one by one the cells that make him up'

(*SM*, pp. 11–12) – against the 'narcissistic' pursuit, once Costello enters, of philosophical deliberations that belie the conceit of the plot's redemptive arc. It's as though Coetzee is himself taking pleasure in revealing how the novel ends up counselling against its own impulse to console.

As *Slow Man* progresses, these two impulses – one reaching for the protagonist's redemption, the other for the novel's aesthetic self-inspection – start to coincide as Rayment scrutinises what Costello, the interrogative stranger in his life, now means to him:

> What he has said about discarding reticence, about speaking his heart, is not, strictly speaking, true. Even to Marijana he has not really opened his heart. Why then does he lay himself bare before the Costello woman, who is surely no friend to him? There can be only one answer: because she has worn him down. A thoroughly professional performance on her part. One takes up position beside one's prey, and waits, and eventually one's prey yields. The sort of thing every priest knows. Or every vulture. Vulture lore. (*SM*, p. 157)

We are taken through a set of rhetorical manoeuvres in this passage that will be familiar to Coetzee's readers: moving from the opening corrections of the first two sentences, the frank question, focalised by Rayment, sets up the process of self-examination played out in the subsequent diagnoses of Costello's 'professional performance'. Morphologically, too, the passage contracts, its syntax becoming shorter, more minimal (especially in the three last sentences that seem to reduce by step) as Rayment pares his own thoughts back to two bare essentials: firstly, that of admission (that 'she has worn him down'); then of accusation (that she has been invoking '[v]ulture lore' to deal with him). An aspect of this verbal contraction not only draws on but dramatises Beckett's admission that 'there is only one real impression and one adequate mode of evocation. Over neither have we the least control.'[99] A strategy that Coetzee most certainly *is* in control of, though, is that of listing questions directed at the character's most fundamental sense of being.

As in the case of his reflections previously described, reeling off such questions typically becomes a basis for establishing what Rayment does *not* feel like doing. This exemplifies Coetzee's mode of posing alternative existential scenarios throughout *Slow Man* in simple syntax.[100] Rayment's queries about himself are enunciated matter-of-factly, with melancholic resignation; and yet their phrasing is so brief as to sound accusatory, condemning:

> Has he given up? Does he want to die? Is that what it comes down to? No. The question is false. He does not *want* to slash his wrists, does not *want* to swallow

down four and twenty Somnex, does not *want* to hurl himself off the balcony. He does not *want* death because he does not *want* anything. But if it so happens that Wayne Blight bumps into him a second time and sends him flying through the air with the greatest of ease, he will make sure he does not save himself. No rolling with the blow, no springing to his feet. If he has a last thought, if there is time for a last thought, it will simply be, *So this is what a last thought is like*. (*SM*, pp. 26–7, Coetzee's emphases)

Stark, functional questions give way to the more imaginatively fleshed-out projection of what Rayment would do if 'Blight bumps into him a second time' on his bike, a projection that is not only hypothetical but impossible given that Rayment will never cycle again. By looking ahead to this idealised scene in which he lets his own life go, cherishing '*what a last thought is like*', Rayment is looking back regretfully at his failure to take advantage of the most catastrophic outcome of his accident. Caught between imagined deaths – between bemoaning the fact that he survived, and the fatality he knows he'll never be able to orchestrate under circumstances comparable to that original crash – he is pinioned, inert in the face of ungraspable alternatives. Coetzee thus finds in Rayment's speculations about his own apathy towards suicide an occasion for reemploying what he noted in Beckett, as we heard earlier, as that 'impulse toward conjuration, the impulse toward silence'. Conjuring scenarios for how things might otherwise be is an impulse Rayment cultivates throughout the first half of *Slow Man*, periodically suspending it, however, as his daydreams of self-erasure are invariably silenced when the Croatian nurse Marijana tends to his intimate needs. Such moments of care in turn counteract the novel's tendency to philosophical involution, as Coetzee compels us to reflect on the global ramifications of the kind of dependency Rayment is developing, a dependency on someone who is vulnerable in relation to her host state, but who is working nonetheless so selflessly for his welfare.

If anything is subject to 'conjuration', then, it is Rayment's own version of that unconditional care that Marijana demonstrates towards him at the outset, and which he reciprocates for Costello, despite himself, at the end. It may be wise for us not to be taken in by such moments of succour, to regard them in the same light as those 'marked' in Beckett, as S. E. Gortarski notes, 'by an increasing distrust of epiphanic moments, perhaps not the psychological experience but its lasting significance'.[101] At the same time, however, the very stillness of the episode where Rayment reconsiders his offer of simple aid to Costello compels us to dwell on its implications. Typographically, in this instance, Coetzee slows the reader's pace, suspending the action to elicit contemplation. If there's a tinge of sentimentality to what Rayment does in letting his guard down, equally the moment 'signifies' what Shameem Black has recently theorised as 'the conditions under which the sentimental makes sense as a productive ethical response'.[102] Those conditions have a formal underpinning too, because they are themselves conjured by the scene's carefully paced arrangement and by our concomitant response to its graphically minimal presentation on the page:

His watch shows 3.15. Three hours yet to dawn. How on earth will he kill three hours?
There is a light on in the living-room. Elizabeth Costello lies asleep at the table she has annexed, her head cradled in her arms atop a mess of papers.
His inclination is to leave her strictly alone. The last thing he wants to do is wake her and open himself to more of her barbs. He is weary of her barbs. Half the time he feels like a poor old bear in the Colosseum, not knowing which way to turn. The death of a thousand cuts.
Nevertheless.
Nevertheless, ever so gently, he lifts her and slips a cushion in under her head.
(*SM*, pp. 236–37)

That the novel's first edition is set in Monotype Bembo only enhances the visibly frugal arrangement of this sequence on the page. Coetzee's typography thereby complements the combination of scenic stasis and Rayment's hesitancy. The moment is fragmented into its component shifts through his indecision, caution and, finally, sympathetic resolve. As a visual correlative to the duration of inner thought, the largest paragraph here is the one in which Rayment is most absorbed in his own self-protection, an 'inclination' for wariness suddenly curtailed by the isolated 'nevertheless'. This adverb cuts in like a caesura, a pause in which he reconsiders the ethical consequences of maintaining his standpoint as a defensive onlooker. When repeated, 'Nevertheless' thus becomes the tipping point at the head of a sentence in which Rayment changes his mind by offering with the cushion a gesture of solicitude.

Coetzee has written that Beckett's 'stories typically draw themselves out to such length that they become the fictional properties of their narrators, who dramatize the conflicting impulses toward illusion and silence by dramatizing themselves as thaumaturges of their stories'.[103] This notion, that anxious moments of narratorial self-reflexivity protract plots at 'such length', may not sound like a template for minimalism, let alone for formal thrift. And yet, as *Slow Man* demonstrates, Coetzee's work sits economically '[s]ide by side', in his own words, 'with this process of doubt' that Beckett was so intent on repeating, probing and exacerbating.[104]

Rearticulating what gives him most stylistic 'delight' in Beckett, Coetzee takes an additional pleasure in paring back his own modes of picturing the interplay of epistemic uncertainty and ethical compromise.

To be sure, after the publication of his third fictionalised memoir, *Summertime*, in 2009, Zadie Smith's conclusion may hold true that Coetzee has 'retreated, spectacularly, to the cannibalisation of the autobiographical', exemplified by his 'rather anaemic later works', as she puts it, where 'the essayistic and self-referential' reign supreme.[105] He is equally aware, however, of the dangers of undermining the enchantments of novel-reading when writerly self-reflexivity runs amok. To this extent, Coetzee has no qualms about protesting his misgivings towards Beckett's late works, as the feeling of reading them 'is an uncomfortable one because they offer us none of the daydream gratification of fiction'.[106] His caution towards the involutions of *Lessness* (1969) shows his awareness of the drawbacks of fiction offering nothing more than an overtly 'destructive commentary upon itself', thereby disqualifying Smith's implication that he has resorted to plundering his own biography for self-indulgent ends.[107] Games of meta-textual self-analysis are not what Coetzee inherits from Beckett's legacy; it is, more arrestingly, the 'lulling plangencies' that we hear in a style guided by circular, often agonistic, thoughts, a style epitomised by *Disgrace*: 'His mind has become a refuge for old thoughts, idle, indigent, with nowhere else to go. He ought to chase them out, sweep the premises clean. But he does not care to do so, or does not care enough'.[108] That we might begin to 'care enough' for David Lurie's capacity for remorse is uncomfortable indeed, given how sparely Coetzee triggers such sympathy, how impartial his clues are to Lurie's sexual motivations early in the novel when compared to the shocking attack on him resulting in the rape of his daughter that sends him on an anguished path to penitence. Such minimalism, though, befits not only the arid farmstead where Lurie retreats to his daughter, but also the tradition out of which Coetzee's *oeuvre* has evolved. If Beckett's fictions can sometimes seem like 'miniature mechanisms for switching themselves off',[109] the traits of compression and contraction they harbour are the very things that turn Coetzee's prose on.

MODERNIST REPOSSESSIONS

In the end, then, perhaps it was the 'element of the stuffed shirt' in Ford that proved all too decisive, sealing Coetzee's disaffection.[110] These intimations of privilege, though, fall short of explaining why Ford's sensibility remained both a point of intrigue and a catalyst for his subsequent dialogue with later modernists. As Coetzee has admitted, 'questions of influence upon my novel-writing are not for me to answer'.[111] If we follow his cue here, as this chapter has done, by taking it on ourselves to draw his map of inheritance, the mapping process is likely to remind us that influences follow indirect paths, skirting in and out of the inheritor's career. 'Most writers absorb influence through their skin', asserts Coetzee; faced with Beckett's eminent legacy, however, he wanted to engage in a more active form of artistic repossession. He needed 'to get closer to a secret', a supremacy that 'I wanted to make my own', but with the aim 'eventually' to 'discard' it.[112] By contrast, although his contact with Ford began with disappointment, it has periodically returned – disrupting any picture we may have of his smooth route from one renounced influence to the next.

It is precisely because Ford turned out to be such an admirable yet enigmatic paragon that he left such an enduring mark on Coetzee's page, even as Beckett emerged as the more suitable subject for his work in structural linguistics. As I have tried to show, Coetzee and Ford synchronise explorations of thrift's cultural uniqueness with the promotion of rhetorical economy, compelling us to rethink the way we connect social and stylistic commitments, especially when we're tracing modernism's afterlives. Sensing precisely that intersection of frugality and form in *Parade's End*, William Carlos Williams was alive to the dualities in Ford's vision, namely his predilection for memorialising great literary precedents while tirelessly appealing for new formal innovations. As Williams concludes: '*Transition* was the biggest word of the quarter century with which the story deals, though its roots, like those of Groby Great Tree, lie in a soil untouched by the modern era'.[113] Something of a tension for Williams, this confluence of transitions and restitutions becomes for Coetzee integral to what Ford does with style itself. The dissolution of feudal hierarchies and jurisdictions is complemented in *Parade's End* by Ford's withdrawal of authorial intrusions of a comforting kind. Allowing free indirect discourse to prevail instead, Ford presents landownership and its sacrifice in such a focalised way as to allow his reader no recourse to an appeasing commentator. For Coetzee, this perspectivism is accompanied by a sense of reserve which is entirely idiomatic: 'Together with a new-found simplicity and directness of emotion come a return to unambiguous portrayal of character, often through third-person narration, that makes *Parade's End* the most "English" of Ford's major novels' (FMF 6.17). Perhaps we should remember here Coetzee's distinction between his initial attraction to Ford's aesthetics and his longstanding affinity with Tietjens's ethics. It's a distinction that is more dialectical than he would have us believe, since it highlights the complicated yet mutually constitutive contact between writerly and socio-political priorities.

An odd trinity at first glance: Ford, Beckett and Coetzee nonetheless set an instructive example for analysing modernism's late-twentieth- and twenty-first-century revitalisations. This seems all the more pertinent at a time when postmodernist notions of appropriation and pastiche now seem inappropriately prescriptive for the task of following modernism's continuance. As we saw in the previous chapter, Ondaatje approaches the principles of Cubist art not as gallery of devices to be emulated or reproduced in a novelistic format, but as a peculiarly 'perfect' paradigm for creativity itself, one that reinvigorates the way readers relate ethically to fiction's provocations of perception. So it is in the case of Coetzee's homage to Ford and Beckett, for the notion of *homage* itself does more than simply offer us, critically speaking, a middle road between influence and originality; neither, for that matter, does it fit comfortably with categories of intertextual parody so often attributed to contemporary novelists in ways that elide the restorative (rather than subversive) outcomes of their returns to earlier working methods. Ford and Beckett alike would be the first to deny that experimental writers today can only deal with influential role models by knowingly dispersing them with the help of metafictional ploys. Coetzee shows how self-reflexivity can work in the service of more urgent and unsettling ends, as his veiled homage to very different modernists provides the occasion for a politically subtle series of recuperations.

CHAPTER 4

The dead hand of modernism: Ian McEwan, reluctant impressionist

It has been more than ninety years since, in *The Craft of Fiction*, Percy Lubbock pondered how '[n]othing, no power, will keep a book steady and motionless before us, so that we might have time to examine its shape and design'. This admission comes at the start of a book that sounds as though it's going to pursue a systematic – as opposed to merely appreciative – account of novelistic technique. Lubbock hedges around this prospect of methodical criticism, however, by conceding that all we 'can hope to possess' in finishing a novel is a 'cluster of impressions'.[1] A decade later, we hear Virginia Woolf declaring along similar lines that 'a novel is an impression' rather than 'an argument',[2] a statement that echoes, as she acknowledges, Thomas Hardy's famously defensive 1892 Preface to *Tess of the D'Urbervilles*, where he vindicated his story of Tess's plight as series of impressions that refuse to be pressed into the service of polemic.[3] Together, Lubbock and Woolf highlight the fluid status of the impression itself as a category distinct from impressionism as a mode. In so doing, they distinguish between using the impression as a kind of critical metaphor and impressionism's formal consequences for the novel. Unsurprisingly, then, the term's slipperiness, its susceptibility to analogy, was compounded when early-twentieth-century writers took the more explicit step of debating whether to call *themselves* impressionists. In this respect, Ford Madox Ford was the most self-conscious, not least in his commentaries about what it means for novelists to identify with artistic impressionism in the first place. In his essay 'On Impressionism' from 1914, for instance, Ford pitches his discussion of impressionism in pragmatic terms, while evaluating how effective this mode might be from the reader's point of view, rather than promoting it from a writerly standpoint as some cutting-edge device. 'Always consider the impressions that you are making upon the mind of the reader', advises Ford, 'and always consider that the first impression with which you present him will be so strong that it will be all that you can ever do to efface it'.[4]

As a writer who has been praised more often for the first impressions left by his thrilling openings than for his hurried endings, Ian McEwan is an appropriate case study for tracing impressionism's late-twentieth-century legacy. Yet as we will see, his relationship to the particular phase in modernist fiction of which impressionism was part is not so straightforward. His affiliation to literary modernism is one that he both acknowledges and denies: sometimes adopting, at other times parodying, the sentiments and strategies that early-twentieth-century experimenters sought to advance. At the same time, however, impressionism's future does at least appear secure in his hands, despite it comprising an inheritance that at times he has preferred to disavow. For even a cursory glance across McEwan's career confirms that his fiction has exploited the dramatic and philosophical uses of perceptual experience that were so key for the likes of Ford, Conrad and Woolf. As Jesse Matz has noted, '[t]o get in the impression not just sense perception but sense that is thought, appearances that are real, suspicions that are true and parts that are whole – this was the "total" aspiration of the Impressionist writer'.[5] It is an aspiration that befits McEwan's work too, despite the fact that his reservations about the modernist project has become increasingly apparent.

Indeed, McEwan isn't the easiest of novelists today to align with any single tradition or genre. Pitched somewhere between the psychological thriller, the novel of ideas, and a more sensuous register that resembles what Zadie Smith coined 'lyrical realism',[6] McEwan nonetheless continues to evoke the conundrums of perception and judgment that lay at the heart of literary impressionism. In more obvious ways, modernist connections are as apparent in setting as in style. We can see this most explicitly in allusions that the Bloomsbury-based *Saturday* (2005) makes to urban 'single-day' novels from Woolf and Joyce. Similarly, *The Comfort of Strangers* (1981) and *Black Dogs* (1992) adopt the formal economy and perspectivism of the Jamesian novella – the former sharing also the Venetian scene of *The Aspern Papers* (1888). Despite his proximity to these modernist templates, though, McEwan has equally wanted, in his words, to 'make a strength out of a kind of ignorance'. This will-to-unawareness implies that he has tried to distinguish himself from any influencing tradition or precedent by cultivating his sense of having 'no roots',[7] to rebel against what he calls the 'overstuffed, overfurnished English novel',[8] as though he has had 'to invent a literature' of his own[9] – in sum, to remain autonomous and match that autonomy in his approach to form.

In light of this impulse to 'write without supports', as he calls it,[10] several questions arise. How has McEwan been able to walk so close to the boundaries of modernism in both method and locale, to pursue what he describes as a 'constant element of self-reinvention', while still being cautious about the perceived insularity of high-modernist aesthetics?[11] How can he admit to being drawn as a young writer to Kafka because he offered 'a freedom from the English novel', only to praise Victorian fiction for the way it 'brought the form to its point ... of perfection'?[12] How can he take such a quintessentially impressionist interest in what he calls 'the fine print of consciousness', while at the same time cursing 'the dead hand of modernism'?[13] Spurred rather than stalled by these seemingly incompatible compulsions, this chapter explores what it is about modernism that McEwan cannot do without.

RELUCTANCE AND AFTER

By providing some answers to those questions, in what follows, my aim is not to resolve McEwan's contradictions. Instead, I will show how his fiction both thematises and formally embodies them within the world of dramatic events. By focusing on key instances from what is widely regarded as McEwan's 'mature' corpus from *The Child in Time* (1987) onwards, I want to discover why he has chosen to foreground 'the creation of character' – a task for which the 'great nineteenth-century novels are', in his opinion, 'unsurpassed'[14] – while at the same time developing his commitment to what is surely the modernist novel's most recognisable impulse: which is to 'remain faithful', in McEwan's phrase, 'to the sensuous, telepathic capabilities of language as it transfers thoughts and feelings from one person's mind to another's'.[15] Grouping together *The Child in Time* (1987), *Atonement* (2001) and *Saturday*, I have singled out novels that are not only deeply concerned with the representation of thought; they also reflect in noticeable ways on their own construction, while demonstrating how impressionist methods of rendering consciousness have become the expressive medium for McEwan's epistemological and ethical concerns. With their double-edged impulse to evoke the subjective lives of characters while subtly drawing our attention to the virtuosic methods by which they do so, these texts enable me to extend this book's overarching contention. For a certain generation of contemporary novelists of which McEwan is part, the legacy of postwar metafiction has stimulated a reassessment of the politics and potential of earlier twentieth-century innovations – the surviving promise of modernist fiction re-emerging from the creative disappointments of postmodernism.

Yet McEwan has had a feisty relationship with that promise. In furthering his effort to 'write against what [he] saw', early in his career, 'as the prevailing greyness of English style and subject matter',[16] his appeal to modernism for more colour has not always been convivial. Here I tend to agree with Laura Marcus, who sees that McEwan does not 'attempt merely to reproduce the modernist text' by offering 'a parody or pastiche of it'; on the contrary, she sees that he 'acknowledges the debt even as he calls attention to the necessary and inevitable distance between his own time and that of the modernist novelist'.[17] That historical 'distance' could simply be for McEwan another way of reasserting his own creative autonomy, of course, even though the very notion of autonomous form, as recent theorists have pointed out, should not be construed as implying that 'the aesthetic exists outside of time and history'.[18] My own sense is that McEwan has been watchful of this temptation to set his writing apart from all that modernism stood for, and he resists it by refusing to regard the technical achievements of modernist narration as reusable relics of literary history. Reluctant though he may be to compromise his stature as a writer without 'roots', the relation between *debt* and *distance*, to adopt Marcus's useful terms, persists as a dialectical feature not only of his craft but also thematically, expressed in the issues of inheritance and self-determination, artistic tradition and scientific progress, that his characters often find themselves debating.

McEwan is hardly the first postwar writer to have allowed that dialectic to become part of his work. Saul Bellow is a key precursor here, and it's surely no coincidence that a line from *The Dean's December* (1982) appears in *Saturday*, one of the novels Henry Perowne vaguely recites but whose author he fails to pin down. Bellow appeals to McEwan because his fiction occupies a pivotal moment in the postwar period, at once overcoming the anxieties of inheriting high modernism, while foreseeing the futility of that metafictional 'anti-illusionism', to recall Coetzee's term, perpetuated through the 1960s and 1970s. To borrow Philip Roth's observation from Chapter 1, Bellow aimed 'not only to infuse fiction with mind but to make *mentalness itself* central to the hero's dilemma'.[19] Similarly, McEwan's own longstanding interest in neuroscience has only intensified his attention to the importance of handling narrative perspective not as a neutral lens, but as an intensifier of events and a reason for experimenting with language. For McEwan, the ambition is to represent 'what it's like to be conscious, or sentient, or, fatally, only half-sentient'.[20] I will consider how these aspects of consciousness shape McEwan's narration later. Here, though, I simply want to emphasise that he is becoming all the more intriguing as a writer who is reluctant to find himself aligned with what he may well view as the institutional elitism of the modernist project, even though his compositional aims belie a deep kinship with those of early-twentieth-century impressionism.

Nowhere more pointedly does McEwan express this sort of reluctance than in *Atonement* (2001). Briony Tallis's *Two Figures by a Fountain* has a 'crystalline' style that, as we later discover, comprises Part I of the novel. In a fictionalised editorial response to her submitted manuscript for *Two Figures*, Cyril Connolly reflects that it 'owed a little too much to the techniques of Mrs Woolf'.[21] The moment would appear to consolidate McEwan's distaste for all things high modernist, but, in fact, it indexes a more indeterminate attitude. Granted, we might assume that the legacy of Woolf's attempt to 'delve into mysteries of perception' in order to 'present a stylized version of thought processes' (*A*, p. 312) is merely performing a cameo role in *Atonement*, a charade that turns out to be short-lived. (Part II switches forward in time to chart the allied withdrawal from France in a lean third-person register that casts off the lush free indirect style of Part I.) Likewise, we could assume that McEwan is using the ornamental language of *Two Figures* to mock a style that's already sounding outdated, at least to a critic like Connolly, because it's being outmoded by that new realism of the interwar years – practised through the 1930s by Elizabeth Bowen and Rosamond Lehmann, both of whom McEwan has at times paid tribute to when reflecting on *Atonement*'s inspirations.[22] In a recent survey of *Atonement*'s modernist affiliations, Richard Robinson repeats this conclusion about McEwan's reservations. Connolly or 'C. C.', as McEwan figures him, is used as a 'key influence', writes Robinson, 'in diverting Briony from Woolfian modernism, emerging as a Tiresias-like critic who already knows what the younger Briony cannot bring herself to confront. Briony infers that Connolly's criticism of her story relates to its moral evasiveness, that she has hidden behind her modernist style and "drown[ed] her guilt" in streams of consciousness'.[23] Following this argument, we might speculate that McEwan is offering something of a literary-critical historiography: his indictment of Briony's aestheticised and self-gratifying way of observing domestic intimacies, blinkered as she is in Part I to Robbie's social alienation from the Tallis household, reveals McEwan siding with the real-life Connolly of *Enemies of Promise* (1938). Posing there as a critic of the fate of literature approaching mid-century, Connolly ponders 'what sort of writing ... is likely to last'. He does so by contrasting 'the realist, or vernacular style of rebels' (McEwan, for one, began his career in rebellious defence of realism's capacity to enter psychosexual domains) with 'the Mandarin' mode that preserves the lyricism of *fin-de-siècle* dandyism,[24] a mode whose supposed indolence is very much in keeping with McEwan's damning picture of Briony's flights of fancy. Inspired by her interest in the romanticised *prospect* of writing, Briony is hindered by her own lyrical style from developing a more ethically reflective manner of describing the social realm of action and accountability – or rather, devastatingly, she develops it too late.

Now, we could make any one of these assumptions, and thereby feel confident about McEwan's misgivings towards the perceived artificialities and ethical inadequacies of high-modernist fiction, were it not for the fact that he cannot entirely undermine Briony's allegiance to the Woolfian novel of consciousness – because that's precisely the kind of novel he wants for himself. As proof of this paradox, McEwan reveals affinities with the very mode he tries not to inherit, by making remarks about his own craft that very nearly echo word-for-word Connolly's concession to Briony, that the 'vagaries and unpredictability of the private self' *do* come together to make a 'worthy subject in itself' (*A*, p. 312). Just as Briony receives the positive feedback that her strengths lie in 'present[ing] a stylized version of thought processes', so McEwan has said that the impulse overarching his career is 'to present, obviously in a very stylized way, what it's like to be thinking'.[25]

However much he might like to distinguish himself from the iconicity of writers like Woolf, the doctrine of internal perspective that McEwan subscribes to – together with his way of working from the 'bottom up', in his phrase, by showing us what a character's sentient mind is like from the inside out – more than adequately suggests that his affinities with impressionism are stronger than Briony's pastiche of Woolf implies.[26] Robinson may be right to say that '[a]t the age of eighteen, Briony is a modernist down to her bootstraps – and in 1940, a modernist out of time'.[27] But this doesn't automatically mean that McEwan himself is unwilling to see modernism back *in* time. He knows that contemporary writers 'can't retreat to the nineteenth-century' any more than they can retreat to the creative scene of 1922; he knows too that they 'now have a narrative self-awareness that we can never escape', an awareness that they 'don't want to be crushed by'.[28] Emerging between these polarities – with Victorian realism out of reach and postmodern self-reflexivity out of fashion – modernist aesthetics have become vital again. To those writers from McEwan's generation for whom 'narrative self-awareness' soon ran its course,[29] we could apply what Woolf said about Henry James being 'much at present in the air' to the way modernism has persisted because its solutions remain pertinent, solutions 'looming large and undefined in the consciousness of writers, to some an oppression, to others an obsession, but undeniably present to all'.[30]

How it is that specifically impressionist methods have loomed large for McEwan is a question we can only begin to answer (paradoxically again) by addressing how he has distinguished those methods as his own. 'A work of art has to be self-generated',[31] he insisted in 2007. This assertion raises the issue of how McEwan has reconciled his belief in artistic freedom from extra-literary obligations with his sense that 'serious' fiction should 'have some muscularity of intellect'.[32] Of course, such split priorities were central to early-twentieth-century fiction, underwriting modernism's negotiation between 'merely' aesthetic and utilitarian conceptions of the novel's purpose.[33] Squaring those priorities, as McEwan's body of work shows, is an ongoing and open-ended task for novelists today. It's a task that situates his work in a context of debates about artistic autonomy, debates that offer, for this chapter's purposes, a more sophisticated way of thinking about McEwan's response to modernism per se, than readings that gauge his ability to emulate earlier twentieth-century narrative techniques as period-styles. As I will go on to show here, his assertion about the need for art to be 'self-generated' points to a productive tension in his work. McEwan invites us to entertain 'a view of the novel', in Martin Ryle's phrase, as a form 'which sees its autonomy as an aesthetic object as *qualified by* its referential dependence on the social milieu'.[34] If McEwan's fiction often 'actively solicits a political reading',[35] it also draws our attention to the formal inventiveness by which it initiates that very process of solicitation. That this invitation to read for the political in McEwan's writing is itself a product of his formal dexterity strikes to the heart of his concern with modernism's outstanding possibilities – however reticently he might acknowledge his inheritance of them. By virtue of that concern, McEwan shares with each of the writers considered in this study an impulse to move beyond postmodern fiction's self-involved reflexivity. In his later fiction, he has tried to combine a commitment to the novel's autonomy with his conviction that imaginative literature can at the same time maintain an 'engagement with the world'.[36] It's this endeavour – to preserve the novel from being reduced to the service of purely instrumental ends, yet without compromising its ability to offer social critique – which poses a challenge that McEwan greets with prototypically impressionist solutions.

AUTONOMY AND INSTRUMENTALISM

The house of fiction McEwan has built since *The Child in Time* contains three distinct levels, allowing room for the realist, the modernist and the metafictionist in ways that encourage these occupants to meet and embrace each other's differences. He has inhabited this house from the start, as he implies in remarks as far back as 1978 about the purpose of innovation. Reflecting in *The New Review* on the abstruse literary 'experimentation of the late Sixties and early Seventies', he suggests that 'there can be surely no more mileage to be had from demonstrating yet again through self-enclosed "fictions" that reality is words and words are lies. There is no need to be strangled by that particular loop – the artifice of fiction can be taken for granted'.[37] That McEwan is discussing how writers might move forward in the aftermath of postmodernist priorities for experimentation (priorities described rather sardonically by McEwan as 'busting up your syntax and scrambling you page order') makes it all the more significant that he decides to reach back. The road ahead, as he sees it, involves the writer's recuperation of that core impressionist investment in evoking 'states of mind and the society that forms them'.[38] Significantly, his sentiments closely echo those of John Barth published four years earlier: 'if you acknowledge and embrace the artificial aspect of art which you can't get rid of anyway, then it doesn't really follow, for example, that you have to abandon certain kinds of literary devices simply because they're metaphors for notions that are no longer viable'.[39] In a similar fashion, McEwan emphasises 'content' as the proper justification for experimenting with form, unconvinced as he is that the postmodern vogue for 'busting up' the novel will continue to be seen as innovative in years to come.

Woolf herself might have agreed with him. Committed to the inseparability of felt perceptions and their formal representation, she viewed the novel to be at its most original when embodying in design the affective content it describes. Likewise, she made it clear that novelists cannot simply co-opt fresh subject-matter and convey it in a predetermined manner, worrying in 'The Narrow Bridge of Art' (1927) that '[o]n all sides writers are attempting what they cannot achieve, forcing the form they use to contain a meaning which is strange to it'.[40] In essence, McEwan and Woolf share the same worry about the will-to-innovation compromising the indissolubility of substance and mode, action and expression. 'Meaning' appears 'strange' in relation to its form when a writer isolates experimentation from social content, rather than seeing inventiveness as intimately bound up with the ethical or social situations that characters encounter and to which they emotionally react. McEwan and Woolf thus also partake in comparable ideas of formal autonomy whose 'manifestation as organic form', as Jonathan Loesberg has pointed out, is often 'criticized as an impossible attempt to give material shape to transcendent design'.[41] To assume, however, that the commitment *not* to treat manner apart from matter (in the way that McEwan and Woolf both imply) is necessarily idealistic would be to misrepresent what the interaction of form and content means to writers who allow, quite intentionally, the 'material shape' of their narrative to be designed *by* the mental processes they focalise. Depictions of thought, for McEwan and Woolf, determine formal decisions; and 'form' in turn, attests McEwan, 'is total in its embrace'.[42]

To the extent that they hold such principles in common, McEwan and Woolf thus recall Adorno's contention that '[a]esthetic success is essentially measured by whether the formed object is able to awaken the content [*Inhalt*] sedimented in the form'.[43] For McEwan, as for Woolf, 'states of mind' provide not merely a focus of description; they are the lifeblood of description. Finding dynamic links between sensation and intellection is a task that compels both writers, despite their historical distance. They are links that provide the basis for interior characterisation and thereby the very content that is 'sedimented in the form' of free indirect style. This content – which is really the affective and cognitive content of characters' perceptions – may be 'awaken[ed]' at the level of the sentence, or on the larger scale of a sequence whose structure emulates the patterns of focalised thought. While it's commonplace to note that the representation of sensation, attention or emotional lability fragments the structures of modernist fiction, the 'idea' persists, as Adorno reminds us, of form as the concept that 'made the wholeness and autonomy of the artwork possible' in the first place.[44] Even for the most daring writers, at either end of the twentieth century, who 'would like to do away with unity altogether', the structural open-endedness of the works they produce 'necessarily regain[s] something comparable to unity insofar as this openness is planned'.[45] By talking of plans, of course, Adorno foregrounds matters of technique; but, again, he understands it not as evidence of craft's separation from, or superiority over, matter – as though a writer's technical aspirations could ever be divorced from what she seeks to dramatise. Indeed, form itself 'converges with critique',[46] insists Adorno, in a phrase that complements McEwan's notion that experimentation should have much 'to do with content'. It is by virtue of this convergence that 'artworks prove self-critical',[47] a prospect that dovetails with McEwan's inclination to 'feel that every sentence contains a ghostly commentary on its own processes'.[48] We can, therefore, note several affinities between Adorno's defence of aesthetic autonomy and what McEwan sees as the viability of writing formally inventive fiction whose originality derives from its social (hence, extra-aesthetic) engagements.

The point of highlighting these shared sentiments is not simply for the convenience of framing McEwan's ambitions with a vocabulary that has been applied so influentially to modernist practices. Undeniably, this *is* one critical payoff, insofar as McEwan's attraction to 'self-generated' art sounds directly in touch with Adorno's claim that form 'is the relation of parts to each other and to the whole as the elaboration of details'.[49] This framework, though, also reveals how McEwan revives for his own time what Charles Altieri has called 'modernist claims for autonomy'.[50] For McEwan has answered some of the most pressing issues facing writers in the wake of postmodernism by restarting discussions that circulated at the heart of modernism's own attempts to describe the relation of aesthetics to politics: namely, discussions about that 'twofold essence', as Adorno terms it, that inheres in all art, but which distinguishes novelists who negotiate the double status of what they publish as 'both an autonomous entity and a social fact'.[51]

Far from flying in the face of modernism's 'dead hand', then, McEwan has taken on its legacy to provide answers for the question of where novelistic experiment should go next, especially after the withering appeal of postmodern self-consciousness. He has come to realise that 'you can never quite escape' today the residue of metafictional reflexivity, suggesting that '[a]t best you can take it for granted' – in a statement that echoes his predictions for the *New Review* in 1978 – 'and not become enslaved to self-reference'.[52] In a comment that is all the more timely in light of *Atonement*, McEwan insisted that he has become 'drawn to some kind of balance' between writing a novel that is 'self-reflective', and one that 'accepts' the premise of its own capacity to create that 'illusion' of inhabiting the perceptual range, habits and dispositions of someone who is essentially unknown to us.[53] Critics have interpreted the pertinence of McEwan's emphasis on this 'balance' in different ways, satisfying a range of theoretical ends. One point of consensus, however, is that novels such as *Atonement* offer important interventions in, not to say convenient examples for, the recent discourse of literary ethics. He not only raises ethical questions diegetically, by pursuing the consequences of characters' moral errors of judgment, but also on a hermeneutic level, as he invites readers at once to contemplate their own expectations of fiction itself as a moral medium and to speculate about the nature of authorial accountability.

McEwan's amenability to this wellspring of new trends in ethical criticism also has implications for how we frame his relationship to impressionism, giving us pause in turn about the ethics of impressionist narration. *Atonement*, for instance, provides an ideal testing ground for what Dorothy Hale has compellingly explored as the 'novelistic aesthetics of alterity', because the novel strives to connect formal innovation and moral provocation in a way that 'derives from Henry James's acute awareness that the politicized struggle between art and its ideological instrumentality is constitutive of novelistic aesthetics itself'.[54] Likewise, just as *Atonement*'s formal procedures bear witness to how McEwan has become, in his own words, 'a more traditional writer, or at least a writer much more aware – consciously, expressively aware – of the traditions of the English novel',[55] so at the level of its content, the novel adopts a combative stance on where the ethical capacities of impressionism potentially fall short.

Picking up on the *Atonement*'s implicit self-critique in this respect, Alistair Cormack argues that in Part I of the narrative 'the exemplary modernist text we encounter is being subtly subverted'. McEwan does this, in Cormack's view, by compelling us to acknowledge Briony's *Two Figures by a Fountain* as the absorbing yet stultifying pastiche that it is. For Cormack, McEwan 'is not using his novel to challenge the ideological functions of a novelistic discourse assaying verisimilitude, but rather to attack static, morally disengaged, plotless modernism'.[56] This is a stark conclusion to reach, one that both homogenises modernism's capacities for moral engagement and underestimates how intensely McEwan is drawn to writing itself as what he calls 'a self-pleasuring act'.[57] Cormack suggests that the 'Woolf-like modernism' of *Atonement*'s opening part should only be 'regard[ed] as an imitation by an absent author-demiurge (McEwan) of one character's own modernist reconstruction of the event'.[58] Does that mean, then, we are not supposed to admire Part I for what it is, only as a sustained and ultimately searing accusation levelled against a style deprived of responsibility? The answer depends on whether we feel compelled to read with the grain of McEwan's metafictional chastisements of ethically blinkered modernism; or whether in fact we're willing to entertain the possibility that, for all its self-awareness, what *Atonement* most reflexively reveals is just how far McEwan (inadvertently) admits that much of the novel's emotive force is enabled and intensified by the very formal dynamics that his plot is designed to criticise and whose influence he would prefer to disavow.

Ultimately, there is nothing unethical about the way Briony writes, only about what, on that fateful evening, she does. If Woolfian free indirect discourse *is* such an amoral mode, as Cormack implies, then the adult

Briony may have surely been inclined to edit Part I accordingly as another act of retrospective atonement, thereby matching, in bluntly realist terms, the sentiments of her adult remorse. In other words, the novel solicits a surface reading which concludes that the success of McEwan's ethical ambition depends on the success of his subversion of modernist aesthetics. This position, however, neglects the complex and contradictory ways in which McEwan might be drawn to impressionism's methods of rendering interiority, precisely because such methods allow his reader psychological access to Briony's impetuousness as a child – an insider's view, so to speak, of those fleeting impressions that she turns into devastating judgments. In short, it is not high-modernist perspectivism that's on trial here, but the horrific misapprehensions of a girl whose actions McEwan invites us to observe, even while we remain powerless to indict her. It's an invitation conveyed by nothing other than his impressionist use of internal focalisation, as it encourages us to share the cognitive space of Briony's rash decisions that later become the subject of her penitence.

Atonement, then, demonstrates that McEwan aims to do more than simply ironise his own literary heritage by betraying the amorality of high modernism. Instead, the novel typifies how he writes at the confluence of what seem like extremes: where Victorian realism's commitment to character and modernism's commitment to sensory experience intersect with the breed of postmodern self-reflexivity that McEwan – like the other writers considered in this book – has never been drawn to anyway. Poised at that intersection, *Atonement* offers something of an arena for these modes, an arena where inheritance and innovation, morality and metafiction, are brought together in sophisticated colloquy. By entertaining these seemingly conflictive properties, *Atonement* remains, in McEwan's own words, his most visible 'attempt' yet on behalf of the post-millennial novel 'to discuss where we stand'.[59]

ACCOUNTABLE IMPRESSIONS

Consumed in the romance of her writerly enterprise, young Briony was fatally ignorant of the ethical repercussions of imagination. Though hardly unique, McEwan's message is that fiction needs to incorporate into its own formal elegance an awareness of its accountability to the lived world it simulates. As we shall see in the next and final chapter, his implication that there remains an indissoluble link between virtuosity and answerability, experimental ambition and ethical responsibility, is one shared by Toni Morrison, who asserted in 2005 'that the practice of great art is the practice of knowledge *unseduced by* its own beauty'.[60] It is a principle that's elegantly encapsulated in the 'dream' McEwan confided to Zadie Smith in the same year as Morrison's claim, a dream that, for him, 'we [writers] all have': 'to write this beautiful paragraph that actually is describing something but at the same time in another voice is writing a commentary on its own creation, without having to be a story about a writer'.[61] That dream has been realised with varying success, of course, if we bear in mind the way *Atonement* implies various commentaries on its own making while also offering a podium for Briony's authorial self-interrogation. By the end of the novel, we have learned to view any 'beautiful paragraph' with due suspicion, mindful of the ethical ramifications of *how* she describes the actions she recalls. Elsewhere, however, McEwan's dream is more subtly achieved, especially in episodes that can enthral us simply by their own stylisation and yet still do justice to the moral, political and emotional exigencies that inspire them. Although it's true that McEwan subscribes to the 'characteristic modernist idea', in Jonah Siegel's words, 'that the most important manifestation of an aesthetic object is a reflection on its own formal qualities', it's certainly not the case that this 'is, paradoxically, a way to do away with the pressures of the material, to make matter into concept'.[62] McEwan endorses that idea of formal self-reflection, yet without seeing it as an escape-route either into the self-ironising strategies of postmodern fiction or into an autonomous literary-aesthetic realm freed of obligations to social critique. Far from relinquishing 'the pressures of the material', McEwan is at his most self-conscious when laying bare the methods by which he folds those pressures into our phenomenological experience of events.

Such is the level of attentiveness that McEwan commands, suspended as we often are between what is unsettling in a scene and the enchantment of reading its execution. At this point, let us make our first visit to *Saturday* – a novel that I will return to later in a more critical fashion – to see how McEwan repudiates the postmodern exaggeration of self-consciousness to extend modernist forms of narrative reflexivity, while at the same time retaining his reader's enthrallment. Supremely gifted in love and intellect, domestically and professionally fulfilled, Henry Perowne is a figure ripe for satire. *Saturday* is notoriously ambiguous, however, about whether we should respond sympathetically or sardonically to its neurosurgeon protagonist. Nowhere more audible is this ambiguously ironic voice than in the novel's carefully choreographed opening scene. In a sequence that is typically unnerving but somehow teasing as well, the restless Perowne leaves his bed and gazes in darkness as a flaming cargo plane descends over

London. Watching from the upper floor window of his Fitzrovia townhouse, Perowne is monarch of all he surveys, and McEwan hints at the imperiousness of his elevated viewpoint over the world beyond his terrace. Here the novel's overarching themes of observation and understanding, sensation and intellection, intersect with the issue of Perowne's helplessness before (what he assumes is) an impending disaster. Dominic Head is right to suggest that 'McEwan's work reveals the legacy of modernism to the extent that it vividly enacts a form of double consciousness in which knowledge and experience co-exist'.[63] But that model of consciousness in Perowne's case now faces an ethical compromise, when he becomes aware of his own simultaneous distance from, yet enthrallment by, a spectacle that deserves horror instead of fascination:

So despite the apologetic posture, the mild manner and an inclination to occasional daydreaming, it's unlike Perowne to dither as he does now – he's standing at the foot of the bed – unable to decide whether to wake Rosalind. It makes no sense at all. There's nothing to see. It's an entirely selfish impulse. Her alarm is due to go off at six thirty, and once he's told her the story, she'll have no hope of going back to sleep. She'll hear it anyway. Now that the shutters are closed and he's in darkness again, he understands the extent of his turmoil. His thoughts have a reeling, tenuous quality – he can't hold an idea long enough to force sense out of it. He feels culpable somehow, but helpless too. These are contradictory terms, but not quite, and it's the degree of their overlap, their manner of expressing the same thing from different angles, which he needs to comprehend. Culpable in his helplessness. Helplessly culpable. He loses his way, and thinks again of the phone. By daylight, will it seem negligent not to have called the emergency services? Will it be obvious that there was nothing to be done, that there wasn't time? His crime was to stand in the safety of his bedroom, wrapped in a woollen dressing gown, without moving or making a sound, half dreaming as he watched people die. Yes, he should have phoned, if only to talk, to measure his voice and feelings against a stranger's. (*S*, pp. 22–3)

Gradually changing key, these present-tense impressions begin by eliciting our sympathy; but the proleptic questions become perfunctory, forestalling any compassion we may be tempted to develop towards Perowne 'in his helplessness'. McEwan thus merges the eloquence of his protagonist's self-vindicating speculations with an underlying sardonicism. Where the passage opens with a measured notation of traits ('posture', 'manner', 'inclination'), it soon peals into paratactic digressions (aptly enough, in the very sentence that begins to highlight Perowne's 'contradictory terms'), digressions that offer a syntactic correlative to his faltering self-image. At the level of intonation, then, McEwan achieves his twinned aims: conveying in a 'stylized way what it's like to be thinking' self-contentedly as Perowne does, while also hinting at the sense in which such contentment – detected here in a man bearing witness to the spectacle of catastrophe – reveals 'how much perception is distorted by will'.[64]

In *Saturday*, McEwan showcases what Maggie Gee, as we saw in the Introduction, called the virtue of 'concealing complexity under a surface ease'; but he ultimately takes it to a more interrogative level. We are constantly invited to speculate on both the provenance and object of scrutiny in *Saturday*, a scrutiny of its protagonist's privilege that's thinly veiled behind a pristine exhibition of McEwan's attention to the 'reeling, tenuous quality' of Perowne's impressions. Beneath the novel's counterfeit serenity, the suggestion is that *Saturday* undercuts its own ostensible endorsement of Perowne's worldview. Hinting at his own choreographed role-play as an external narrator, McEwan alternates modes with impersonal grace, modulating between the sympathetic focalisation of Perowne's inner 'turmoil' and the more steely, sage-like impartiality of a prosecutor, overseeing an ethically suspect scenario of inaction. Capturing this contrariness between the depicted scene and the mordancy of its depiction, McEwan's voice operates at a sly remove, insinuating a 'commentary on its own creation' but without intruding in this most suspenseful of openings. With this register, he builds into the narrative's tonal composure a means of sanctioning against the reader's passive observance of events, summoning us to the breach of this novel's self-inquiry where our immersion often coincides with moral discomfiture.

Tangible *moments* of intensity such as these, of course, recall what would become, in Leo Charney's words, the 'defining trope of the modern'.[65] If, however, the impression of such moments, as Woolf contended, makes one 'aware that we are spectators and also passive participants in a pageant',[66] McEwan turns the passivity of spectatorship into a motivation for critique, disturbing the reader's pleasure in the facile way he conveys such moments from the outset. We may regret this disturbance, as our gratifications are dispelled. Yet that is the point. It reveals the critical edge McEwan gives to the impressionist rendering of ephemerality. These moments of perception can certainly become 'sculpturesque', in Woolf's term;[67] and yet, McEwan wouldn't want us *not* to appreciate the equally sculptured language that articulates them. Sculptures are rarely made entirely for their own sake, and we should think twice before mistaking their apparent autonomy as proof that they are irrelevant to the 'pageant' of social life – together with the passing and pressing time of that life, which the sculptured moments of impressionist fiction are so well-suited to evoke.

'MODERNISTS HAVE THEIR USES AFTER ALL': IMPRESSIONS OF TRAGIC TIME

If *Atonement* and *Saturday* stand out in McEwan's career as laboratories for examining both the fate of character in fiction and the future of formal reflexivity, then they certainly do not stand alone. More than a decade before, central topics of intellectual and popular-cultural discussion were even more thoroughly (some would say, schematically) played out in *The Child in Time*. As someone in mourning while sitting on a government subcommittee of childcare experts, though still traumatised by the abduction of his daughter Kate, Stephen Lewis has a propensity for introspection and sudden bouts of distraction. His periods of wandering reflection establish the structural logic of a narrative that, in its subjectivism, bears all the hallmarks of impressionist fiction. As Stephen thinks back to what-might-have-been, had he not left home that morning for the supermarket where Kate was abducted, McEwan generates pathos by having Stephen re-enact, like a Joycean negative epiphany, the reversal in all its gradual stages:

Later, in the sorry months and years, Stephen was to make efforts to re-enter this moment, to burrow his way back through the folds between events, crawl between the covers, and reverse his decision. But time – not necessarily as it is, for who knows that, but as thought has constituted it – monomaniacally forbids second chances.[68]

McEwan provides details of an action that never happened – Stephen's return to his wife, Julie, in bed through 'the folds' and 'covers' – but which somehow makes that reversal more tangible, as though it really *is* a recollection and not the hypothetical 'decision' that it will forever remain. As a make-believe 'moment', rather than a lived one from the past, it is ultimately what intensifies the tragic regret Stephen experiences here in this remorseful fantasy of reversal.

Even at this early stage in the novel, then, time itself steps in as the antagonist. While McEwan personifies temporality in ways that recall the hammering chimes of Big Ben in *Mrs Dalloway* (1925), unlike Woolf, he makes less of the distinction between official clock time and the personalised rhythms of everyday experience. *The Child in Time* is, in this sense, McEwan's answer to the way '[p]ostmodernist fiction', in Barry Lewis's estimation, 'does not just disrupt the past but corrupt the present too', parodying 'the linear coherence of narrative by warping the sense of significant time, *Kairos*, or the dull passing of ordinary time, *Chronos*'. The former, as Lewis argues, is 'strongly associated with those modernist novels which are disposed around moments of epiphany and disclosure', whereas postmodern fiction tends to 'chuckle at such solemnities'.[69] What's distinctive about *The Child in Time*'s impressionist rendition of diurnal experience is that it turns the tables on Lewis's literary-historical binary, as McEwan brings the seemingly unremarkable 'passing of ordinary time' into sharp focus at precisely those moments in the novel which we're invited to consider as the most ethically and emotionally 'significant'.

Quotidian duration serves not only as an elastic framing device reflected in the novel's episodic form, as well as a cerebral foe that Stephen is forever battling in episodes of remembrance; it also becomes a subject of debate between Stephen and his physicist friend Thelma. In his grief, he looks to Thelma for intellectual companionship, which she in turn reciprocates as her husband Charles withdraws into a domestic fantasy of boyhood innocence. Warmly mocking Stephen's belief in literary accounts of time's 'patterned movement' (*CT*, p. 44), she spars with him by reviving the 'two cultures' divide: "As far as I can make out, you think that some local, passing fashion like modernism – modernism! – is the intellectual achievement of out time. Pathetic!'" (*CT*, p. 45). Such debates might seem performative to the reader, if not exaggerated; and we wonder whether McEwan is half-sharing Thelma's scoff at modernism, even as Stephen campaigns to free literature from that citadel of scepticism to which Thelma consigns it. I will come back to this tension in McEwan's allegiances later, when returning to *Saturday* where – just as Thelma's physics often claims the upper hand to Stephen's aesthetics – rational, neuroscientific accounts of consciousness compete with more perceptual, phenomenological depictions of experience which link McEwan to impressionism. *The Child in Time* may thus be seen as a forerunner to *Saturday* in that it stages these contradictory sides of its creator. Just as, in *Saturday*, Daisy Perowne defends her family by stunning their attacker when reading aloud one of her poems, so Stephen defends himself against Thelma's quantum mechanics by reciting Eliot's famous meditation on time in the opening three lines of 'Burnt Norton' – to which Thelma replies, 'your modernists have their uses after all' (*CT*, p. 118).

Away from the arena of scientific discovery and debate, however, McEwan never loses sight of the affective dimensions of time. To evoke such dimensions, *The Child in Time* is structured around the forces that govern Stephen's retrospection, again pointing to the interdependency of personal tragedy and public temporality, private mourning and the merciless onward motion of daily routine. Hampering his capacity to recall minor details, time also becomes an anthropomorphic presence that taunts him with alternative versions of the here-and-now. Stephen feels perpetually tempted to imagine the present as it might otherwise be by re-analysing the past, returning to the shopping scene of Kate's disappearance where he longs to 'move his eyes, lift them against the weight of time, to find that shrouded figure at the periphery of vision, the one who was always to the side and slightly behind, who, filled with a strange desire, was calculating odds, or simply waiting' (*CT*, p. 16). Such attempts to push back against the 'weight' of actual events and rewrite the script that leads up to Kate's abduction only exacerbate Stephen's periods of mournful daydreaming. In turn, these periods are encapsulated by the novel's very form, as its structural digressions into protracted flashbacks seem to conspire with the 'monomaniacally' obliterative progress of everyday time.

Architecturally, then, *The Child in Time*'s temporal progression works, or appears to work, independently of its protagonist. Time is the one sovereign agent in a novel whose very unfolding seems to occur autonomously around and in spite of Stephen's sense of will. Yet it also reveals how the symbolic structures of time notate across the novel a series of 'aesthetic alternative[s]', to borrow Mark Wollaeger's words, to institutionalised routine, but without allowing the novel to 'surrender to subjectivism'.[70] In effect, alternative temporal states provide opportunities for Stephen to objectify and reassess his own subjective apprehension of the present, even as he is pulled longingly towards a past that's impossible to correct. At once friend and foe, time's function in this novel is to persist as a motif with material ramifications, as McEwan urges us to 'acknowledge the social dimension of the modernist aspiration to discover principles of order occluded by a surfeit of naturalistic detail'.[71] In this sense, impressions of time in the narrative have a twofold consequence. They have the capacity to immerse Stephen in mournful retrospection and distract him from making potentially proactive decisions (such as starting to write, or breaking his marital silence by contacting Julie); but also, and more dynamically, they facilitate a defamiliarised view of his involvement in the activities of public office. McEwan never quite allows his protagonist to inhabit London's political sphere at a sufficiently critical remove, and Stephen remains far more reassured than he knows he ought to be by the *idea* of the quango's timetable for meetings that in reality he finds so dull. Purposefully, then, McEwan does not always capitalise on the potential for defamiliarising Stephen's perspective; nor, at an expressional level, is the novel's 'surfeit of naturalistic detail' as frequently undermined as it might otherwise have been. That said, McEwan *does* suspend and interrupt the novel's prevailing realism with Stephen's propensity for distraction. This interruptive rendering of memorial time counterpoints Stephen's personalised sense of passing weeks with the dispassionate flow of diurnal time, in such a way that counteracts the degree of order and efficiency he feels he ought to be cultivating. Even the committee room serves the opposite function that it should; instead of a place for intellectual deliberation, it is a realm of uncontrolled reflection and free association:

> It was the conspiracy of objects – lavatory seat, bed sheets, floor dirt – to remain exactly as they had been left. At home too he was never far from his subjects, his daughter, his wife, what to do. But here he lacked the concentration for sustained thought. He daydreamed in fragments, without control, almost without consciousness. (*CT*, pp. 11–12)

Throughout the first two sentences, the enumerations emulate the principles of accretion and digression that structure the novel as a whole, as McEwan qualifies Adorno's notion that form (in this instance, syntactic form) remains 'the artefact's coherence, however self-antagonistic and refracted' the text itself turns out to be.[72] This antagonism in *The Child in Time* exists between the manner in which Stephen thinks and the disciplined tasks that he tries to involve himself in, from his institutional role in the quango to his professional one as a children's novelist attempting to reignite some semblance of a regular writing routine.

In this passage, McEwan's brilliantly unspecific clause 'what to do' captures in the rhythm of its anapaest the throbbing motion of Stephen's daydreams as they centre on images of Kate. In contrast to the intimacy of that clause, focalised as it is by Stephen, the final staccato sentence feels accusatory (its severity reinforced by the repeated negative preposition 'without'), certainly more distanced and reportorial. This is McEwan at his most teacherly: revealing that however attracted he is to free indirect style, he always reserves an audibly detached voice for perorations and asides. Events at the supermarket 'crime scene' immediately following Kate's disappearance correspond in tone to this depersonalised, documentary register: 'The policemen took out their notebooks and Stephen told his story, which was energetic both in delivery and in attention to detail. He was sufficiently removed from his own feelings to take pleasure in succinctness of expression, the skilful marshalling of relevant facts' (*CT*, pp. 19–20). It is here that McEwan's tragic narrative produces its own version of what Alex Zwerdling identifies in *Jacob's Room* (1922) as Woolf's 'double awareness of the sharpness of grief and its absurdity', an alertness that McEwan exhibits as he tracks Stephen's remorse without letting lyrical impressions console for what is lost, just as Woolf 'worked hard to avoid sentimentalizing her subject and casting her book in the romantic mold'.[73]

It would be as tempting to expand such affinities between McEwan and Woolf as it is to confirm Roth's recent dialogue with Conrad or Coetzee's appreciation of Ford. As we have seen in those previous chapters, however, contemporary novelists create conversations with earlier twentieth-century moments of innovation without compromising their ambition to address the politics of form in ways that are singularly their own. McEwan has been as vocal as any writer in this book about the balance that can be achieved between inheritance and autonomy, insofar as he has become 'a more traditional writer', as we've heard, one who is 'consciously, expressively aware' of the re-emergence of the literary past, yet who shares Roth and Kundera's ethos of making fiction that is traditionally new – utilising the modernist heritage to allow the novel to do what it hasn't quite done before.

IN THE THEATRE OF CONSCIOUSNESS

What is not new, of course, is the quest McEwan's late fiction has undertaken to depict, with considerable immediacy and vivacity, how the mind translates sensations into thoughts. A rather more self-serving motivation for this quest is revealed by McEwan's disclosures in an interview about the underlying aims of his account of the neurosurgical procedure that closes *Saturday*, as Henry Perowne operates on the mind of a villain (Baxter) who hours before had broken into his home and threatened to rape his daughter. 'I knew I wanted to write a major operation at the end', says McEwan, 'but it would really be about writing, about making art'.[74] McEwan has often been criticised for over-hasty or tritely sentimental endings.[75] Additionally, when Perowne falls into a reverie on the mysteries of the human brain – a reverie provoked, yet oddly in no way disturbed, by his operating on a man whose threats he and his family have just endured – such complaints about McEwan's poor endings might seem justified. Their justification is in turn only reaffirmed if we take at face value his claim that the technical complexities of neurosurgery are in fact 'about making art'. To suggest that *Saturday* is an allegory of the novelist's undertaking becomes still more uncomfortable, not to say ethically problematic, in the novel's final stages. Here it seems that McEwan wants (in one of his own favourite phrases) to have it both ways, in setting eloquence and trauma side by side. Memories of Baxter's invasion of Perowne's Fitzrovia townhouse are allayed by his immersion in his own surgical expertise. Moreover, the elegant description of this life-saving procedure parallels the pleasures of artistic 'making' that we know are McEwan's own:

Just like the digital codes of replicating life held within DNA, the brain's fundamental secret will be laid open one day. But even when it has, the wonder will remain, that mere wet stuff can make this bright inward cinema of thought, of sight and sound and touch bound into a vivid illusion of an instantaneous present, with a self, another brightly wrought illusion, hovering like a ghost at its centre. Could it be explained, how matter becomes conscious? He can't begin to imagine a satisfactory account, but he knows it will come, the secret will be revealed – over decades, as long as the scientists and the institutions remain in place, the explanations will refine themselves into an irrefutable truth about consciousness. (*S*, pp. 254–5)

In a passage that is all about the mind, that is focalised in such a perspectival way, that is trying to reproduce at the level of style a correlative to the notions of consciousness that it thematises – given all these efforts on McEwan's part, we might inevitably ask: why does this seem like a *rendition* of literary impressionism yet nothing more?[76] Such misgivings arise because McEwan has chosen to subdue the vital immediacy of reflection that we find in Ford, Conrad and Woolf, replacing that vitality with Perowne's self-contented assurance that experts like him will one day be able to explain where mental impressions come from. Instead of seeing Perowne as a character engaged in the immediate conflicts and divagations of cogitation, we get the rather more serene, yet less dynamic, activity of him romanticising the prospect of neurological discovery. To be fair, McEwan conveys Perowne's wandering sense of wonder in a way that resembles what Jesse Matz – writing on Woolf's impressionism – calls 'that quest for salvific insight' provoked by 'an effort to adumbrate a new faculty, one that has the freedom perceptually to range'.[77] While McEwan may exhibit a degree of the 'earnest Modernism' that for Matz characterises Woolf's 'effort',[78] the 'new faculty' *Saturday* endorses is cognitive rather than phenomenological. Throughout a one-day narrative that does nothing to hide its association with *Mrs Dalloway*, McEwan often repairs those differences between sight and knowledge that Woolf's writing left in dynamic play, in order to show how Perowne's sharp perceptions give way to considered judgements. However much the novel inherits (at the level of mode) certain impressionist features, it does everything to remedy (at the level of character) the perceptual ambiguities that were so important to literary impressionism in the first place.

Saturday, then, undoubtedly gestures to the craft as well as the contexts of impressionism, with its perspectival narration and its Bloomsbury location. Ideologically speaking, however, the novel advertises McEwan's support for the kind of 'hard' psychology that seeks to explain the qualities of ambivalence and obliquity that were crucial for impressionists like Woolf,

James and Conrad. McEwan seems to endorse neurological explanations of perception such as those from Nicholas Humphrey, who has contended that experience itself is a delusion, nothing more than a 'magical mystery show' hosted by the brain.[79] On this model, the 'bright inward cinema of thought', as Perowne pictures it, is just as unreal as that 'ghost' which is one's inner self. Here McEwan contradicts impressionism's investment in the way sensory perceptions construct our experience of the world, by implying instead that consciousness is not linked to sensation but to a cinematic illusion in which we're deceived into thinking that there is a direct correspondence between what we perceive and what we mentally picture. In his effort to unveil the fact that 'consciousness', in Humphrey's words, 'is no more or less than a piece of magical "theatre"', McEwan is left with a dilemma – or, at the very least, with a contradiction.[80] What does it mean to privilege impressions as a mode for representing the consciousness of his characters, only then to undermine the assumption that the pictures of experience our brains paint for us are generated by the impressions we receive? In short, can McEwan be an impressionist and a neurologist at the same time? It appears not; but, paradoxically enough, he continues to need the resources of impressionism in order to engage with what Humphrey and other contemporary science writers have called that 'hard problem' of consciousness. McEwan, therefore, is increasingly facing a situation in which his fiction's style mismatches its ideological content. More than ever concerned with thematising neuroscientific arguments, he creates a tension between the evolutionary materialism underpinning those arguments and the highly phenomenological register with which he charts characters' mental lives.

This contradiction between style and content is not necessarily a fatal flaw in McEwan's enterprise. Recent commentators, though, have seen it as precisely that, detecting in it something more surreptitious. Marco Roth, for instance, has isolated McEwan as a leading culprit of what he calls the rise of the 'neuronovel'. For Roth, neuronovels are becoming more and more widespread, achieving a good deal of popularity among the reading public. As a genre, however, they are deceptive because they *seem* to be partaking of the modernist fascination with felt impressions, when in fact they are using descriptions of sensory experience as a way of drawing pathological conclusions. More worryingly, in Roth's view, is the tendency for writers like McEwan to make black-and-white distinctions between healthy and unhealthy minds, in ways that also suggest that novelists today can only be experimental if their focalising characters are to some extent psychologically disabled:

[T]o ground special perceptions and heightened language in neurological anomaly ends up severely circumscribing the modernist project. The stylistic novelty and profound interiority of *Ulysses* or *To the Lighthouse* were called forth by normal protagonists – an ad salesman, a housewife – and were proposed as new ways of describing everyone and anyone from the inside out. Modernism seemed revolutionary as long as it threatened to become general; the neuronovel refashions modernism as a special case, odd language for describing odd people, different in neurological kind, not just degree, from other human beings. In this way, the 'experimental' writing of neuronovelists actually props up rigid social conventions of language use. If modernism is just the language of crazy, then real men must speak like Lee Child.[81]

Although Roth has a point here about the dangers of pastiche, insofar as the worst thing that can happen to impressionism is that it's revived nowadays in a medically-inflected language of rational cognition, at the same time, I am not sure that the label 'neuronovel' does any kind of justice to recent developments in the representation of consciousness. Nor does it answer the question of *why* contemporary writers might be redeploying impressionist strategies to stage ethical scenarios that involve observation and misperception (such as the one we saw at the heart of *Atonement*). Moreover, as a label, 'neuronovel' joins a raft of other terms for new tendencies in fiction – like James Wood's 'hysterical realism' – which are nothing more than polemical nicknames that generalise the novel's development by reducing style down to a symptom of writerly angst.[82] In this way, Roth also criticises the neuronovel for the way it has become a source of artistic capital, a source that is easily tapped by McEwan while anxiously sought by his less-established peers. 'Most novelists', he claims, 'have grounds for fearing that Ian McEwan, tribune of the healthy brain, will defeat them in the combat over readers and their money. To put all this more simply, the neuronovel tends to become a variety of meta-novel, allegorizing the novelist's fear of his isolation and meaninglessness, and the alleged capacity of science to explain him better than he can explain himself.'[83] Roth could have nuanced this rather melodramatic conclusion by invoking Thomas Hardy's 'The Science of Fiction' (1891), where Hardy dealt eloquently in appeasing the 'fear' that writers might legitimately feel about the fate of fiction in a culture drawn to scientific explanations. Aside from the fact that Roth's commentary is not unprecedented, what he does suggest is that we need to continue to pursue more precise accounts of the evolving rhetoric of neural cognition in fiction today, including the role such rhetoric plays as a catalyst for innovation – not least for a writer as capable as McEwan, who presumably has no need for such catalysts to begin with.

Saturday is the kind of novel that invites such an account, as it navigates that path between impressions and judgements, between sensation and understanding. Yet it's also a novel about *why* we should continue to take pleasure at all in reading what Philip Roth, as we heard in Chapter 1, celebrated in Bellow as descriptions of *mentalness*. In the episode from *Saturday* quoted previously, we see that even more than the prospect of uncovering 'the brain's fundamental secret', Perowne savours the idea that the 'wonder will remain'. For now, implies McEwan, it is fiction, more than any other artistic medium, which assists in the act of preserving that 'wonder', that enchantment of experiencing thoughts (and of how they come about) for their own sake. Read sympathetically, then, we could see McEwan as leading the way for impressionism's persistence in contemporary fiction, not only because it allows writers to prove something about how the brain works, but also because it offers a defence of the novel's affecting capacity to simulate perception while probing the ethical ramifications of how characters act towards the social realms they perceive.

In the course of providing that defence, however, McEwan shares more than we might think with precisely those figures involved in the perceiving. For just as he painstakingly reproduces throughout much of his late fiction that 'vivid illusion of an instantaneous present' which fascinates Perowne, so it may be equally tempting for us to hear him ventriloquising Briony Tallis's conviction that '[t]o enter a mind and show it at work, or being worked on, and to do this within a symmetrical design – this would be an artistic triumph' (*A*, p. 282). McEwan has knowingly endorsed this triumphant pursuit, of course, even though he wouldn't agree with Briony's sweeping assertion that the 'novel of the future would be unlike anything in the past' (*A*, p. 282). Both *Atonement* and *Saturday* endorse it as well, even as they engage politically with a world beyond their own aesthetic demonstrations of consciousness, centralising characters who become accountable to the discriminations they make on the basis of self-satisfied perceptions. The question we are left with, though, is whether the mode McEwan exhibits so well, but which is largely centred on individual psychological states, can remain appropriate for our global times. What does it mean for writers like McEwan to prioritise an internalist perspective on the mind, rather than what John Searle terms 'the social element in individual consciousness'.[84] How might this individuated field of vision meet demands on the novel form to look beyond the self, as much as it does beyond the nation? To put it more bluntly, can the phenomenological register of impressionism provide a vehicle for the philosophy of transnationalism, as Laura Doyle has recently called it? As Doyle astutely notes, there has been a good deal of 'talk of resistance and counterproduction', but there are stories yet to be told about 'the radical, *involuntary* interconnectedness of subjects who live in history and together shape, suffer, enjoy, and resist its forces'.[85] Might the very obliquity and perspectivism we expect from impressionist fiction enable novelists today to engage with such instances of 'involuntary interconnectedness', however protean those intersubjective encounters may be?

To single out McEwan as a writer who can re-imagine modernism's role in conveying transnational encounters of the kind Doyle has in mind, would be, I think, to claim too much. There is no doubt that his dialogue modernism yields elegant results, as his late work continues to chart 'the conscious mind as a river through time' along with 'the obstacles that would divert it' (*A*, pp. 281–2). It remains to be seen, however, whether this ongoing artistic pursuit of the 'luminous halo' of experience, in Woolf's famous phrase, will privilege an understanding of that experience in which the individual takes precedence over the intersubjective.[86] In order to do that, McEwan would need to provide narratives that refuse so unhesitatingly to condone – as *Saturday* tacitly does – the intellectual supremacy of characters like Henry Perowne, who have the time to linger over their own subtle impressions, and who move in social domains that reassure them of their own mental acuity; in short, characters who seem to work on behalf of their creator to fulfil the expectation that Henry James himself had of any budding novelist in 1884 – to become 'one of th[ose] people on whom nothing is lost'.[87]

At the same time, McEwan's ambiguous treatment of this capacity in characters – because he supports and satirises them with equal measure – points to one of several ideological schisms that are, as Rita Felski and Jonathan Eburne have recently shown, as productive for thinking more broadly about modernism's continuation as they are for pinpointing local contradictions in a given work.[88] McEwan adds a tint of pathos to his portrait of the privileged Perowne, who eschews novel reading only to become someone 'on whom nothing is lost' except for fiction's edifying demonstration of the importance of imaginative empathy. That pathos is played out at a compositional level as well, disclosed by the way *Saturday*, much like *Atonement*, embodies an 'awareness of the schism between aesthetic innovation and political transformation'.[89] Appearing all the more fraught by virtue of its own formal grace, the affinity of McEwan's fiction with impressionism may be more explicit than he would prefer; but it nonetheless exemplifies precisely the kind of contemporary modernism which is 'suspended between direct political engagement and an aesthetic autonomy that remains vital for the imagining of a radically alternative future'.[90] In the next and final chapter, Toni Morrison demonstrates her own virtuosic version of this suspenseful modernism, one that, in her phrase, 'keeps you on the edge' as a reader – complementing as she does those writers we have encountered so far, whose creative conversations with modernism's past keep it right on the edge of the novel's unfolding present.[91]

CHAPTER 5

'License to strut': Toni Morrison and the ethics of virtuosity

According to Woolf, '[t]he writer's task is to take one thing and let it stand for twenty: a task of danger and difficulty'.[1] In the novel published a year before this assertion, Woolf shows us how that principle of doing less in order to symbolise more might work. Reaping multiple rewards from minimal means is 'a task' that governs many of the motifs introduced in *Mrs Dalloway*. Motifs, that is, which are not always ethereal, like the 'flow of the sound' from streets whose echoes so frequently spark memories for Peter Walsh; not always tactile either, as they sometimes are for Clarissa, when she 'plung[es] her hand into the softness' of her evening gowns just as, seconds before, she had 'plunged into the very heart of the moment' of reflection where 'she alone knew how different' her inward self was to the one she 'composed so for the world'.[2] Such motifs can also figure more explicitly as traits and attitudes, manifesting themselves in beliefs that characters nurture inwardly but which typify external, distinguished qualities for which others admire them. Motifs in Woolf's world embroider not only moments of being or experiences that happen *for* characters; they play as significant a role in describing what characters *are*, naming what they do as much as what they feel. Nowhere more satirically does Woolf elaborate a single motif to 'let it stand for twenty' than in her portrait of William Bradshaw, the imperious consultant who seems to specialise as intensely in his own public distinction as in any medical matter, ever the 'master of his own actions' especially when 'the patient was not'.[3] The passage that introduces him is memorable as one of Woolf's most sardonic:

Proportion, divine proportion, Sir William's goddess, was acquired by Sir William walking hospitals, catching salmon, begetting one son in Harley Street by Lady Bradshaw, who caught salmon herself and took photographs scarcely to be distinguished from the work of professionals. Worshipping proportion, Sir William not only prospered himself but made England prosper, secluded her lunatics, forbade childbirth, penalized despair, made it impossible for the unfit to propagate their views until they, too, shared his sense of proportion.[4]

This was also a memorable portrait for Toni Morrison. In her master's thesis presented to Cornell exactly thirty years after *Mrs Dalloway* appeared, Morrison isolates that episode 'as one of the few where the author noticeably intrudes'. She describes it as 'an intense passage', made all the more so when Woolf flouts the modernist credo of impersonality by stepping forward precisely in order to show her 'strong feeling', in Morrison's view, 'against those who would make detachment and independence impossible'.[5] The audible intrusion of a condemning yet also mocking voice exemplifies, for Morrison, a strategic move: one that sees Woolf suspending the novel's free indirect discourse to lend it a sardonic edge – imposing on it precisely in order to indict the 'one who *does* impose his will'.[6]

Interestingly, this is the one place in Morrison's thesis where she foregrounds the implications of style and idiom. We might think this uncharacteristic of her subsequent critical writings, so alert as they are to matters of technique, alongside the political responsibilities that accompany a writer's formal decisions. The stylistic dexterity to which she is drawing our attention in that episode, tells us less about Morrison in her mid-twenties as a student admiring Woolf than it does about her values as the innovator she would become. Two decades after she submitted her thesis, *Song of Solomon* (1977) pays homage to that dictum from Woolf. Letting one symbol stand for twenty becomes, for Morrison, a means of introducing us to the everyday reflections of Milkman Dead's mother, Ruth:

Hurriedly, then, she began to set the table. As she unfolded the white linen and let it billow over the fine mahogany table, she would look once more at the large water mark. She never set the table or passed through the dining room without looking at it. Like a lighthouse keeper drawn to his window to gaze once again at the sea, or a prisoner automatically searching out the sun as he steps into the yard for his hour of exercise, Ruth looked for the water mark several times during the day. She knew it was there, would always be there, but she needed to confirm its presence. Like the keeper of the lighthouse and the prisoner, she regarded it as a mooring, a checkpoint, some stable visual object that assured her that the world was still there; that this was life and not a dream. That she was alive somewhere, inside, which she acknowledged to be true only because a thing she knew intimately was out there, outside herself.[7]

The proliferation of analogies for the watermark elevates a passage that started in domestic routine to the register of a refrain. Each sentence brings with it a new turn on the original motif: transforming the 'stable visual object' that Ruth knows it to be, into something personalised yet entirely inanimate. Morrison repeats and elaborates that image, her paratactic phrases simulating in their construction the very sentiment they disclose – the sentiment that repetition can be reassuring, as the routine of Ruth's glance to the watermark surely is. Meanwhile, Morrison's lighthouse analogy works less convincingly as an allusion to Woolf's 1927 novel, than it does as the opening voice of a duet in which the simile of the exercising prisoner joins in counterpoint. Ruth sits between two analogies that couldn't be more different; but like a fugue, the dissonance between the lighthouse keeper and the prison inmate is suddenly reconciled, as the two figures seem to combine to generate further metaphors ('a mooring, a checkpoint'), just as a fugue's disparate voices work contrapuntally to provide new harmonies. Morrison thus evokes the fleeting consolation Ruth claims in things 'outside herself' with a register that takes us somehow beyond the literary – registering Morrison's own 'effort', as she called it a decade after *Song of Solomon*, 'to be *like* something that has probably only been fully expressed perhaps in music'.[8]

Now, we could go on in this vein: closely reading, or rather closely listening to, this reprise of rhetorical features that reveal Morrison's kinship with Woolf. This is indeed how critics have often approached Morrison's relation to modernism, with the view to showing, as David Cowart has done for Faulkner and Joyce, how Morrison's 'debt' to such writers 'is considerable, not only in the centrality of [her] character's brooding on the past but in the very syntax in which the author describes it'.[9] This process of tracing echoes as evidence of Morrison's indebtedness to canonical modernists may well be rewarding to some degree, where the aesthetic payoff for the reader takes the form of that pleasure-pursuit of spotting affinities. This would seem to be what Harold Bloom had in mind, when he diagnosed Morrison's inheritance only then to explain away her inventiveness. 'Every strong writer', as Bloom infamously put it, 'welcomes the opportunity to be an original, and Morrison's literary achievement more than justifies her sly embrace of African-American cultural narcissism'.[10] Such remarks are as vacuous as they are offensive, not least because Morrison has in various places expressed disdain for the assumption that her compatibility with modernist fiction can be gauged simply in terms of identifiable influences, as though tradition means little else to her than a bank of stylistic reserves. By regarding Morrison's creativity as never entirely her own, certainly not self-generated, Bloom begins to sound like a victim of his own vocabulary, a vocabulary of strength and submission, icons and unconscious imitators, which detracts from how vitally modernism persists in Morrison's practice by insinuating instead that she is prone to emulation even at her most daring.

What interests me in this chapter, therefore, as throughout the study it concludes, is not the way a writer 'inherits' modernist tendencies en route to fulfilling her own aims or as a means of garnering artistic capital as an experimenter. Nor am I concerned with rehearsing, in Morrison's case, an influence-based account of her modernist lineage, despite the implication of some of her most devoted critics: that we should praise her ability to navigate, and in so doing transcend, high-modernism's legacy *as* the very mark of her singularity in contemporary literary culture.[11] While Mark McGurl may be correct to say that '[i]n the wake of the Nobel Prize ... it should be safe to point out how much Morrison learned from Joyce and Faulkner and Woolf when she studied them at school', insofar as significant 'aspects of her work ... are difficult to imagine without the models offered by such works as *As I Lay Dying*', it is precisely the viability of imagining-without-models that I want to entertain here.[12]

It seems crucial to do so, if 'Morrison Studies' is to move forward.[13] Rather than spotting modernism's lessons as the moments where Morrison is at her most innovative, we would do well to trace the debates she herself conducts about the purpose and responsibilities of formal audacity, while highlighting the virtuosic procedures she forges to include the reader in that debate on ethical terms. In adopting this approach, I am sympathetic to Michael Nowlin's 1998 review of *Unflinching Gaze* – probably the most significant collection devoted to Morrison's Faulknerian heritage. Nowlin reflects that she 'has entered the oracular space once occupied by Faulkner' himself, entering 'precisely because of her remarkable dexterity with literary language', insofar as she 'seems these days to be a living *refutation* of the death of the author'. Combining her own formal esteem with her visible role as a spokeswoman for the wider critical work that fiction should perform, Morrison leaves us 'hard pressed', admits Nowlin, 'to renounce those modernist notions of heroic authorship that have shaped twentieth-century Anglo-American literary criticism'.[14] This talk of heroics, of course, points to a rather different side of Morrison's prestige, the institutional prestige brought by the academic praise of her work and its subsequent canonisation, to say nothing of her former position as Robert F. Goheen Chair in the Council of the Humanities at Princeton. The values she places on the status of this acclaim – and, in turn, our use of that institutionalised praise in the picture we form of her literary-historical stature – need to be distinguished from those qualities of *revision* and *discovery* that Morrison has cultivated as a 'not easily-taken-in reader' of her own writing.[15] Therefore, what informs my account of the modernist character of Morrison's ambitions are the risks she undertakes at the level of style, rather than her continued lionisation as a figurehead for the contemporary literary scene, mindful as I am of her fear that '[w]hat has happened ... is that writing has become almost a celebrity thing in the sense that people don't want to *write*; they want to *be authors*. And that's quite different'.[16]

However inexorable, then, Morrison's public eminence now seems, it can also be a licence for analytical inexactness. Celebrity profiling, as Aaron Jaffe has recently shown, can make the cultural face of distinction appear seamlessly connected to what makes the work itself so distinctive from the perspective of its internal components and procedures. What Jaffe describes as that 'ubiquitous tissue of promotion' that surrounded 'modernism's crowning successes', belied a network of acclaim that was 'not necessarily concerned with putting the aesthetic artefacts themselves first'.[17] This idea that public prominence may ultimately detract from the particularities of those artistic practices being praised, surely corresponds with Nowlin's estimation that 'Morrison is a current darling of multiculturalists ... though her intense preoccupation with literary form' does 'forc[e] the question of literary value that such critics often pretend indifference to'.[18] Nowlin's worries at the end of the 1990s are very much of their time, given the recent surge of interest in placing aesthetic responses within political frameworks. Nevertheless, there is some recuperative work to be done if we are fully to understand how technical pre-eminence and social commitment coincide for a writer like Morrison, for whom that 'question of literary value' seems indissolubly linked to questions of ethical accountability.

To her, these intersections of form and conviction, craft and critique, are constitutive of the 'best art', since 'you ought to be able to make it unquestionably political and irrevocably beautiful at the same time'.[19] In turn, to approach this sense of the inseparability of virtuosity and responsibility entails a micro-level of analysis that hasn't always flourished in scholarship on contemporary fiction.[20] Although the rise of a so-called New Formalism in recent years may help to provoke such a methodological prioritisation of technique, Morrison suggests that the interface of aesthetics and politics is not a choice but a prerequisite for an ethically attuned practice of reading, a practice that Morrison herself summons and theorises when she calls for a closer attention to the 'details of how certain sentences get written and the *work* I hope they do'.[21]

As I have tried to demonstrate in this book by approaching very different late-twentieth- and twenty-first-century novels, it's this micro-focus that allows us to pursue what writers' stylistic ambitions reveal about the politico-ethical ramifications of literary tradition coexisting with innovation. In Morrison's case, one of those ambitions uncovers a paradoxical sensibility at the heart of her work; or, at least, it *seems* like a paradox for a writer who wishes to lead the novel towards new horizons. I am thinking here of the importance she has placed on economy, where ideas of cutting back, of deliberate understatement, become her basis for invention, if not the measure of rhetorical flair. As we heard in Chapter 3, Morrison insisted in her 1992 *Paris Review* interview that the 'sense of knowing when to stop is a learned thing', implicitly part of the writer's 'experience' of what 'it mean[s] to be thrifty with images and language'.[22] It's her insistence that '[y]ou shouldn't overgratify, you should never satiate',[23] that will form the basis of my examination of her peculiar counterpointing of discipline and audacity, control and virtuosic improvisation.

This dialectal balance of seemingly contrary imperatives spotlights an idiomatically modernist dilemma about the coordination of craft and intuition, where the writer faces a choice between taking command of the novel form or setting it alight. As one solution for coordinating such choices, Morrison's call for economy as a foundation for inventiveness is nothing new, as revealed by early advocates of minimalism like Fitzgerald, Hemingway and, as we have seen, Ford Madox Ford. Sixty years after Fitzgerald outlined how fiction ought to be constructed from carefully 'selected moments', the ethos of leaving out in order to symbolise more struck a chord with Morrison:

The difficulty for me in writing – *among* the difficulties – is to write language that can work quietly on a page for a reader who doesn't hear anything. Now for that, one has to work very carefully with what is *in between* the words. What is not said. Which is measure, which is rhythm and so on. So, it is what you don't write that frequently gives what you do write its power.[24]

Going on this evidence, we can clearly hail Morrison as a beacon for all contemporary novelists who consider that less is definitely more, a sentiment pointedly expressed by the opening narrator of *Love* (2003) who observes that 'silence is looked on as odd and most of my race has forgotten the beauty of meaning much by saying little'.[25] What's significant is that her earlier comments about the importance of 'what you don't write' come just a year after she published *Jazz*, the novel she still regards as her 'best book' precisely *because* of its verbal adventurousness.[26] '[T]he challenge' in writing it, as Morrison recalls in her new foreword, 'was to expose and bury the artifice and to take practice beyond the rules'. A narrative fashioned from what she calls that 'process of invention, of improvisation, of change',[27] *Jazz* was itself an oracle of sorts. For its stylistic panache anticipated the global recognition that Morrison deserved and soon achieved when she won the Nobel the following year – the very same year, we note, she spoke so forthrightly about the virtues of thrift. In a fittingly ironic turn of events, supreme international recognition and media attention coincided with a time when Morrison was reflecting on the difficulties of writing quietly on the page.

If the audacity of *Jazz* marked a hiatus for Morrison, stirring thoughts about how she could 'practice thrift' over the next phase of her career, the Nobel Prize itself turned the tables again. As she would recall in 2008, with the award came a new sense of formal freedom – the feeling of finally having the 'license to strut'.[28] Certainly the publishers were keen to cheer on this notion that Morrison was now fully sanctioned to swagger. When *Paradise* appeared in 1998, her return was heralded by Knopf on the flap of the first edition as a 'bravura performance'. That very image of choreographed ostentation, however, could not be further removed from Morrison's belief, iterated on the pages of the *PMLA* in 2005, 'that the practice of great art is the practice of knowledge *unseduced by* its own beauty'.[29] Against the backdrop of this friction between the tenor of world acclaim and the tenacity of her own compositional obligations, Morrison emerges as a novelist fully aware of the ethical implications of extending modernist innovations in art that 'sharpens us, makes us vulnerable, makes us fierce, coherent'.[30] At the same time, she shows how artistic esteem for novelists today, as it did for their precursors, can assume separate public and private faces, where the promotional fruits of cultural prestige may not provide us with any logical index to a writer's personal benchmarks of satisfaction. In turn, this reorients our attention to novelists' motivations for taking risks with form, as we're prompted to explore how far they choose to pursue innovation for its own sake, such that it becomes the 'only activity', where Morrison is concerned, 'that I engage in wholly for myself'. That a writer so in touch with the modernist heritage as Morrison can also find ways of being '[w]holly free' sheds new light on what the most virtuosic contemporary writers understand the value of that inheritance to be.[31]

We, thus, need a more *active* sense of how Morrison not only responds to but also re-imagines the critical work of modernist methods. Otherwise we run the risk of inadvertently endorsing the famously condescending assuredness with which Bloom announced that 'literary tradition chooses an authentic writer, more than the other way around', such that '[s]omething of Virginia Woolf's aestheticism lingers on in Morrison's style and vision, altogether (I think) to Morrison's benefit'.[32] As later sections will argue, we should be less compelled by vague intimations of how any particular modernist writer 'lingers on' into contemporary fiction, than by Morrison's own hope that her work, like jazz itself, 'forces you to appreciate its artifice and to linger on its invention and to recognize how well practiced the performer is'.[33]

'NOT *LIKE*': READING MORRISON BEYOND INFLUENCE

If the modernist 'tradition chooses' its late-twentieth- and twenty-first-century heirs, then surely it's more enriching 'to appreciate' how they spend their inheritance than simply to track-down to whom they are creatively beholden. If anything still 'lingers' around Morrison's career, it is the irony that although her increasing stylistic verve has given her a facility for self-reinvention with every new novel, this appears only to have nurtured an escalation of commentaries on what Philip Weinstein calls Faulkner's 'claims on her attention'.[34] In this field of comparisons, the tendency is for critics to explain Morrison's technical competence by recourse to influence, thereby becoming insensitive to why Morrison might 'want to break away', in her words, 'from certain assumptions that are inherent in the conception of the novel form'.[35] To offer an appreciation of artifice and invention of the kind Morrison applauds is not to say that we should avoid analysis in favour of descriptive summary. It does suggest, however, that we follow her own advice here by particularising her formal ambitiousness, and 'how well practiced' it is, without reducing those ambitions to the traits of a neo-modernist in whose style we can 'hear' the 'unmistakable rhetorical performances' of great precursors.[36] In fact, something to bear in mind is the way Morrison refuses to confuse self-differentiation with creativity – where breaking from the past is proof of innovation – refusing, in turn, to subject her most dominant forebears, namely Faulkner and Woolf, to iconoclasm. Using as a guideline her belief that 'one looks through history for signs of renewal',[37] we can begin to see how Morrison surpasses those comparisons with Faulkner, especially, the very comparisons her writing continues to attract even as it invites more aesthetically precise responses. This is because she manages such affinities without succumbing to them, upholding 'a strong connection to "ancestors"', as she describes them – in a phrase that deliberately invokes Bloom's terminology only to invert its logic of influence as combat between forerunner and heir – an African American ancestry with profound heritage of its own, while at the same time 'giving [her]self permission to write books that do not depend on anyone's liking them'. All of which amounts to an effort 'to write better' and thereby 'solve certain kinds of problems' *through* that act of writing.[38]

'Get it all down. Take chances. It may be bad, but that's the only way you can do anything really good'.[39] This may have been Faulkner's compositional starting-point, but it's not one, as I have implied, that befits Morrison's virtuosity. If she is prone to 'take chances', the risks in question are likely to be taken with understatement, compelled as she is by 'the absences, the spaces around the words'.[40] Recognising such comparisons between aesthetic priorities can be enlightening; but there is only so much critical mileage to be gained in pursuing close readings of diverging imperatives. One would do better to question the usefulness of defining influences through semblances at all – as, indeed, Morrison has famously done:

> I am not *like* James Joyce; I am not *like* Thomas Hardy; I am not *like* Faulkner. I am not *like* in that sense. I do not have objections to being compared to such extraordinarily gifted and facile writers, but it does leave me sort of hanging there when I know that my effort is to be *like* something that has probably only been fully expressed perhaps in music, or in some other culture-gen that survives almost in isolation because the community manages to hold on to it. Sometimes I can reflect something of this kind in my novels. Writing novels is a way to encompass this – this something.[41]

It is a memorable cluster of correctives, often quoted yet not always, we should note, in full.[42] Morrison plots a journey from influential counterparts to reach her own comparison with music, a journey that this chapter will try to reproduce in its movement from her modernist inheritance – as we've plotted it back to her study of Woolf – to the deployment of certain modernist strategies through the expression of that unique 'something' which she tries to 'encompass' as her own. To carry out this inquiry, I will take my cue from Morrison herself, aligning with her own sense of what it takes to do justice to the particularity of a literary work. A bulwark of theoretical frames may be enabling, she says, in excavating content, but it takes another approach to understand how a novel is formed. In criticism written especially on 'any subject about women', she complains, 'half of it' tends to be 'sociology or some other -ology before you get to simply see what is beautiful, and why, and what the criteria are, the criteria for that book'.[43] Following this appeal to take the work on its own terms, this chapter argues that Morrison's work asks what might happen if modernism 'took as its creative task', as she puts it, 'and sought as its credentials those recognized and verifiable principles of Black art'? How would the modernist commitment to obliquity change and progress if it were reemployed, in her words, 'to write literature that was irrevocably and indisputably Black?'[44] I pursue the implications of these questions but without the kind of predeterminations that extract stock political responses from her novels. Instead, the following sections take major compositional tendencies, values or ideals identified by Morrison herself over the past three decades. Under the headings they provide, I will bring together moments in her *oeuvre* from *Jazz* onward: the career phase that most aptly showcases a writer who is at once drawn to modernist conceptions of renewal, while at the same time sustaining her own phase of rebellion and creative individuation in the process of allowing herself the 'license to strut'.

We begin with *possession* and *aloofness*: two aspects of her reactivation of the impersonal aesthetic that modernist writers adopted in various guises but eventually adapted too for changing political conditions. Depersonalisation is a flexible idiom for Morrison. It facilitates her 'total possession' of creative processes,[45] without compromising her 'job', in Michael Silverblatt's terms, of overseeing 'a vast staff of arrangers', who 'get everything immaculately in place and then disappear' – leaving us, as readers, to think through our proximity to the kinds of prejudices her densely textured narratives evoke from angles that alternatively elicit our sympathy and indignation.[46] Turning to a more phenomenological aspect of engaging with Morrison's texts, I then move on to her term for the compositional process by which character, plot and symbolic patterns are interrelated, as details about them accumulate in what she calls the 'undertow' of successive events: *crystallisation*. These terms are highly suggestive of Morrison's allegiance to the idea of form as processual – as something to be performed rather than attained and admired. Once the novel is performatively conceived as such, we can trace the ways in which different narrative parts crystallise into a whole, a whole that's maintained by the text's underlying flow of motivic patterns and connections. It is a form of cohesion provided by many memorable networks of symbolism in her novels, especially when 'different facets' work together to refract the 'light', as she puts it, 'looking at one simple thing', usually an object or seemingly ordinary event that springs open into a larger web of implications.[47] Finally, I will close by considering the importance Morrison has placed throughout her career – though more insistently in recent years – on readerly *involvement*. That her narratives solicit an 'affective and participatory relationship' with the reader on both linguistic and thematic levels seems indisputable;[48] so it's surprising to hear that she is left 'breathless' when 'told', especially with respect to later novels like *Paradise*, 'that this is "difficult" writing'.[49] Here we are invited to consider how Morrison turns high modernism's famous defence of difficulty around, in order to make fiction *work upon* us and make us aware too that it is doing so – a two-tiered impulse that corresponds with McEwan's effort, as the previous chapter explored, to write paragraphs that are beautiful in and of themselves but that also offer an ethically alert 'commentary on their own creation'.

If Morrison never loses faith in fiction's capacity to re-envision the world of racial persecution, political hegemony and social injustice, then *Paradise* itself implies that the process of testing alternative visions of community without violence can only be demanding, and the novel reinforces those demands via the challenging claims it makes on the reader's attention. As we will see, by allowing her devotion to 'that feeling of dislocation and inventiveness and startling change' to implicate rather than alienate her reader,[50] Morrison invites from us a 'visceral' in addition to a 'cognitive, intellectual response to how this whole thing is put together'.[51] That 'whole' of which she speaks also encompasses indirectly, and more challengingly still, those imagined alternatives to the situations, acts and historical consequences of the inhumanity she evokes between factions of prejudicial intolerance. The potential for modernist narration to engage us viscerally and intellectually is thus in keeping with her motivation to draw us emotionally *and* reflectively into her fiction, so that we recognise how her work 'should not even attempt to solve social problems', as she maintains, though 'it should certainly try to clarify them'.[52]

Uniting the sections that I've briefly sketched above will be the intersection Morrison values between practised methods and inspired advancements: in effect, the connection between a concern with craft she inherits from those modernists she most admires and a virtuosic distinction that is all her own. 'The point is', she declared a year after publishing *Sula* (1973), 'that it doesn't look like it's sweating'. This early, well-documented endeavour to ensure that her prose conceals its underlying technical 'effort' is worth bearing in mind as we rethink the relevance of modernist innovation for Morrison's vision for the contemporary novel.[53] If it's so crucial for her that 'the seams can't show',[54] then what kind of room for daring experimentation does this leave? Can her conscious perfectionism of technique really go hand in hand with risk-taking improvisation? Yes, of course it can, it would be tempting to say. There we could let the case of Morrison and modernism rest, were it not for the fact that she unsettles our readerly presuppositions as dynamically as she handles narrative form. She asks us to extend the rigour with which we read, just as she sees that the novel's purpose 'really is about stretching' the expectations its audience may have about precisely what formal innovation enables fiction politically to do'.[55]

This convergence of heritage and invention in Morrison's style compels us to partake too in that process of 'stretching' our assumptions concerning the ethics of virtuosity. Just before doing so, however, there is one thing we *can* conclude about this intersection that helpfully contextualises Morrison's place in this book. For just as Ondaatje was attracted to Cubism as a point of connection between impressionism and Futurism, between inherited and emergent modes, Morrison likewise takes the view that to write inventively in dialogue with tradition should not be understood as a contradiction. Instead, such a dialogue is, to borrow her own eloquent notion, the sign of a creative *confluence* – a place where the modernist commitment to revitalising form flows directly into what is most idiosyncratic about her aesthetic and political aims.[56]

POSSESSION AND ALOOFNESS

'I am not experimental', announced Morrison, around the time she started writing *Beloved* (1987), 'I am simply trying very hard to recreate something out of an old art form in my books'.[57] It is a startling statement if we take her negation of literary experiment at face value, as it sounds out of sync with the awesome intervention in contemporary literary culture that *Beloved* would make four years later. In its context, however, her assertion is appropriate for a time when a particularly extravagant brand of metafiction flourished under the aegis of Salman Rushdie, Julian Barnes and Angela Carter – to name only its British exponents – in an age of fictional self-reflexivity when the aping of (potentially nostalgic) traditionalism was preferable to any impulse 'to recreate something out of an old art form'. Even though Morrison echoes Carter's own preference for 'putting new wine in old bottles', it's unlikely that she would share Carter's enthusiasm for the way the 'pressure of the new wine makes the old bottles explode'.[58] A writer who was never enamoured by trends through the 1970s and 1980s towards fiction's parodic self-examination, Morrison's increasingly idiosyncratic style would, at the same time, become increasingly commensurate with modernism's distinctive articulation of obliquity as basis for developing political and ethical perspectives. Among the facets of material and mental life her fiction 'registers' – to borrow Rebecca Walkowitz's useful typology of modernist style – are 'the limits of perception and waning of a confident epistemology, the conflict between the exhaustive and ineffable, the appeal of the trivial, the political consequences of uniformity and variousness in meaning, the fragmentation of perspectives, and the disruption of social categories'.[59] A more problematic feature that goes unmentioned here – one that critics find unpalatable because of its connection to the more imperious elements of high-modernist formalism – is that of impersonality. I have written elsewhere on the need to see how narratorial depersonalisation can represent a somewhat more ideologically agile move on the novelist's part.[60] Despite the vaunted austerity of its role in T. S. Eliot's poetics and in Wyndham Lewis's externalised modes of narration, impersonality came to mean something quite different to late modernist women writers on the Left. They tactically appropriated Eliot's famous injunction that 'the more perfect the artist, the more completely separate in him will be the man who suffers and the mind which creates', by using it in fiction at the radical end of modernism's political spectrum.[61] Morrison is very much in keeping with this narratological appropriation and political rotation of impersonality, but for different reasons. To her, it has become a prerequisite for composition itself, characterising a process that 'has to be very private and very unrelated'.[62] Being at once involved in, and detached from, even the most intimate moments of plotting and stylisation is the challenge she poses herself. 'I have to feel', she said as far back as 1976, 'as if it's being done almost in a very separate womb of my own construction',[63] while admitting at the same time to 'lik[ing] that risk' of maintaining the 'formality and repetition' that is sometimes suited to the narration of characters' recursive memories.[64] Clearly, 1976 marked a time in which such thoughts of immersion and detachment loomed large for Morrison as she discussed her procedures, as in another interview from that year she likens her writing process to a state of double consciousness: combining 'total possession and total aloofness at the same time'.[65]

To explore how this double consciousness of absorption and impersonality affects not only her working methods but also her published text, I will turn to opening sections of the novel Morrison regards, more than any other, as having a life of its own, and whose very mode would encapsulate the dangerous age it evoked: *Jazz*.[66] More so than its predecessors, this was a novel that fulfilled Morrison's search for a narrative register that could embody the interaction of unplanned and 'constructed aspect[s] of the writing process'.[67] If these paradoxical aims seem commensurate with Ondaatje's work, not only do they remind us of his alternation between conscious artistry and spontaneity, but also of how that alternation could be realised dramatically – played out, we recall, in the specialised professions of his characters as they combine learned skill and pure intuition.

Likewise, for Morrison, her need to remain 'very conscious ... of trying to blend that which is contrived and artificial with improvisation',[68] was duplicated by *Jazz* on a diegetic level, as its narrative 'pull[ed] from the material or the people the compositional drama of the period, its unpredictability' (*J*, p. xviii). Much of our technical interest in this novel, therefore, cannot be divorced from this theme of conscious improvisation that *Jazz* stages in diegetic respects that are then reciprocated by its linguistic virtuosity. In tracing how this poetics of unpredictability is sustained, however, we're not simply reminded of Morrison's insistence on the inseparability of content and craft. It also reveals why those 'two contradictory things' that she calls 'artifice and improvisation' point to a similarly paradoxical cooperation between immersion and impersonality, enchantment and distance – antinomies of engagement that are as relevant to how we read and respond to *Jazz* as to the way it is written.

If such equivalences do exist between the way composer and listener engage with *Jazz*, it should come as no surprise for a novelist who admits that the reason why she tries 'to bring the reader in as co-author or a complicitous person really stems from my desire to be engaged as a reader myself'.[69] Indeed, Morrison's narrator is so imposing as to require that she take a seat among the novel's audience, as though she could be anything but depersonalised – standing aloof as her suave commentator steps in, sweeping across the opening setting of Harlem, as '[d]aylight slants like a razor cutting the buildings in half' (*J*, p. 7). Just as *Jazz*'s narration, as Morrison told Salman Rushdie, 'begins to love its language and love its point of view',[70] so it rhythmically partakes in the qualities of '[i]mprovisation, originality, change' that Morrison hoped the novel would not simply be 'about' but rather 'would seek to become' (*J*, p. xviii). And just as the city can only be evoked through dizzying turns and descents in perspective, so the task of chronicling this scene of urban change demands a meter that matches that chronicler's appetite:

At last, at last, everything's ahead. The smart ones say so and people listening to them and reading what they write down agree: Here comes the new. Look out. There goes the sad stuff. The bad stuff. The things-nobody-could-help stuff. The way everybody was then and there. Forget that. History is over, you all, and everything's ahead at last. (*J*, p. 7)

The resolute iambics at the head of this passage ('at last') dissolve into the amphibrachic fourth, fifth and sixth sentences. Here, in each of its repetitions ('the sad stuff', 'The bad stuff', 'could-help-stuff'), the phrase rises to a punchy refrain, as the middle adjectives ('sad' and 'bad') – or in the case of its final recurrence, a verb ('help') – emulates in tempo the will-to-lay-to-rest all that 'History' traumatically represents. As the narrator implies, though not without with a tinge of scepticism counterpointing the ebullience, metropolitan modernity becomes an emblem of spiritual futurity as well as architectural progress and racial democratisation, reorienting the attention of those who occupy it away from what's 'over'. An existential (and admittedly utopian) reorientation, Morrison reproduces it on a lexical level too, shifting the deixis from 'then and there' to '[a] city like *this* one'. Indeed, that impulse to celebrate 'the new' culminates again in the rhythm that expresses it, as the contrasting meters working across this passage alternate in the final sentence, before they resolve on the iamb of that adamant announcement ('at last') with which the narrator began.

Such metrical interplay, then, between alternating phrases of two and three syllables produces a rhythmic equivalent to what Morrison calls those 'two contradictory things' lying at the centre of her own creative process: 'artifice and improvisation'.[71] The novel thus enacts, at the level of its syntax, something like that intermingling of order and expressivity, impersonal expertise and self-possessed extemporisation, that Morrison finds in jazz performance itself, where the harmonically consonant tonalities of a background motif may be ruptured by the discords of virtuosic solos. Like her desire to remain aloof from the tenor of her narration but only after being wholly possessed in its construction, she embraces contradictory states of refinement and free-play, where discipline meets risk. Meter is at once the compositional focus and showcased product of such contradictions. Scholarship on contemporary fiction, however, has devoted less time than it might to the semantic importance of meter, not only because it demands a discrete scale of attention that's assumed to be too localised for analysing how language is manipulated over the kind of extended narrative duration we confront in a novel, but also because of the tendency for critics to regard rhythm – along with its accompanying effects on euphony and emphasis – merely as an aspect of how prose *works* rather than what it *means*.[72] In Morrison's case, to assume that such features have little bearing on interpretation simply won't do. As *Jazz* amply demonstrates, meter's influence on how we interpret her choices about diction and idiom becomes crucial: crucial for understanding how the novel embodies the 'compositional drama of the period'; how its 'structure' can, as Morrison hoped, '*equal* meaning' and not simply embellish it (*J*, p. xix); and finally how she herself reoccupies in this narrative the modernist template of the conscious artist, 'who practices and practices and practices in order to be able to invent and to make his art look effortless and graceful'.[73] If the vernacular of her second novel, *Sula* (1973), allowed Morrison 'to manipulate language' by operating 'credibly and, perhaps, elegantly with a discredited vocabulary',[74] then *Jazz* set her a different challenge of evoking musical vocabularies in ways that would preserve their aliveness – rather than simply documenting jazz as the cultural institution it would become. *Jazz*'s discourse, then, compelled her to 'manipulate language' as she had done in *Sula*, but this time from the standpoint of a calculating improviser who, though aloof, ultimately repossessed that linguistic virtuosity as her own.

CRYSTALLISATION AND UNDERTOW

One of the things that Morrison found 'technically just astonishing' in Faulkner is his ability to withhold the fact of race, revealing it obliquely, 'hint[ing]' at it through the very '*structure* of the book', so that ultimately 'the structure is the argument'.[75] While Morrison has not quite remained loyal to this innovation, insofar as she makes no attempt to shroud matters of colour or diffuse them via her characters' perspectival restrictions or misperceptions, she has retained an affinity with the modal obliquity for which Faulkner's narration is notorious. She matches, if not in manner, exactly, then certainly in ambition, the idea of containing an argument latently in novelistic structure, whereby an event's importance is borne out in the very form of its conveyance. As a process running throughout her work, but one that more recently became more prominent for *Love*, she has likened this evolving relation between structure and meaning to 'the way crystal forms. You know you have a small piece and then it expands to another. And another layer comes on in a different shape, but it's all the same material'.[76] Without wanting to imply that Morrison's preferred unit of composition is the paragraph, in what follows, I will introduce episodes from *Paradise* that demonstrate how that 'crystalline growth' can occur within the space of several lines.[77] Condensed at this paragraphic level, we not only find again Morrison's commitment to form as processual – where each 'small piece' of a novel 'expands to another' while remaining part of 'the same material' – but also her invitation for the reader to enter what she identifies, on various occasions, as a novel's *undertow*: that region of deep engagement where we start to make connections precisely because of what's understated, through comparisons that are not immediately self-evident.[78]

Undertow implies that fictional narratives, open as they are to innumerable re-readings, are oriented towards flow and change rather than completion and resolution. Undertow also offers a lens through which to approach the way Morrison foregrounds the performative potential of form, insofar as she emphasises how a novel's construction (at a syntactical level or in the larger, organisational terms of an entire chapter) visibly shapes the sense of what it conveys. For her, form is never simply a scaffold but an active agent of depiction, seen forming what it shows. Along these lines, meaning itself becomes apparent through what form *does*, its ethical implications mobilised by the way our formal encounter with the narrative *happens*. It is this conception of form's performativity that crystallisation captures so aptly for Morrison. The term enables us to pinpoint not only how composite her creative procedures are; it facilitates a model for reading the aesthetic and political undertows of her work in full awareness of how she reforms the very modernist protocols from which her strategies are partly sourced.

Consider this instance of crystallisation in *Paradise*. Early in the novel, Morrison draws our attention to the ambiguous aura of what will become a central historical landmark for the narrative.[79] It's the spot where Ruby's founders first gathered to eat, where that town's laws were debated, and where the fatal decision by its patriarchs is taken to storm the refuge of an outlying convent. As she unravels the life story of an emplacement that is both a publicly honoured monument and a domestic appliance, she crystallises the link between the functions it serves and the ominous collective fate it foresees:

An oven. Round as a head, deep as desire. Living in or near their wagons, boiling meal in the open, cutting sod and mesquite for shelter, the Old Fathers did that first: put most of their strength into constructing the huge, flawlessly designed Oven that both nourished them and monumentalized what they had done. When it was finished – each pale brick perfectly pitched; the chimney wide, lofty; the pegs and grill secure; the draft pulling steadily from the tail hole; the fire door plumb – then the ironmonger did his work. From barrel staves and busted axles, from kettles and bent nails, he fashioned an iron plate five feet by two and set it at the base of the Oven's mouth. It is still not clear where the words came from. Something he heard, invented, or something whispered to him while he slept curled over his tools in a wagon bed. His name was Morgan and who knew if he invented or stole the half-dozen or so words he forged. Words that seemed at first to bless them; later to confound them; finally to announce that they had lost.[80]

The image of the oven opens out like a fan, from the simple noun of the opening sentence to the anthropomorphic virtues elaborated, just two sentences later, by the sudden enlargement of the vision of a thing that 'both nourished them and monumentalized what they had done'. This very sense of figurative and syntactic extension is a feature of what Morrison means by crystallisation, as she gradually builds up the portentousness of the description of an object that will become the novel's symbolic centrepiece.

So, while it eventually becomes a cipher of all this community 'had lost', Morrison initially names the oven and categorises its functions through purely functional similes, offering a catalogue of components (brick, chimney and pegs) that notes, again in practical terms, the materialisation of what was a 'flawlessly designed' idea. In this enumerative sequence, Morrison's use of semicolons seems reminiscent of Woolf's free indirect discourse with its preference for extending one observation fluidly into the next through clausal subordination, as though Woolf were trying to resist the grammatical finality of the period. Although this scene isn't being processed and inflected by a specific focalising consciousness, Morrison's taxonomical sentences share Woolf's desire to sustain the continuity of successive perceptions. The oven, after all, is a monument of progressive development and consolidation, a witness to Ruby's settlement as a generational ideal, and at this stage in the novel Morrison preserves the beneficent image of it as such. To do so, she turns description into something accretive with the help of semicolons, unfolding in miniature a serial account of the oven's epic construction. By the time we reach the closing sentence, however, she also insinuates the graver changes, by giving pause between details of distinct consequences. This is where Morrison departs from Woolf's narration. For the semicolons now serve a rather different purpose: effecting fragmentation rather than fluidity, they reproduce grammatically the theme of Ruby's broken utopian ambition that the novel dramatises as a whole. 'Symbolic value' surrounding the town's domestic and ideological hub, as Danielle Russell has noted, 'supersedes practical concerns', when 'this former emblem of communal cohesion creates a quiet, but insidious division', as the 'evolving needs of the community are not reflected in the static symbol' just as the oven begins increasingly to advertise, over time, its own 'failure to fit into the cultural landscape'.[81] Such an inversion of symbolic value is reflected at the level of syntax too. Semantically speaking, the final sentence in this passage is constructed so as to be the most portentous: three verb-led phrases sweep across Ruby's history, from its initial sanctification, subsequent confusion, and its most recent demise, where words 'that seemed to bless' now appear to condemn.

By beginning with a celebratory catalogue of the oven's manufacture, before closing with the dire relevance now acquired by its cryptic message-plate, Morrison has not only taken that 'small piece' of Ruby's townscape and moved with it across generations; she also enables the changing implications of the oven and the very form of their expression to become interdependent. Figuration and phraseology thus crystallise each other here, while Morrison, within the space of a paragraph, turns the oven into an oracle of Ruby's moral disintegration, culminating in that day of violence against the convent women with which the novel proleptically begins: 'They shoot the white girl first' (*P*, p. 3). This startling opening sentence epitomises Morrison's preference for working *in medias res*. Such a mode requires that bold declarative observations or statements about already-unfolding actions are fleshed-out, so that the details such sentences condense can be unravelled. It's as though Morrison sets up opportunities for rewinding events, in effect, inviting us to view her crystalline formations in reverse. This is, of course, part of the kind of participatory reading experience that she values and cultivates, the dynamics of which I will be considering in the next section. For now, though, I want to explore the extent to which *in medias res* provides an ideal mode for Morrison, because it suits the way that in crystallisation, as Michael Silverblatt observes, 'the structure should emerge almost on its own'.[82] That's very much what it feels like to read events *in medias res*, where things happen almost on their own, without intrusive authorial comment, and where characters might take actions or savour perceptions without us being aware of what is motivating them to do so.

For Morrison, though, *in medias res* is not simply a means of intensifying her narration's obliquity by upholding the Jamesian priority of *showing* events rather than *telling* them – though her fiction *does* reaffirm that qualitative distinction as well. Nor is it a style for perpetuating our bewilderment, as high-modernist fiction is often assumed to do, loosening our interpretive grasp on why events are being narrated in the order that they are. Quite the contrary. *In media res* works in perhaps more basic terms for Morrison as a mode that reproduces in the reader the very condition that it names: plunging us into the perceptual density, pace and immediacy of a given moment, it activates our receptivity to scenes that are already underway. Swept along into the undertow of such moments, all our senses are imaginatively engaged by the array of textures seen, felt and smelt in the course of what happens:

The first drops were warm and fat, carrying the scent of white loco and cholla from regions north and west. They smashed into gentian, desert trumpets and slid from chicory leaves. Plump and slippery they rolled like mercury beads over the cracked earth between garden rows. As they sat in kitchen light, Lone, Frances and Sut DuPres could see, even smell, the rainfall, but they could not hear it, so soft, so downy, were the drops. (*P*, p. 281)

The immediate itemisation ('the first drops') places us in a position of knowing that the narrator is outlining an event that has already been set in motion. As is the case with that opening observation in *Paradise* ('They shoot the white girl first') – an observation mimicked in the first sentence, in the previous quote, though reset here in the past tense and in a situation whose pastoralism directly counters the novel's violent opening – the reader is having to catch up, or at least keep pace, with a scene that began before we arrived and for which Morrison holds all background detail in reserve. By this stage in the narrative, though, we are sufficiently aware of the impending violence confronting those women sharing the convent that the beauty of this happenstance deluge appears like a fragile lull before the storm of a more brutal kind, wrought by human design. Ultimately, the rhetorical effect of a scene that offsets natural events against imminent vengeance is one of suspense. Morrison explores the sensorium created by rainfall in ways that make the figures, 'sat in kitchen light', seem inert if also helpless – a direct contrast to how vigorously the cloudburst affects the very women who are facing attack:

> The rain's perfume was stronger north of Ruby, especially at the Convent, where thick white clover and Scotch broom colonized every place but the garden. Mavis and Pallas, aroused from sleep by its aroma, rushed to tell Consolata, Grace and Seneca that the longed for rain had finally come. Gathered in the kitchen door, first they watched, then they stuck out their hands to feel. It was like lotion on their fingers so they entered it and let it pour like balm on their shaved heads and upturned faces. Consolata started it; the rest were quick to join her. There are great rivers in the world and on their banks and the edges of oceans children thrill to water. In places where rain is light the thrill is almost erotic. But those sensations bow to the rapture of holy women dancing in hot sweet rain. They would have laughed, had enchantment not been so deep. If there were any recollections of a recent warning or intimations of harm, the irresistible rain washed them away. (*P*, p. 283)

Animating, benevolent, yet dangerously consoling, the 'rain's perfume' connects events across narrative time, just as it carries scent across geographical space. Part of the symbolism's undertow that extends from one episode to the next, precipitation also functions as a motif that's comparable to the figure of the oven whose history, as we saw previously, Morrison unpacks like a Russian doll. Moreover, like *Jazz*'s more explicitly rhythmic motifs, such as the alternation of iambic and amphibrachic phrases, the rain in *Paradise* also forms the basis of a riff – a riff played out through radically different similes ('mercury' and 'lotion') into equivalent substances that seem entirely appropriate to how droplets feel and move. Visceral as 'those sensations' may be for Morrison's heroines, the scene also works on the reader in a similar fashion, proving the conviction she had about *Jazz*'s register that '[w]hen it's tactile, your emotions are deeply involved'.[83]

This is a conviction that originated well before *Jazz*, though, stemming from Morrison's longer running aim, first recorded in the late 1970s, to eliciting an 'emotional' as well as an 'intellectual response' from her readers. Her 'job' in turn, as she called it, 'is to do both at the same time', something she accomplished through the ensuing two decades, even if the intellectualism of high theory in that period made it difficult for her critics to mention their emotions.[84] Curious though it may seem, nowhere is that affective dimension more evident and relevant than in the very moments where we find Morrison most testing, most resistant to critical assimilation. In turn, because she 'identifies race as a productive element of ... modernist form', in Urmila Seshagiri's phrase, 'a central organizing aesthetic category instead of merely a social problem',[85] one of the challenges we experience in reading Morrison's prose is the way it asks us to participate in what it does, before we start interpreting what it says.

'TO HAVE THE READER WORK': DIFFICULTY AND PARTICIPATION

Should we not recognise this voice? Or more to the point, what is it about this voice that impresses on us the need to recognise its singularity as well as its provenance?

But I have seen the City do an unbelievable sky. Redcaps and dining-car attendants who wouldn't think of moving out of the City sometimes go on at great length about country skies they have seen from the windows of trains. But there is nothing to beat what the City can make of a nightsky. It can empty itself of surface, and more like the ocean than the ocean itself, go deep, starless. Close up on the tops of buildings, near, nearer than the cap you are wearing, such a citysky presses and retreats, presses and retreats, making me think of the free but illegal love of sweethearts before they are discovered. (*J*, p. 35)

My citation reveals the source, of course. Regardless of such giveaways, however, the inflections of that voice are not easily forgotten by a reader who has listened to its Harlem chronicle; and especially not forgotten, perhaps, by the reader who can hear its primary place among the many other registers of Morrison's *oeuvre*. *Jazz* stands out in important respects, as much as for Morrison herself as for her audience. From her point of view, this is because the novel's language fulfilled an ambition she expressed over a decade before its release. That lilting timbre of its scenic descriptions and their consonance between nouns and adjectives ('surface' and 'starless'); the surprising half rhymes ('near' and 'wearing', 'love' and 'discovered') that throw into relief an image of the city as a realm of affiliations at once acoustic and libidinal, since rhyme performs in miniature the linking of public space with private feelings that jazz represents for nocturnal life at large; and finally, the narrator's endlessly inventive reach for comparisons ('like the ocean'), a narrator so suavely in charge, as we saw earlier in this chapter, of the urban panoramas he or she conveys – these are just some of the idioms through which *Jazz* evokes yet also *shares* sensory experiences, idioms that Morrison long believed are vital for a novel's ability to connect with its reader. 'To make the story appear oral', she famously asserted, 'meandering, effortless, spoken', is not only 'to have the reader *feel* the narrator without *identifying* that narrator, or hearing him or her knock about', but thereby also 'to have the reader work *with* the author in the construction of the book'.[86] That the degree to which readers contribute to a book's 'construction' remains immeasurable makes this an ambitious plea. The quantification of readerly engagement, though, is not what Morrison is valuing or debating; it is the intensity and ethical import of that participation which counts.

In the context of describing how readers are affected by modernist fiction, it's more common to hear talk of the difficulties a reader faces than what Morrison calls those 'holes and spaces [that] the reader can come into'.[87] This implies that her model for participatory reading redefines what we mean by difficulty from stylistic and interpretive angles, as it questions the familiar notion of difficulty as deliberate exclusion we might associate with high modernism – be it the fragmentation and polyphony of *The Waste Land* or the puns and neologisms of *Finnegans Wake*. As Morrison implies, through her continual insistence on having her audience do the work, no text is *inherently* difficult; what it does to normative critical procedures and expectations, however, may well cause it to appear so. This is in keeping with recent work by modernist scholars on the perceived challenges posed by formal innovation, which reveal in and of themselves more about our own preconceptions than about any conventions the text may be subverting. As Leonard Diepeveen has observed, 'difficulty' itself is an arbitrary benchmark for identifying what authentically 'modernist' narration is like, because it is 'not a property of the difficult work at hand, but a reading protocol that is radically affect-based'.[88] This chimes with Morrison's sense that difficulty is manifested not in any aspect of narrative discourse so much as in the process of being 'put', as her readers, 'into the position of being naked and quite vulnerable' but 'nevertheless trusting'.[89]

It is that dual state of vulnerability and trust that she has endorsed across her career, because it replicates within the reading experience the combination of risk and openness that informs her creative practice. To assume that pose of trusting vulnerability is not only to establish a 'very intimate acquaintance with the people in the book, without any prejudices', but also an 'intimacy that's so complete, it humanizes [the reader] in the same way that the characters are humanized from within by certain activity, and in the way in which I am humanized by the act of writing'.[90] Here was Morrison in 1981; and this ideal of an affective correspondence between acts of writing and reading persists, not simply as a projection of a model reader, but as a kind of manifesto for the vocabulary she hopes readers will employ.

What is so challenging about that 'intimate acquaintance' Morrison invites is that it establishes, to recall Diepeveen's term, a new 'reading protocol'. The difficulties of achieving that intimacy thus become for Morrison a way of resisting critics who have, in her view, been content to see '[o]ther kinds of structures ... imposed on my works', when in fact she has been 'trying hard to use the characteristics of the art form that I know best, and to succeed or fail on those criteria rather than on some other criteria'.[91] The highly theoretical tendencies of the decade in which Morrison was speaking here immediately come to mind as the focus of that resistance. Yet the commitment to taking her fiction on its own terms, as this chapter has argued, still provides a valuable, and indeed necessary, intervention today, even if the critical tables have tilted in recent years towards novelistic aesthetics with an accompanying caution about the limits of reading contemporary fiction for instrumental ends. Nearly thirty years later, Morrison's claim that her 'writing expects, demands participatory reading'[92] is pertinent for what much scholarship on the novel now 'expects', as the ethics of reading has become instituted as one way of questioning that role in evaluation of predetermining 'criteria' of which Morrison was so critical.

However much Morrison raises the bar for her readers, she also makes similar demands of herself. Rhetorical thrift, as we have seen, is one such stipulation, just as it provoked Coetzee to reassess minimalism as medium for political critique. Likewise Morrison's insistence that the novelists should 'never satiate' speaks, in turn, to the level of readerly participation she aims to cultivate and which is also demanded, as we saw in Chapter 4, by McEwan's ambivalently satirical late style.[93] As in Coetzee's morally uncompromising fictions of shame and imperial violence, so for Morrison the act of rhetorically cutting back is a catalyst for drawing us ethically in. However much she echoes Faulkner's claim that we should not be surprised to find him difficult because he deliberately wants to 'say it all in one sentence, between one Cap and one period',[94] Morrison's most testing passages may in fact turn out *not* to be those where she 'tr[ies] to say a lot in a line', but instead where she writes 'in a very economical way' in order to 'provoke' as well as 'evoke'.[95] Showing less and less is a means of establishing an interpretive situation in which she can, at first, 'rely very heavily on the reader to know a *lot* about what he *does* know', before then proceeding to undercut that knowledge as events unfold.[96]

Unsettling critical expectations just as contrapuntal melodies disorient the ear is an overarching imperative for *Jazz*. The novel exemplifies Morrison's preference for writing in an 'economical way', as it follows inroads to the 'click of dark and snapping fingers' (*J*, p. 227) that are the thematic scene and formal source of its narration:

It's good they don't need much space to dance in because there isn't any. The room is packed. Men groan their satisfaction; women hum anticipation. The music bends, falls to its knees to embrace them all, encourage them all to live a little, why don't you? since this is the it you've been looking for. (*J*, p. 188)

Aside from a brief mention that this 'room is packed', there are no other scenic details, only actions recorded as 'the dancers hesitate, have a moment of doubt', and melodies personified as 'the music will solve and dissolve any question' (*J*, p. 188). Indeed, 'the it' of the musical envelope that's enfolding Morrison's huddled dancers takes precedence over any asides about facial features or atmospheric mood. Such orientational embellishments are made redundant. Like a solo improvisation that refuses to return to its tonic chord, Morrison's parataxis delays and defers any final predication. Motion rather than resolution is what counts. Despite the accumulation of details one expects with parataxis, however, she doesn't give us more than we apparently need to know or that we should expect to know. She aligns us instead with the restricted yet suggestive perspective of those, like Dorcas, who have entered a 'market where gesture is all: a tongue's lightning lick; a thumbnail grazing the split cheeks of a purple plum' (*J*, p. 192). We are within the crowd, and Morrison prevents her narrator from rising like a periscope above it to offer a vantage point over the scene. This may be descriptively partial; we may find it unsatisfying, if not momentarily confusing. Like the effect of episodes *in medias res* in *Paradise*, though, Morrison's point is that the rewards of perspectival constriction are more compelling for us than the full revelations of third-person narrative could ever be. We are left with a partial, cramped, suitably 'dissolv[ing]' view of a setting in which boundaries are elided and replaced by gestural invitations to intimacy. Spartan though her depiction may be, fleeting though her attention to human form remains, she fixes our imaginative attention on all that we might have 'been looking for' in this scene but has yet to be shown. Our dissatisfaction with absent detail is assuaged, as the process of reading through those gaps enacts the solution to such 'moment[s] of doubt', just as the music does for dancers.

What it takes 'to make a truly aural novel', as Morrison rightly anticipated over a decade before *Jazz*, is the introduction of 'many places and spaces for the reader to work and participate'.[97] Like many of the convictions we have considered in this chapter as in those that precede it, Morrison's plea for readers to be as intensely engaged in style as she is in composing it has certain precedents. Where Emerson made clear in 'History' (1841) that 'the student is to read history actively and not passively',[98] so Angela Carter insisted over a century later that '[r]eading is just as creative an activity as writing and most intellectual development depends upon new readings of old texts'.[99] What unites these very different writers – working in eras that bookend modernism as it is usually periodised – is the contention that the challenges readers face have a bearing beyond the private world of reading itself, and that active reading contributes to the 'intellectual development' of responses towards the aesthetic medium to which we attend. For A. Alvarez, this amounts to 'a two-way pact: the writer makes himself heard and the reader listens in – or, more, accurately, the writer works to find or create a voice that will stretch out to the reader, make him prick up his ears and attend'.[100] Morrison, as we've seen, has taken pains to cultivate that kind of attention to voice, even if it's actually her gaps and silences that compel us to listen in. In this way, her thrifty prose reveals that there is a difference between associating difficulty, on one hand, with the cognitive strain of reading semantically opaque or dense prose, and the kind of pleasure we take in deciphering a complex mix of meters or deciding what grammatical components make a line sound as virtuosic as it does. What the participatory challenges that Morrison poses reveal is that difficulty is not simply a matter of accessibility. It speaks, instead, to that broader metacritical debate about the appropriate *scale* on which we can read the legacy of modernist innovations and their ethical efficacy – from the smallest syntactic unit to the wider cultural reception of a writer's prestige.

MODERNISMS HELD IN RESERVE

Such methodological questions of scale spotlight one of Morrison's more controversial beliefs, voiced as far back as 1981, that '[i]f there were better criticism, there would be better books'.[101] Some twenty-five years later, she reiterates that appeal. 'In trying to break open the critical language you have to take risks',[102] she asserts, echoing Woolf's advice in 1917 that to practice 'creative criticism' one needs 'to be free to make one's own laws and to be alert to do it afresh for every newcomer'.[103] Morrison is certainly no newcomer, and her pre-eminence often makes it difficult for the critic to gain analytical purchase on a body of work that seems to invite nothing more than respectful appreciation. I have tried nonetheless to work in the spirit of those interpretive risks of which she speaks. In so doing, my effort has not only been to do justice to Morrison's formal virtuosity, but also to convey at least something of the experience of being that 'fastidious and not-easily-taken-in reader who', in her mind, is willing 'to participate in the text a lot'.[104] For us to read in this fashion – even if we are not always likely to be as 'fastidious' or indeed 'smart enough' as Morrison would like us to be[105] – seems especially important at a time when literary critics, cultural theorists and art historians alike are considering more sensitively than ever the notion that 'modernism necessarily transcends', in Peter Osborne's phrase, 'its own historically inaugural ... form'.[106] As a writer committed to making her reader work and who invites us to take interpretive risks just as she does with technique, Morrison is living proof of that transcendence. This is not to argue that we should understand Morrison's practice as a 'modernist' one entirely without recourse to identifiable influences or paradigmatic moments of early-twentieth-century novelistic experiment; it is, rather, to take seriously the remarks of one of her key precursors, Zora Neale Hurston, who in 1934 suggested that '[w]hat we really mean by originality is the modification of ideas'.[107] Hurston points to how we might gauge artistic exemplariness not by how decisively it negates past achievements or resists tradition, but rather by how artists extend the scope of what is possible for their chosen medium. Throughout this book we have seen that this scope's extension involves, and indeed solicits, a state of creative impiety that motivates contemporary writers not to parody what they inherit but to allow practical conversations to flourish with modernism as a historically located project. Working at the confluence of innovation and inheritance, novelists confront that project as a precedent to be redeveloped rather than revered, precisely in order to discover not only why modernism meant so much to the novel but also what it might still become.

In light of Hurston's contention, we can see how modernism's continuance in the work of Coetzee, Kundera, McEwan, Morrison, Ondaatje and Roth is often generated by their 'modification of ideas', by their impulse, as Morrison puts it, 'to take ordinary assumptions and to push them to their logical conclusions',[108] to reckon with the novel's past accomplishments without preserving them in ideological amber. These writers share Morrison's will to perpetuate modernism beyond – if also because of – the legacy of postmodernism's era of artistic self-involution. They have sought to keep fiction formally alive and politically alert, just as, for her, jazz 'always keeps you on the edge'. To write on that edge requires the cultivation of what Morrison identifies in her own prose as a dynamic kind of incipience: 'the feeling that there's some more'. What better way to prospect for modernist futures than by detecting this 'feeling of something held in reserve' within the novel today, as writers 'sense that there is more – that you can't have it all right now'?[109] This commitment speaks beyond the corpus of this book, casting a wider spotlight on modernism's reach into the contemporary scene as it reappears in incipient formations: in those ways of making that persist precisely because they 'never fully satisfy',[110] presenting the novel with possibilities that are currently held in reserve.

Notes

INTRODUCTION

1 Charles Ruas, 'Toni Morrison' (1981), in Danille Taylor-Guthrie (ed.), *Conversations with Toni Morrison* (Jackson: University Press of Mississippi, 1994), p. 112.
2 Urmila Seshagiri, 'Modernist Ashes, Postcolonial Phoenix: Jean Rhys and the Evolution of the English Novel in the Twentieth Century', *Modernism/Modernity*, 13: 3 (2006), p. 492.
3 Raymond Williams, *The Politics of Modernism: Against the New Conformists* (London: Verso, 1990), p. 35 (Williams's emphasis).
4 Ibid., p. 35.
5 Ibid., p. 34.
6 Ibid., p. 32.
7 For a reapplication of Williams's influential model of residual, dominant and emergent formations, see Cyrus R. K. Patell, 'Representing Emergent Literatures', *American Literary History*, 15: 1 (2003): pp. 61–9.
8 Reassessing the contemporary relevance of modernist ideas of autonomy in relation to what 'art as an institution promises', Lambert Zuidervaart observes that by 'attacking a problematic marginalization of non-aesthetic concerns within the modern art world, postmodernism overlooks what makes art both intrinsically worthwhile and societally important' (*Art in Public: Politics, Economics, and a Democratic Culture* (Cambridge: Cambridge University Press, 2011), p. 224).
9 Mark McGurl, *The Novel Art: Elevations of American Fiction after Henry James* (Princeton: Princeton University Press, 2001), p. 9 (McGurl's emphases).
10 Liam McIlvanney and Ray Ryan, 'Introduction', in McIlvanney and Ryan (eds.), *The Good of the Novel* (London: Faber and Faber, 2011), pp. vii–viii.
11 Janice Radway, 'Zines, Half-Lives, and Afterlives: On the Temporalities of Social and Political Change', *PMLA*, 126:1 (January 2011), p. 143.
12 Derek Attridge, *J. M. Coetzee and the Ethics of Reading: Literature in the Event* (Chicago: University of Chicago Press, 2004), p. 5.
13 Amy Hungerford, 'On the Period Formerly Known as Contemporary', *American Literary History*, 20:1–2 (Spring/Summer 2008), p. 418.

14 J. M. Bernstein, 'Modernism as Aesthetics and Art History', in James Elkins (ed.), *Art History versus Aesthetics* (London: Routledge, 2006), p. 266.
15 Ibid., p. 256.
16 Ibid., p. 256.
17 Samuel Otter, 'An Aesthetics of All Things', *Representations*, 104 (Fall 2008), pp. 116–17.
18 Ibid., p. 118.
19 Attridge, *J. M. Coetzee and the Ethics of Reading*, p. 12.
20 Rebecca L. Walkowitz, *Cosmopolitan Style: Modernism Beyond the Nation* (New York: Columbia University Press, 2006), p. 4.
21 Ibid., p. 6.
22 Michel Foucault's 'What Is Enlightenment?', quoted in Walkowitz, *Cosmopolitan Style*, p. 6.
23 Susan Stanford Friedman, 'Definitional Excursions: The Meanings of Modern/Modernity/Modernism', quoted in Walkowitz, *Cosmopolitan Style*, p. 6.
24 For a shrewd discussion of the radical politics that have been associated with experimental modes, including those strategies that are perceived to represent an ideological and aesthetic break from literary realism, see the opening two chapters of Andrzej Gasiorek's *Post-war British Fiction: Realism and After* (London: Arnold, 1995).
25 Timothy Brennan, 'Running and Dodging: The Rhetoric of Doubleness in Contemporary Theory', *New Literary History*, 41:2 (Spring 2010), p. 294 (Brennan's emphasis).
26 Milan Kundera, *The Curtain: An Essay in Seven Parts*, trans. Linda Asher (London: Faber and Faber, 2007), p. 81; Walkowitz, *Cosmopolitan Style*, p. 8.
27 Jonathan Franzen, 'Jonathan Franzen on the Social Novel'. http://www.fifthestate.co.uk/2009/01/25th-estate-jonathan-franzen-on-the-social-novel/ [Accessed on 10 February 2011].
28 Leslie A. Fiedler, 'The Death and Rebirths of the Novel: The View from '82', in Ihab Hassan and Sally Hassan (eds.), *Innovation/Renovation: New Perspectives on the Humanities* (Madison: University of Wisconsin Press, 1983), p. 28.
29 Ibid., pp. 28–29.
30 Hungerford, 'On the Period Formerly Known as Contemporary', p. 415.
31 Gerhard Hoffman's thoughts on what comes 'after postmodernism' have some bearing here, when he considers that the 'mixtures of concepts, approaches, and styles make the post-postmodern changes in fiction appear less radical and much less clear than suggest the announcement and celebration of a new realism as the latest stage of literary development' (*From Modernism to Postmodernism: Concepts and Strategies of Postmodern American Fiction* (Amsterdam and New York: Rodopi, 2005), p. 624).
32 Maggie Gee, 'Re: Contemporary Fiction: The Legacies of Modernism'. Unpublished email to David James, Friday 23 September 2005, 11:19:36.
33 Ibid.

Notes to pages 12–18

34 David Tracy, 'Fragments: The Spiritual Situation of Our Times', in John D. Caputo and Michael J. Scalon (eds.), *God, the Gift and Post-Modernism* (Bloomington: Indiana University Press, 1999), p. 174.
35 Andrzej Gasiorek and Patrick Parrinder, 'Introduction', in Gasiorek and Parrinder (eds.), *The Oxford History of the Novel in English, Volume 4: The Reinvention of the British and Irish Novel 1880–1940* (Oxford: Oxford University Press, 2011), p. xxiii.
36 Ibid., p. xxiii.
37 Leonard Wilcox, 'Baudrillard, Don DeLillo's *White Noise*, and the End of Heroic Narrative', in Hugh Ruppersberg and Tim Engles (eds.), *Critical Essays on Don DeLillo* (New York: G. K. Hall, 2000), p. 198.
38 Walkowitz, *Cosmopolitan Style*, p. 18.
39 Angela Leighton, *On Form: Poetry, Aestheticism, and the Legacy of a Word* (Oxford: Oxford University Press, 2007), p. 262.
40 Ibid., p. 33.
41 Ibid., p. 263.
42 Isobel Armstrong, *The Radical Aesthetic* (Oxford: Blackwell, 2000), p. 165.
43 Ibid., p. 165.
44 Toni Morrison, 'Rootedness: The Ancestor as Foundation' (1984), in Carolyn C. Denard (ed.), *What Moves at the Margin: Selected Nonfiction* (Jackson: University Press of Mississippi, 2008), p. 59.
45 Andreas Huyssen, *After the Great Divide: Modernism, Mass Culture, Postmodernism* (Basingstoke: Macmillan, 1986), p. 162.
46 Ibid., p. 174.
47 John Barth, 'The Literature of Replenishment' (1980), repr. in Michael J. Hoffman and Patrick Murphy (eds.), *Essentials of the Theory of Fiction* (London: Leicester University Press, 1996), p. 276.
48 As Madelyn Jablon has warned, reflecting on Linda Hutcheon's narratology, metafiction hardly means the same thing to all writers of a certain generation: 'scholars of African American literature must assume the task of redefining such terms as "metafiction" and "mimesis as process"', and, henceforth, 'this task necessitates a redefinition of the thematization of self-consciousness in literature', one 'that is distinct from parody because African American writers create thematically self-conscious fictions that are neither parody nor an acknowledgement of literature's "usedupness"' (*Black Metafiction: Self-Consciousness in African American Literature* (Iowa City: University of Iowa Press, 1997), p. 31).
49 Charles Altieri, 'Why Modernist Claims for Autonomy Matter', *Journal of Modern Literature*, 32: 3 (2009), p. 3.
50 Linda Hutcheon, 'Gone Forever, But Here to Stay: The Legacy of the Postmodern', in Pelagia Goulimari (ed.), *Postmodernism: What Moment?* (Manchester: Manchester University Press, 2007), p. 16.
51 Ibid., p. 17.
52 Ibid., p. 17.

53 Pericles Lewis, *Religious Experience and the Modernist Novel* (Cambridge: Cambridge University Press, 2010), p. 6.
54 Gasiorek, *Post-war British Fiction*, p. 193.
55 Ibid., p. 192.
56 Fredric Jameson, *A Singular Modernity: Essay on the Ontology of the Present* (London: Verso, 2002), p. 5.
57 Caroline Levine, *Provoking Democracy: Why We Need the Arts* (Oxford: Blackwell, 2007), p. 147.
58 Jameson, *A Singular Modernity*, p. 210.
59 Tyrus Miller, *Late Modernism: Politics, Fiction, and the Arts Between the World Wars* (Berkeley: University of California Press, 1999), p. 19.
60 Tim Mayers, *(Re)Writing Craft: Composition, Creative Writing, and the Future of English Studies* (Pittsburgh: University of Pittsburgh Press, 2005), p. 44.
61 Mark McGurl, *The Program Era: Postwar Fiction and the Rise of Creative Writing* (Cambridge, MA: Harvard University Press, 2009), p. 217.
62 Ibid., p. 220.
63 Ibid., p. 228.
64 Ibid., p. 247.
65 Elissa Schappell, 'Toni Morrison: The Art of Fiction' (1992), in Carolyn C. Denard (ed.), *Toni Morrison: Conversations* (Jackson: University Press of Mississippi, 2008), p. 82.
66 McGurl, *The Program Era*, p. 320.
67 Ibid., p. 315.
68 Hungerford, 'On the Period Formerly Known as Contemporary', p. 418.
69 Nicholas Wroe, 'A Life in Writing', Interview with Ian McEwan, *The Guardian*, Review, 6 March 2010, p. 11.
70 Robert Stepto, 'Intimate Things in Place: A Conversation with Toni Morrison' (1976), in Taylor-Guthrie (ed.), *Conversations with Toni Morrison*, p. 23.
71 Ibid., p. 23.
72 Cary Fagan, 'Where the Personal and Historical Meet: Michael Ondaatje', in Beverley Daurio (ed.), *The Power to Bend Spoons: Interviews with Canadian Novelists* (Toronto: The Mercury Press, 1998), p. 115.
73 Ibid., p. 121.
74 Ibid., p. 117.
75 Clarence Major, 'Necessary Distance: Afterthoughts on Becoming a Writer', in Bernard W. Bell (ed.), *Clarence Major: Portraits of an African American Postmodernist* (Chapel Hill: University of North Carolina Press, 2001), p. 71.
76 Ibid., p. 72.
77 Margaret Reynolds and Jonathan Noakes, 'Interview with Ian McEwan' (2001), in Reynolds and Noakes (eds.), *Ian McEwan: The Essential Guide* (London: Vintage, 2002), p. 20.
78 Derek Attridge, 'Ethical Modernism: Servants as Others in J. M. Coetzee's Early Fiction', *Poetics Today*, 25: 4 (Winter 2004), p. 653.

79 Schappell, 'Toni Morrison', p. 81.
80 Morrison, 'Rootedness', p. 59.
81 Tom Gunning, 'Re-newing Old Technologies: Astonishment, Second Nature, and the Uncanny in Technology from the Previous Turn-of-the-Century', in David Thorburn and Henry Jenkins (eds.), *Rethinking Media Change: The Aesthetics of Transition* (Cambridge, MA: MIT Press, 2003), p. 51.
82 Radhika Jones, 'Peter Carey: The Art of Fiction' (2006), in Philip Gourevitch (ed.), *The Paris Review Interviews: Vol. II* (New York: Picador, 2007), p. 440.
83 Kundera, *The Curtain*, p. 15.
84 Ibid., p. 78 (Kundera's emphases).
85 Harold Bloom, *The Anxiety of Influence: A Theory of Poetry* (Oxford: Oxford University Press, 1973), p. 5.
86 Henry Widdowson, *Practical Stylistics* (Oxford: Oxford University Press, 1992), p. 56.
87 Ibid., p. 56.
88 Paul H. Fry, 'How to Live with the Infinite Regress of Strong Misreading', *Modern Language Quarterly*, 69: 4 (December 2008), p. 441.
89 Bloom, *The Anxiety of Influence*, p. 96.
90 J. M. Coetzee, 'He and His Man' (2003), repr. in John Sutherland (ed.), *Nobel Lectures: 20 Years of the Nobel Prize for Literature Lectures* (Cambridge: Icon Books, 2007), p. 58.
91 Ibid., p. 60
92 Ibid., pp. 60, 61.
93 Ibid., p. 62.
94 Ibid., p. 62.
95 Toni Morrison, 'James Baldwin: His Voice Remembered; Life in His Language' (1987), in Denard (ed.), *What Moves At the Margin*, p. 90.
96 Coetzee, 'He and His Man', p. 62.
97 Ibid., p. 62.
98 Michael Roth, *The Ironist's Cage: Memory, Trauma, and the Construction of History* (New York: Columbia University Press, 1995), p. 16.
99 Ibid., p. 17.
100 Gertrude Stein, notebooks, quoted in Leon Katz, 'The First Making of *The Making of Americans*', Doctoral Diss. Columbia University, 1963, p. 161.
101 Toni Morrison, *Playing in the Dark: Whiteness and the Literary Imagination* (Cambridge, Mass.: Harvard University Press, 1992), p. xi.
102 Joe David Bellamy, 'Preface', in *The New Fiction* (Urbana: University of Illinois Press, 1975), p. xi.
103 Ibid., p. xii.
104 Kundera, *The Curtain*, pp. 77–8.
105 Gertrude Stein, *Three Lives*, repr. in *Writings, 1903–1932* (New York: Library of America, 1998), p. 102.
106 Julie Sanders, *Adaptation and Appropriation* (London: Routledge, 2006), pp. 154–5,

107 Ibid., p. 38.
108 Letter to Robert Ross, 22 October 1986, quoted in Ross, '"It cannot *not* be there": Borges and Australia's Peter Carey', in Edna Aizenberg (ed.), *Borges and His Successors* (Columbia: University of Missouri Press, 1990), p. 45.
109 Richard Walsh, *The Rhetoric of Fictionality: Narrative Theory and the Idea of Fiction* (Columbus: Ohio State University Press, 2007), p. 130.
110 Max Saunders points to this self-promoting gesture when taking stock of the Jamesian turn exemplified by David Lodge and Colm Tóibín. Saunders suggests that '[o]ne reason is potential narcissistic, seeking to aggrandise the author's self by association with "the Master"', and therefore '[t]o be able to represent the interiority of such a fierce literary intelligence and complex sensibility is a supreme challenge for a writer' ('Master Narratives', *The Cambridge Quarterly*, 37: 1 (2008), p. 127).
111 Michael Wood, *Yeats and Violence* (Oxford: Oxford University Press 2010), p. 97.
112 William Faulkner, 25 February 1957, *Faulkner in the University*, ed. Frederick L. Gwynn and Joseph L. Blotner (Charlottesville: University Press of Virginia, 1995), pp. 20–1.
113 Siri Hustvedt, 'My Father Myself', *Granta* 104 (2008), p. 72.
114 Ibid., p. 73.
115 Laura Marcus, 'Ian McEwan's Modernist Time: *Atonement* and *Saturday*', in Sebastian Groes (ed.), *Ian McEwan: Contemporary Critical Perspectives* (London: Continuum, 2009), p. 85.
116 E. M. Forster, *Aspects of the Novel*, ed. Oliver Stallybrass (London: Penguin, 2005), p. 142.
117 Zadie Smith, 'E. M. Forster, Middle Manager', in *Changing My Mind: Occasional Essays* (London: Hamish Hamilton, 2009), p. 15.
118 Ibid., p. 22.
119 Paul B. Armstrong, 'Two Cheers for Tolerance: E. M. Forster's Ironic Liberalism and the Indirections of Style', *Modernism/Modernity*, 16:2 (2009), p. 283.
120 Rob Nixon, 'Preparations for Travel: The Naipaul Brothers' Conradian Atavism', *Research in African Literatures*, 22 (1991), p. 179.
121 David Lodge, 'Towards a Poetics of Fiction: An Approach Through Language', in *The Novelist at the Crossroads, and Other Essays on Fiction and Criticism* (London: Routledge and Kegan Paul, 1971), p. 66.
122 Lodge, 'The Novelist at the Crossroads', in *The Novelist at the Crossroads*, pp. 17–18.
123 John Haffenden, 'Martin Amis', in Haffenden (ed.), *Novelists in Interview* (New York and London: Methuen, 1985), p. 4.
124 Martin Amis, rev. of *Diversity and Depth in Fiction*, by Angus Wilson (1984), in Amis, *The War Against Cliché: Essays and Reviews 1971–2000* (London: Jonathan Cape, 2001), p. 79.
125 Jeanette Winterson, *Art Objects: Essays on Ecstasy and Effrontery* (London: Jonathan Cape, 1995), p. 11.

126 Ian McEwan and Olivia Manning, 'The State of Fiction: A Symposium', *The New Review*, 5: 1 (Summer 1978), p. 51.
127 D. J. Taylor, *A Vain Conceit: British Fiction in the 1980s* (London: Bloomsbury, 1989), p. 7.
128 Winterson, *Art Objects*, p. 55 (my emphasis).
129 Lodge, 'The Novelist at the Crossroads', p. 4.
130 Ibid., p. 22 (Lodge's emphases).
131 Thomas LeClair, 'An Interview with Don DeLillo' (1982), in Thomas DePietro (ed.), *Conversations with Don DeLillo* (Jackson: University Press of Mississippi, 2005), p. 7.
132 Ibid., p. 6.
133 Rosa González, 'The Pleasure of Prose vs. Pornographic Violence: An Interview with Ian McEwan', *The European Messenger*, 1: 3 (Autumn 1992), p. 40.
134 Alan Hollinghurst, 'Introduction' to Henry James, *The Ivory Tower* (New York: Review, 2004), p. xvii.
135 Henry James, 'The Art of Fiction' (1884), in *Literary Criticism: Essays on Literature, American Writers, English Writers*, ed. Leon Edel (New York: Library of America, 1984), p. 53.
136 LeClair, 'An Interview with Don DeLillo', p. 7.
137 James, 'The Art of the Novel', p. 61; 'The Future of the Novel' (1899), *Literary Criticism*, p. 105.
138 LeClair, 'An Interview with Don DeLillo', p. 7.
139 Thomas Hardy, 'The Profitable Reading of Fiction' (1888), repr. in Michael Millgate (ed.), *Thomas Hardy's Public Voice: The Essays, Speeches, and Miscellaneous Reviews* (Oxford: Clarendon, 2001), p. 80.
140 'A Different Window: reading European fiction', with A. S. Byatt, Aleksandar Hemon and Tom McCarthy, chaired by Daniel Hahn. Southbank Centre, London: 7.45pm. A report on the event by John Dugdale appeared in 'The Week in Books', *The Guardian*, Review, 6 February 2010, p. 5.
141 Aleksandar Hemon, 'Last Exit', *Bookforum*, 16:5 (February/March 2010), p. 11.
142 Quoted in Dugdale, 'The Week in Books', *The Guardian*, Review, 6 February 2010, p. 5.
143 Jameson, *A Singular Modernity*, p. 3.
144 Pamela L. Caughie, 'Introduction', in Caughie (ed.), *Disciplining Modernism* (New York: Palgrave Macmillan, 2009), p. 3.
145 See, for instance, Dorothy J. Hale's incisive commentary of the emerging conversations between narrative ethics, Jamesian theories of the novel, and the positive reassessment of formalist criticism in 'Aesthetics and the New Ethics: Theorizing the Novel in the Twenty-First Century', *PMLA*, 124: 3 (May 2009): pp. 896–905. For an application of conceptions of alterity to a more globalised map of novelistic strategies see Shameem Black's *Fiction Across Borders: Imagining the Lives of Others in Late Twentieth-Century Novels* (New York: Columbia University Press, 2010).

146 Douglas Mao and Rebecca L. Walkowitz, 'The New Modernist Studies', *PMLA*, 123:3 (May 2008), p. 738.
147 My objective in this book has been to emphasise the specific strategies of contemporary writers who recuperate and reanimate modernist strategies, regardless of their salience for the theorisation of *transnationalism* – a term that has already become overdetermined, as several commentators in a timely issue of *Novel* have remarked. See especially Rita Barnard's and Nancy Armstrong's contributions to 'Theories of the Novel Now, Part 1', *Novel: A Forum on Fiction* 42:2 (Summer 2009).
148 Huyssen, 'High/Low in an Expanded Field', *Modernism/Modernity*, 9:3 (September 2002), p. 363.
149 Ibid., p. 365.
150 Thomas Doherty, 'On Critical Humility', *Textual Practice*, 23: 6 (December 2009), p. 1029.
151 Henry James, Letter to Howard Sturgis, 8 November 1903, repr. in Susan E. Gunter and Steven H. Jobe (eds.), *Dearly Beloved Friends: Henry James's Letters to Younger Men* (Ann Arbor: University of Michigan Press, 2004), p. 131.
152 Echoing this plea for thinking positively about the relation between formalism and historicism, Daniel Hack has recently argued that the 'goal ... is not to trade textual interpretation for the methods of book history and reception studies – close reading for distant reading, in [Franco] Moretti's shorthand – but rather to show that each needs the other if we are to understand as fully as possible either a text's intrinsic features or its cultural impact, let alone the relationship between the two' ('Close Reading at a Distance: *Bleak House*', *Novel: A Forum on Fiction*, 42: 3 (Fall 2009), p. 421).
153 Jahan Ramazani, *A Transnational Poetics* (Chicago: University of Chicago Press, 2009), p. 99.

CHAPTER 1. ADVANCING ALONG THE INHERITED PATH

1 George Eliot, 'Shadows of the Coming Race', *Impressions of Theophrastus Such*, repr. in Charles Lee Lewis (ed.), *Essays of George Eliot* (New York and Boston: Caldwell, 1884), p. 399.
2 T. S. Eliot, 'Tradition and the Individual Talent' (1919), in *The Sacred Wood: Essays on Poetry and Criticism* (London: Faber & Faber, 1997), p. 41.
3 Ibid., p. 40.
4 Ibid., p. 41.
5 Michèle Roberts, 'The Need to Blow Up Sheds', rev. of *The Creative Feminine and Her Discontents: Psychotherapy, Art and Destruction*, by Juliet Miller, *The Guardian, Review*, Saturday, 10 May 2008, p. 8.
6 Carol Shields, 'Narrative Hunger and the Overflowing Cupboard', in Edward Eden and Dee Goertz (eds.), *Carol Shields, Narrative Hunger, and the Possibilities of Fiction* (Toronto: University of Toronto Press, 2003), p. 33.

Notes to pages 44–53

7 Ian McEwan, 'In Prose of Science'. *The Age*, 22 April 2006. http://www.theage.com.au/news/arts/in-prose-of-science/2006/04/20/1145344217780.html [Accessed 1 July 2006].
8 Jorge Luis Borges, *Labyrinths: Selected Stories and Other Writings* (London: Penguin, 2000), p. 236.
9 Eliot, 'Tradition and the Individual Talent', p. 40.
10 Kundera, *The Curtain*, p. 81.
11 Milan Kundera, *The Art of the Novel*, trans. Linda Asher (New York: HaperCollins, 2000), p. 6 (Kundera's emphases).
12 Milan Kundera, *Testaments Betrayed*, trans. Linda Asher (London: Faber & Faber, 1995), p. 75.
13 Ibid., p. 75 (Kundera's emphases).
14 Ibid., p. 76.
15 Ibid., p. 75.
16 Asher Z. Milbauer and Donald G. Watson, 'An Interview with Phillip Roth' (1988), in George Searles (ed.), *Conversations with Philip Roth*, (Jackson: University Press of Mississippi, 1992), p. 250.
17 Philip Roth, *The Facts* (New York: Farrar, Straus and Giroux, 1988), p. 157.
18 Milbauer and Watson, 'An Interview with Phillip Roth', p. 250.
19 Ibid., p. 250.
20 Kundera, *The Art of the Novel*, p. 83.
21 Philip Roth, *American Pastoral* (London: Vintage, 1998), p. 35.
22 Jay L. Halio, 'Deadly Farce in the Comedy of Philip Roth', in Ben Siegel and Jay L. Halio (eds.), *Playful and Serious: Philip Roth as a Comic Writer* (Newark: University of Delaware Press, 2010), p. 220.
23 Roth, *American Pastoral*, p. 20 (Roth's emphasis).
24 Ibid., p. 34.
25 James, 'The Art of Fiction', p. 53 (James's emphasis).
26 Roth, *American Pastoral*, p. 20.
27 Joseph Conrad, Preface to *The Nigger of the 'Narcissus'* (1897), repr. in Edward Garnett (ed.), *Conrad's Prefaces to His Works* (New York: Haskell House, 1971), p. 52.
28 Philip Roth, *Nemesis* (London: Jonathan Cape, 2010), pp. 140–41. Hereafter *N*.
29 Dorothy Richardson, Foreword to *Pilgrimage* (London: Virago, 1979), vol. I, pp. 10, 11.
30 Kevin Bell, *Ashes Taken For Fire: Aesthetic Modernism and the Critique of Identity* (Minneapolis: University of Minnesota Press, 2007), p. 2.
31 Ibid., p. 10.
32 Philip Roth, 'Age Makes a Difference', interview by Hermione Lee, *The New Yorker*, 1 October 2007. http://www.newyorker.com/reporting/2007/10/01/071001fa_fact_lee [Accessed 31 May 2010].
33 Kundera, *The Art of the Novel*, p. 66.
34 James, 'The Future of the Novel', in *Literary Criticism*, p. 105.
35 Unable to decide whether to associate Roth with the 'disjunctive irony' of modernism or the 'suspensive irony' of postmodern 'randomness', Debora

Shostak moves beyond this typology of post/modern traits – drawn from Alan Wilde's *Horizons of Assent* (1981) – to pose a series of questions about the extent to which Roth is ventriloquising his own reflexive personas: 'Is he finally liberated by the freedom of the fluid boundaries around self and world, impersonating all possible positions while holding none, and merely embedding within the manifold possibilities of representation a simulacrum of referentiality? Or is he more a realist than a post-modernist, lending mimetic weight to current theories of subjectivity as a way to prove their power to define the essence of the self? Is he impersonating a realist or rendering the reality of impersonation?' (*Philip Roth: Countertexts, Counterlives* [Columbia: University of South Carolina Press, 2004], p. 190).

36 Hermione Lee, *Philip Roth* (London: Methuen, 1982), p. 82. For Lee, Roth is, despite his segues into the big American novel of the national condition, an economical writer at heart. His 'admiration for the long short stories of Chekov ('The Dual'), Kafka ('The Burrow') and Henry James ('The Middle Years'), suggests that the novella is his ideal form, and that his longer fictions are, essentially, extended short stories' (p. 82).

37 Kundera, *The Art of the Novel*, p. 95.
38 Ibid., p. 73.
39 Ibid., p. 73.
40 Ibid., p. 72.
41 Ibid., p. 90.
42 Ibid., p. 92.
43 Ibid., pp. 88, 90.
44 Carlos Fuentes, 'The Other K', in *Milan Kundera and the Art of Fiction: Critical Essays*, ed. Aron Aji (New York: Garland, 1992), p. 17.
45 Fred Misurella, *Understanding Milan Kundera: Public Events, Private Affairs* (Columbia: University of South Carolina Press, 1993), p. 193.
46 Milan Kundera, *The Unbearable Lightness of Being*, trans. Michael Henry Heim (1984; New York: HarperPerennial, 2009), p. 59.
47 Kundera, *The Art of the Novel*, p. 34.
48 Kundera, *The Unbearable Lightness of Being*, p. 221.
49 Kundera, *The Art of the Novel*, p. 43 (Kundera's emphases).
50 Philip Roth, 'Milan Kundera' (1980), *Shop Talk: A Writer and His Colleagues on their Work* (London: Vintage, 2002), p. 93.
51 Roth, 'Milan Kundera', p. 94; James, 'The Art of Fiction', p. 60.
52 Sanford Sternlicht, *Masterpieces in Jewish American Literature* (Westport: Greenwood, 2007), p. 111. Notwithstanding the contrasting modernists they adopt as precursors, and their opposing sympathies towards the 'psychological novel', there are tonal links between Roth and Kundera that are more obvious than those affinities in craft I explore in this chapter. These links also associate Roth with Kafka for reasons similar to those that have drawn Kundera to Kafka. As Morton P. Levitt notes, 'the tensions [in Kafka's work] between comic impulse and satiric vision, between reason and immoderation, between grotesque inventiveness in detail and matter-of-factness in

language', such tensions become a 'metaphor for Roth of human and artistic potential' ('Roth and Kafka: Two Jews', in *Critical Essays on Philip Roth*, ed. Sanford Pinsker [Boston: G. K. Hall, 1982], p. 246).

53 Ford Madox Hueffer, 'English Literature of Today – II', in *The Critical Attitude* (London: Duckworth & Co., 1911), p. 97.
54 Milan Kundera, 'The Legacy of *The Sleepwalkers*', trans. Alfred J. MacAdam, *Partisan Review*, 51 (1984/5), p. 728.
55 Virginia Woolf, Letter to Harmon H. Goldstone (16 August 1932), *Letters of Virginia Woolf*, ed. Nigel Nicolson, 6 vols. (London: Chatto and Windus, 1979), v. p. 91.
56 See Mark McGurl, *The Novel Art: Elevations of American Fiction After Henry James* (Princeton: Princeton University Press, 2001), chap. 1.
57 Kundera, *The Art of the Novel*, p. 44.
58 Ibid., p. 221.
59 James, 'The Art of Fiction', p. 50.
60 Kundera, *The Art of the Novel*, p. 29.
61 Ibid., p. 29.
62 Joseph Conrad, *The Shadow-Line*, ed. Jacques Berthoud (London: Penguin, 1986), p. 43.
63 Ibid., p. 120.
64 Kundera, 'The Legacy of *The Sleepwalkers*', p. 728.
65 Milan Kundera, 'The Novel and Europe', trans. David Belles, *New York Review of Books*, 19 July 1984, p. 18.
66 Ford Madox Ford, 'Literary Portraits – III', *Tribune*, (10 August 1907) repr. in Max Saunders and Richard Stang (eds.), *Ford Madox Ford: Critical Essays* (Manchester: Carcanet, 2002), p. 35.
67 Hana Píchavá, *The Art of Memory in Exile: Vladimir Nabokov and Milan Kundera* (Carbondale: Southern Illinois University Press, 2002), p. 110.
68 Philip Roth, 'Rereading Saul Bellow' (2000), introduction to Saul Bellow, *Herzog* (London: Penguin, 2003), p. xvii.
69 Milan Kundera, *The Book of Laughter and Forgetting* (London: Faber & Faber, 2000), p. 221.
70 Ibid., pp. 225–26.
71 Milan Kundera, *Slowness*, trans. Linda Asher (New York: HarperPerennial, 1998), p. 39.
72 Roth, 'Milan Kundera', p. 94.
73 George Plimpton, 'Philip Roth's Exact Intent' (1969), in Searles (ed.), *Conversations with Philip Roth*, p. 35.
74 Ibid., p. 35.
75 Ibid., p. 35.
76 Kundera, *The Book of Laughter and Forgetting*, p. 15.
77 Max Saunders, *Self Impression: Life-Writing, Autobiografiction, and the Forms of Modern Literature* (Oxford: Oxford University Press, 2010), p. 18 (my emphasis).
78 Philip Roth, *Indignation* (London: Jonathan Cape, 2008), p. 55.

79 Kundera, *The Book of Laughter and Forgetting*, p. 119.
80 Ibid., p. 118.
81 Roth, *American Pastoral*, p. 35.
82 Kundera, *The Art of the Novel*, p. 29.
83 Ibid., p. 29.
84 Kundera, *The Unbearable Lightness of Being*, p. 39.
85 Ibid., p. 221.
86 Kundera, *The Book of Laughter and Forgetting*, p. 227.
87 Clive Sinclair, 'Doctor or Pornographer? Clive Sinclair Talks to Philip Roth about his New Book', in Searles (ed.), *Conversations with Philip Roth*, p. 191.
88 Gustave Flaubert, Letter to Louise Colet, 16 January 1852, *The Letters of Gustave Flaubert, Volumes I & II: 1830–1880*, ed. and trans. Francis Steegmuller (London: Picador, 2001), p. 213.
89 Kundera, *The Art of the Novel*, p.142.

CHAPTER 2. THE PERFECT STATE FOR A NOVEL

1 Fernand Léger, 'Notes on Contemporary Plastic Life' (1923), in Edward F. Fry (ed.), *Functions of Painting* (London: Thames and Hudson, 1973), p. 27.
2 Fernand Léger, 'The Origins of Painting and Its Representational Value' (1913), *Functions of Painting*, p. 3.
3 Sam Solecki, 'Interview with Michael Ondaatje' (1984), in Solecki (ed.), *Spider Blues: Essays on Michael Ondaatje* (Montreal: Vehicule Press, 1985), p. 325.
4 Ibid., p. 328.
5 The broader methodological advantages and pitfalls of 'interartistic comparison' are thoughtfully considered by Wendy Steiner in *The Colors of Rhetoric: Problems in the Relation Between Literature and Painting* (Chicago: Chicago University Press, 1982), where she warns that the 'act of naming a style [for comparison across artistic media] is burdened with presuppositions' (p. 177), and that any 'matching of technical elements' must be set critically alongside a 'comparison of ideologies' concerning the objectives and expectations of such an internally diverse 'movement' as Cubism was (p. 179).
6 Milena Marinkova, 'Framing Fame: Michael Ondaatje's Cinema of Affection and Liminality', *Moving Worlds*, 10:2 (2010), p. 7.
7 Robert McCrum, 'The Divided Man', interview with Michael Ondaatje, *The Observer Magazine*, 28 August 2011, p. 28.
8 Ibid., p. 30.
9 Laura Doyle, 'Notes Toward a Dialectical Method: Modernities, Modernisms, and the Crossings of Empire', *Literature Compass*, 7:3 (2010), p. 209.
10 Ibid., p. 209.
11 Quoted in Jesse Matz, 'Cultures of Impression', in Douglas Mao and Rebecca L. Walkowitz (eds.), *Bad Modernisms* (Durham: Duke University Press, 2006), p. 313.

12 Martin Heidegger, *Poetry, Language, Thought*, trans. Albert Hofstader (New York: Harper & Row, 1971), pp. 152, 154.
13 Michael Ondaatje, *In the Skin of a Lion* (1987; New York: Vintage, 1997), p. 34, hereafter *SL*.
14 John Berger, 'The Moment of Cubism' (1969), in *Selected Essays and Articles: The Look of Things*, ed. Nikos Stangos (London: Penguin, 1971), p. 151 (Berger's emphases).
15 Fernand Léger, 'Contemporary Achievements in Painting' (1914), in *Functions of Painting*, p. 15.
16 Léger, 'The Origins of Painting and Its Representational Value', p. 8.
17 Léger, 'Contemporary Achievements in Painting', p. 12.
18 Catherine Bush, 'Michael Ondaatje: An Interview', *Conjunctions*, 15 (1990), p. 97.
19 Henry James, *The Ambassadors*, New York Edition, vol. xxi (New York: Scriber's, 1909), p. xix.
20 Bush, 'Michael Ondaatje: An Interview', p. 97.
21 Linda Hutcheon, 'Michael Ondaatje', in Hutcheon and Marion Richmond (eds.), *Other Solitudes: Canadian Multicultural Fictions* (Toronto: Oxford University Press, 1990), p. 197; Caryl Phillips, 'Introduction: The Gift of Displacement', in *A New World Order: Selected Essays* (London: Vintage, 2002), pp. 129–34.
22 Marinkova, 'Framing Fame', p. 7.
23 Jane Bennett, *Vibrant Matter: A Political Ecology of Things* (Durham, NC: Duke University Press, 2010), p. xi.
24 Hutcheon, 'Michael Ondaatje', p. 200.
25 Bennett, *Vibrant Matter*, p. xi.
26 Dave Weich, 'Michael Ondaatje's Cubist Civil War'. http://www.powells.com/authors/ondaatje.html [Accessed 19 April 2009].
27 Hutcheon, 'Michael Ondaatje', p. 197.
28 Weich, 'Michael Ondaatje's Cubist Civil War'.
29 Interview with Beverley Slopen (1992), quoted in Ed Jewinski, *Michael Ondaatje: Express Yourself Beautifully* (Toronto: ECW Press, 1994), pp. 133–4.
30 Léger, 'The Origins of Painting and Its Representational Value', p. 7.
31 Susan Stanford Friedman, 'Towards a Transnational Turn in Narrative Theory: Literary Narratives, Traveling Tropes, and the Case of Virginia Woolf and the Tagores', *Narrative*, 19:1 (January 2011), p. 7.
32 Ibid., p. 7.
33 Maya Jaggi, 'In Conversation with Michael Ondaatje', *Wasafiri*, 32 (Autumn 2000), p. 10.
34 Solecki, 'An Interview with Michael Ondaatje', p. 324.
35 Bush, 'Michael Ondaatje: An Interview', p. 92 (my emphasis).
36 Ibid., p. 92.
37 Léger, 'Contemporary Achievements in Painting', p. 14; Solecki, 'An Interview with Michael Ondaatje', p. 322.
38 Weich, 'Michael Ondaatje's Cubist Civil War'.

Notes to pages 74–77

39 Solecki, 'An Interview with Michael Ondaatje', p. 322.
40 Jaggi, 'In Conversation with Michael Ondaatje', p. 7.
41 Hutcheon, 'Michael Ondaatje', p. 200.
42 Weich, 'Michael Ondaatje's Cubist Civil War'.
43 Hutcheon, 'Michael Ondaatje', p. 198.
44 Bush, 'Michael Ondaatje: An Interview', p. 92.
45 Michael Ondaatje, 'Author Q & A', *The Borzoi Reader*. http://www.randomhouse.com/knopf/catalog/display.pperl?isbn=9780307266354&view=qa [Accessed 19 April 2009].
46 Interview by Slopen, quoted in Jewinski, *Express Yourself Beautifully*, p. 134; Bush, 'Interview with Michael Ondaatje', pp. 90–1.
47 Sam Solecki, 'An Interview with Michael Ondaatje' (1975), in *Spider Blues*, p. 22.
48 Ondaatje, 'Author Q & A', *The Borzoi Reader*.
49 Eliot, 'Tradition and the Individual Talent', pp. 41, 40.
50 Albert Gleizes and Jean Metzinger, *On Cubism* (London: T. Fisher Unwin, 1913), p. 31.
51 Henri Le Fauconnier, Letter to Alexandre Mercereau, November 1908, quoted by Didier Ottinger, 'Cubism + Futurism = Cubofuturism', in Ottinger (ed.), *Futurism*, exhb. cat. (London: Tate Publishing, 2009), p. 21.
52 Guillaume Apollinaire, *The Cubist Painters*, trans. Peter Read (Berkeley: University of California Press, 2004), p. 25.
53 Jaggi, 'In Conversation with Michael Ondaatje', p. 7.
54 Michael Ondaatje, *Running in the Family* (Toronto: McClelland & Stewart, 1982), p. 190.
55 Eleanor Wachtel, 'An Interview with Michael Ondaatje' (1992), *Essays on Canadian Writing*, 53 (Summer 1994), p. 256.
56 Albert Gleizes, *Modern Art and the New Society* (Belfast: CUBISM, 1984), pp. 9–10 (Gleizes's emphasis).
57 Michael Ondaatje, *The English Patient* (New York: Vintage, 1992), p. 272, hereafter *EP*.
58 Michael Ondaatje, *Anil's Ghost* (Toronto: McClelland & Stewart, 2000), p. 69, hereafter *AG*.
59 Michael Ondaatje, *Divisadero* (New York: Knopf, 2007), p. 136, hereafter *D*.
60 Louis Menand, 'The Aesthete: The Novel and Michael Ondaatje', *The New Yorker*, 4 June 2007 http://www.newyorker.com/arts/critics/books/2007/06/04/070604crbo_books_menand [Accessed 19 April 2009].
61 Jaggi, 'In Conversation with Michael Ondaatje', p. 10.
62 Robert J. C. Young, 'An Evening with Michael Ondaatje', *Moving Worlds*, 10:2 (2010), p. 5.
63 Gail Jones, 'A Poetics of Sense: Michael Ondaatje's *In the Skin of a Lion*', *Moving Worlds*, 10:2 (2010), p. 65.
64 Apollinaire, *The Cubist Painters*, p. 26.
65 Solecki, 'An Interview with Michael Ondaatje' (1984), p. 330.
66 Menand, 'The Aesthete: The Novel and Michael Ondaatje'.

67 Jones, 'A Poetics of Sense', p. 57.
68 Apollinaire, *The Cubist Painters*, p. 26.
69 Léger, 'The Origins of Painting and Its Representational Value', p. 4.
70 Bush, 'Michael Ondaatje: An Interview', p. 91.
71 Milena Marinkova, '"Perceiving [...] in one's own body" the Violence of History, Politics and Writing: *Anil's Ghost* and Witness Writing', *The Journal of Commonwealth Literature*, 44:107 (2009), p. 109.
72 Nicholas Wroe, 'A Life in Writing: John Berger', *The Guardian, Review*, 23 April 2011, p. 13.
73 Berger, 'The Moment of Cubism', p. 135.
74 Metzinger, 'Cubism et tradition', *Paris-Journal* (16 August 1911), p. 5, quoted in Ottinger, 'Cubism + Futurism = Cubofuturism', p. 25.
75 Léger, 'The Origins of Painting and Its Representational Value', pp. 6, 7.
76 Berger, 'Fernand Léger' (1963), in *Selected Essays*, p. 194.
77 Berger, 'Fernand Léger' (1954), in *Selected Essays*, p. 30.
78 Berger, 'The Moment of Cubism', p. 162.
79 Bush, 'Michael Ondaatje: An Interview', p. 97.
80 Ibid., p. 94.
81 Ibid., p. 94.
82 Ibid., p. 95.
83 Steiner, *The Colors of Rhetoric*, p. 182.
84 Stephen Henigan, *When Words Deny the World* (Erin: Porcupine's Quill, 2002), p. 146.
85 Gail Caldwell, 'The Territory Behind', *Boston Globe* 27 May 2007 http://www.boston.com/ae/books/articles/2007/05/27/the_territory_behind [Accessed 31 August 2009].
86 George Bowering, 'Once Upon a Time in the South: Ondaatje and Genre', in Jean-Michel Lacroix (ed.), *Re-Constructing the Fragments of Michael Ondaatje's Works* (Paris: Presses de la Sorbonne Nouvelle, 1999), p. 36.
87 'Michael Ondaatje: An Interview', p. 91.
88 McGurl, *The Program Era*, p. 134.
89 Léger, 'The Origins of Painting and Its Representational Value', p. 4.
90 Raising issues of scale with respect to what constitutes aesthetic response, Roger Scruton has recently argued that we need to pay attention to the way localised 'syntactical structures encode their semantic interpretation', as a starting point for 'show[ing] how, or why, expression in art is a *value* – a mark of aesthetic success, which can be grasped only by someone who is also alert to the overall aesthetic impact of the work that exhibits it' ('Working Towards Art', *British Journal of Aesthetics*, 49:4 (October 2009), pp. 319–20).
91 Woolf, 'How It Strikes a Contemporary' (1923), *The Essays of Virginia Woolf*, ed. Andrew McNeillie (London: Hogarth, 1988), vol. III, p. 358.
92 McEwan, Interview by Smith, *The Believer*, p. 50.
93 Ian Davidson, *Ideas of Space in Contemporary Poetry* (Basingstoke: Palgrave Macmillan, 2007), p. 6.
94 Wachtel, 'An Interview with Michael Ondaatje', p. 256.

95 Jones, 'A Poetics of Sense', p. 57.
96 Ibid., p. 58 (Jones's emphasis).
97 Gleizes, *Spirituality, Rhythm, Form* (Brecon and Ampus: Association des Amis d'Albert Gleizes, 1996), p. 25.
98 Ibid., p. 26.
99 Ibid., p. 25.
100 Chelva Kanaganayakam, 'In Defence of *Anil's Ghost*', *Ariel*, 37:1 (January 2006), p. 7.
101 Margaret Scalan, '*Anil's Ghost* and Terrorism's Time', *Studies in the Novel*, 36:3 (Fall 2004), p. 316.
102 Paul Crowther, *The Language of Twentieth-Century Art: A Conceptual History* (New Haven: Yale University Press, 1997), pp. 38, 39.
103 Mark Roskill, *The Interpretation of Cubism* (Philadelphia: The Art Alliance Press, 1985), p. 147.
104 Douglas Cooper, *The Cubist Epoch* (London: Phaidon, 1970), p. 82.
105 Christopher Green, *Braque, Gris, Léger, Picasso: Cubism and Beyond* (London: Helly Nahmad Gallery, 2001), p. 15.
106 Marinkova, '"Perceiving [...] in one's own body" the Violence of History, Politics and Writing', p. 109.
107 Bush, 'Michael Ondaatje: An Interview', p. 91.
108 Gertrude Stein, 'Portraits and Repetition' (1935), repr. in Catharine R. Stimpson and Harriet Chessman (eds.), *Gertrude Stein: Writings, 1932–1946* (New York: Library of American, 1998), p. 291.
109 Ibid., p. 303.
110 Amédée Ozenfant, *Foundations of Modern Art*, trans. John Rodker (New York: Dover, 1952), p. 55.
111 Steiner, *The Colors of Rhetoric*, p. 179.
112 Friedman, 'Towards a Transnational Turn in Narrative Theory', p. 7.
113 Bush, 'Michael Ondaatje: An Interview', p. 91.
114 Berger, 'The Moment of Cubism', p. 162.
115 Gleizes and Metzinger, *On Cubism*, p. 22.
116 Malcolm Bradbury, 'Modernisms/Postmodernisms', in Ihab Hassan and Sally Hassan (eds.), *Innovation/Renovation: New Perspectives on the Humanities* (Madison: University of Wisconsin Press, 1983), p. 313.
117 Wayne C. Booth, 'Renewing the Medium of Renewal: Some Notes on the Anxieties of Innovation', in Hassan and Hassan (eds.), *Innovation/Renovation*, p. 137.

CHAPTER 3. SPARE PROSE AND A SPARE, THRIFTY WORLD

1 J. M. Coetzee, 'The Poetics of Reciprocity: Interview', in David Atwell (ed.), *Doubling the Point: Essays and Interviews* (Cambridge, MA: Harvard University Press, 1992), p. 67.
2 Ibid., p. 64.
3 Timothy Bewes, *The Event of Postcolonial Shame* (Princeton: Princeton University Press, 2011), p. 139.

Notes to pages 97–101

4 The transnational 'turn' in the New Modernist Studies has facilitated the redefinition of modernism as cosmopolitan in scope and reception, and as a phenomenon that has always been geopolitically implicated. In opposition to what she calls 'the early days of the field', when 'modernism was understood primarily in formalist terms as a loose affiliation of movements coalescing around certain aesthetic rebellions', Susan Stanford Friedman has drawn attention to the widely recognised shift in the discipline towards the study of modernism's multiplicities. While this might arouse fears in some of an endless, and critically vague, process of enlargement, Friedman instead 'advocate[s] a *transformational* planetary epistemology rather than a merely expansionist or additive one, one that builds on the far reaching implications of the linkage of modernism with modernity' ('Planetarity: Musing Modernist Studies', *Modernism/Modernity*, 17:3 (September 2010), p. 474).

5 Simon Gikandi, 'Modernism in the World', *Modernism/Modernity*, 13:3 (September 2006), p. 421. Jahan Ramazani makes a similar case for registering the enabling force of modernist methods for narratives of postcoloniality, arguing that for such writers 'modernism represents not an "imposition of a set of largely uncontested parameters upon a non-European cultural reality," but a multifaceted and mutable resource, amenable to different localizing strategies and syntheses' (*A Transnational Poetics*, p. 105).

6 Attridge, *J. M. Coetzee and the Ethics of Reading*, pp. 17, 18.

7 Ibid., p. 30.

8 Coetzee, 'Kafka: Interview', in *Doubling the Point*, p. 24.

9 Ibid., p. 27.

10 Ian McEwan, 'The State of Fiction: A Symposium', *The New Review*, 5:1 (1978), p. 51.

11 Coetzee, 'Remembering Texas', in *Doubling the Point*, p. 52.

12 Ibid., p. 52.

13 Coetzee, 'Beckett: Interview', in *Doubling the Point*, p. 27; 'Popular Culture: Interview', in *Doubling the Point*, p. 105.

14 Angus Wilson, 'Diversity and Depth' (1958), in *Diversity and Depth in Fiction: Selected Critical Writings*, ed. Kerry McSweeney (London: Secker & Warburg, 1983), p. 132.

15 Attridge, *J. M. Coetzee and the Ethics of Reading*, p. 20. In his lecture 'What is a Classic?' Coetzee's awareness of his own implication in the acquisition, involuntary or calculated, of cultural capital via his extension of tradition becomes clear. Bach could well stand for Beckett in the following question that Coetzee asks himself: 'is there some non-vacuous sense in which I can say that the spirit of Bach was speaking to me across the ages, across the seas, putting before me certain ideals; or was what was really going on at that moment that I was symbolically electing high European culture, and command of the codes of that culture, as a route that would take me out of my class position in white South African society and ultimately out of what I must have felt, in terms however obscure or mystified, as an historical dead end [?]' (in *Stranger Shores: Essays 1986–1999* (London: Random House, 2002), pp. 10–11).

16 Coetzee, 'The Poetics of Reciprocity: Interview', in *Doubling the Point*, p. 64.
17 Coetzee, 'The Works of Ford Madox Ford with Particular Reference to the Novels', M.A. Diss. University of Cape Town, 1963, 2.29. (As the dissertation's pagination is sectioned by chapter, all subsequent parenthetical page references under the abbreviation FMF will be followed by their chapter or appendix number.)
18 Peter Brooker, 'Afterword: "Newness" in Modernisms, Early and Late', in Peter Brooker, Andrzej Gasiorek, Deborah Longworth, and Andrew Thacker (eds.), *The Oxford Handbook of Modernisms* (New York and Oxford: Oxford University Press, 2010), pp. 1031, 1035. This idea of the reciprocity between literary heritage and formal innovation, whether 'contestatory' or convivial, is not entirely unprecedented, of course. Coetzee himself draws on T. S. Eliot's model of the artist's immersion in and responsiveness to tradition as a catalyst for new advancements when discussing what counts as inimitable art, including those artworks whose aura survives. Gauging their present and future impact requires an acute attention to history: 'Historical understanding is understanding of the past as a shaping force upon the present. Insofar as that shaping force is tangibly felt upon our lives, historical understanding is part of the present. Our historical being is part of our present' (*Stranger Shores*, p. 15).
19 Coetzee, *Dusklands* (London: Vintage, 1998), p. 1. Hereafter *D*.
20 Ford Madox Ford, *The Good Soldier*, ed. Martin Stannard (New York and London: Norton, 1995), p. 11.
21 Ford Madox Ford, 'On Impressionism', *Poetry & Drama*, 2:6 (June–December 1914), p. 169.
22 Coetzee, *Youth* (London: Vintage, 2003), p. 53.
23 Wolfe, Letter to F. Scott Fitzgerald, quoted in Andrew Thurnbull, *Thomas Wolfe: A Biography* (London: The Bodley Head, 1967), p. 276.
24 Mark McGurl also quotes Wolfe's anecdotal backlash against economy, when observing that 'the rule of "show don't tell" makes it clear that what is being restrained in the craft of [Hemmingway's] fiction is, precisely, self-expression, enough of which must remain to produce the aesthetic pleasure of its active restraint' (*The Program Era*, p. 102).
25 Schappell, 'Toni Morrison: The Art of Fiction', in Denard (ed.), *Toni Morrison: Conversations*, p. 82.
26 Joyce, Letter to Grant Richards, 5 May 1906, in Richard Ellmann (ed.), *Letters of James Joyce* (London: Faber & Faber, 1966), vol. II, p. 134.
27 Walter Pater, 'Style' (1888), in *Appreciations* (London: Macmillan, 1910), pp. 34, 17.
28 Henry James, Preface, *The Princess Casamassima* (1886; London: Macmillan, 1921), p. xii.
29 G. H. Lewes, *The Principles of Success in Literature*, ed. T. S. Knowlson (London: Walter Scott, 1898), p. 138.
30 Ford Madox Ford, *Return to Yesterday*, ed. Bill Hutchings (Manchester: Carcanet, 1999), p. 53.

31 Ford Madox Ford, *The English Novel: From the Earliest Days to the Death of Joseph Conrad* (Manchester: Carcanet, 1983), p. 11.
32 Ford Madox Ford, 'Literary Portraits – III', *Tribune*, 10 August 1907, repr. in Saunders and Strang (eds.), *Critical Essays*, p. 35; James, Preface, *The Princess Casamassima*, p. xiii.
33 Ford Madox Ford, *The March of Literature* (London: George Allen & Unwin, 1939), p. 843.
34 Ford Madox Ford, *Mightier than the Sword* (London: George Allen & Unwin, 1938), p. 261.
35 Ford, *The March of Literature*, p. 802.
36 Ford Madox Ford, *Thus to Revisit* (London: Chapman & Hall, 1921), p. 211.
37 Coetzee, *Youth*, p. 61.
38 Ford Madox Ford, 'Literary Portraits – XX', *Outlook*, 24 January 1914, quoted by Coetzee, FMF 5.02.
39 David Atwell, 'Editor's Introduction', *Doubling the Point*, p. 13.
40 Coetzee, *Youth*, p. 108.
41 Coetzee, 'Beckett: Interview', p. 20.
42 Ibid., p. 20.
43 Morris Dickstein, *A Mirror in the Roadway: Literature and the Real World* (Princeton: Princeton University Press, 2005), p. 108. Dispensing with the 'postmodern' as a vacuous label for classifying political and narratological dynamics alike, Attridge debates the viability of aligning Coetzee with the relentlessly ethical and existentially penetrating objectives peculiar to writers of the 'late-modernist' moment. See *J. M. Coetzee and the Ethics of Reading*, Chapter 1.
44 Ford Madox Ford, 'A Jubilee', rev. of *Some Imagist Poets*, *Outlook* 36, 31 July 1915, in *Collected Essays*, p. 180.
45 Ford, *The English Novel*, p. 122.
46 Coetzee, 'Beckett: Interview', p. 20.
47 Ford Madox Ford, *Provence: from Minstrels to the Machine* (London: George Allen & Unwin, 1938), pp. 103, 222.
48 J. M. Coetzee, 'Alex La Guma and the Responsibilities of the South African Writer', *Journal of New African Literature and the Arts*, 9:10 (1972), p. 6.
49 Coetzee, 'Beckett: Interview', p. 20.
50 Raymond Williams finds in Sturt a 'fusion of detailed record', one that cuts a path across 'a part-imagined, part observed rural England'. For Williams, *The Wheelwright's Shop* (1923) and *Change in the Village* (1912) offer topographic and sociological retrospectives on countryside work by setting local case studies against a broader synoptic narrative. Moving from discrete customs to transitions in labour on a county-wide and national scale, these texts present a precise 'notation of craft' alongside 'a conventionally foreshortened version of history' (*The Country and the City* (Oxford: Oxford University Press, 1973), p. 261).
51 Coetzee, 'Beckett: Interview', p. 20.
52 George Sturt, *Change in the Village* (London: Duckworth, 1912), p. 9.
53 Ibid., p. 9.
54 Ibid., pp. 9, 10.

55 Ford Madox Ford, *The Heart of the Country* (1906), repr. in *England and the English*, ed. Sara Haslam (Manchester: Carcanet, 2003), p. 175.
56 In Arnold Bennett's retrospect, Sturt was the kind of historian who forever opposed the romanticised equation of 'quaintness' and rural tenacity, retaining 'a steely and everlasting hatred of all sentimentality'. See Bennett's 'introductory memoir' to Sturt's *A Small Boy in the Sixties* (Cambridge: Cambridge University Press, 1927), p. xi.
57 Sturt, *Change in the Village*, p. 94.
58 David C. Gervais, 'Late Witness: George Sturt and Village England', *The Cambridge Quarterly*, 20:1 (1991), p. 42.
59 Ford, *England and the English*, p. 122.
60 Ibid., p. 336.
61 Ford Madox Ford, 'Un Coeur Simple', *Outlook* (5 June 1915), repr. in Sondra J. Stang (ed.), *The Ford Madox Ford Reader* (Manchester: Carcanet, 1986), p. 180.
62 Ford, *Thus to Revisit*, p. 70.
63 Ford, 'Mr Conrad's Writing' (1923), in *Critical Essays*, p. 229.
64 Max Saunders elucidates the wider implications of Ford's tonal and psychological impassiveness: 'In the greatest art the act of will is simultaneously an act of humility; an ontological passivity in the face of the perceived world' (*Ford Madox Ford: A Dual Life* (Oxford: Oxford University Press, 1996), vol. II, p. 213). Ford's own stance is forthright: 'humility is necessary in approaching the study of words and your mind must be utterly cleared of any trace of preconception' ('Un Coeur Simple', in *The Ford Madox Ford Reader*, p. 180).
65 Ford Madox Ford, *A Call* (Manchester: Carcanet, 1984), pp. 18–19. Hereafter *AC*.
66 Thomas Hardy, 'The Art of Authorship' (1890), repr. in Michael Millgate (ed.), *Thomas Hardy's Public Voice: The Essays, Speeches and Miscellaneous Prose* (Oxford: Clarendon, 2001), p. 103.
67 Elizabeth Bowen, 'Postscript to the *Demon Lover and Other Stories*' (1946), in Hermione Lee (ed.), *The Mulberry Tree: Writings of Elizabeth Bowen* (London: Vintage, 1999), p. 95.
68 Ford, *England and the English*, p. 148.
69 J. M. Coetzee, *Life & Times of Michael K* (London: Book Club Associates/Secker & Warburg, 1983), p. 81. Hereafter *MK*.
70 J. M. Coetzee, 'Farm Novel and Plaasroman', in *White Writing: On the Culture of Letters in South Africa* (New Haven: Yale University Press, 1988), p. 65.
71 Ford, *The English Novel*, p. 3.
72 Jim Hansen, 'Samuel Beckett's *Catastrophe* and the Theater of Pure Means', *Contemporary Literature*, 49:4 (Winter 2008), p. 662.
73 Ford Madox Ford, *Parade's End*, ed. Max Saunders (London: Penguin, 2002), p. 178. Hereafter *PE*.
74 Coetzee, 'Farm Novel and Plaasroman', p. 71.
75 Ibid., p. 74.

76 Ibid., p. 75.
77 J. M. Coetzee, 'Idleness in South Africa', in Nancy Armstrong and Leonard Tennenhouse (eds.), *The Violence of Representation: Literature and the History of Violence* (London: Routledge, 1989), p. 136.
78 Ford, *England and the English*, pp. 148–49.
79 Coetzee, 'Idleness in South Africa', p. 135 (Coetzee's emphasis).
80 Ford Madox Ford, 'Les Jeunes and *Des Imagistes*' (1914), in *Critical Essays*, p. 158.
81 Ford, *England and the English*, p. 178.
82 Ford Madox Ford, 'Mr Thomas Hardy and "A Changed Man"' (1913), in *The Ford Madox Ford Reader*, p. 171.
83 Schappell, 'Toni Morrison: The Art of Fiction', p. 79.
84 Coetzee, *Youth*, p. 155.
85 Coetzee, 'Beckett: Interview', p. 20.
86 Ibid., p. 23.
87 Ibid., pp. 25, 27.
88 Ibid., p. 27. See his 1978 essay, 'Samuel Beckett and the Temptations of Style' (1973), in *Doubling the Point*, pp. 43–9.
89 Coetzee, 'Samuel Beckett and the Temptations of Style', p. 44.
90 Samuel Beckett, *Watt*, in *Novels*, Grove Centenary Edition, vol. 1 (New York: Grove Press, 2006), p. 275.
91 Discussing the parallels between the novel's parts, Susan VanZanten Gallagher notes that '[i]n their respective roles as government servants, Dawn explores the psychological interior of the Vietnamese rendered in their mythology, and Jacobus journeys into the physical interior of Africa. As explorers, both are driven to know the unknown, to encompass that unknown both mentally and physically' (*A Story of South Africa: J. M. Coetzee's Fiction in Context* (Cambridge, MA: Harvard University Press, 1991), p. 59).
92 David Attwell, *J. M. Coetzee: South Africa and the Politics of Writing* (Berkeley: University of California Press, 1993), p. 55.
93 Stephen Mulhall, *The Wounded Animal: J. M. Coetzee and the Difficulty of Reality in Literature and Philosophy* (Princeton: Princeton University Press, 2009), p. 160.
94 Coetzee, 'Samuel Beckett and the Temptations of Style', p. 43.
95 Samantha Vice detects a comparable duality in the timbre of *Age of Iron*. 'There is', she writes, 'on the face of it a rather strange cohabitation between the elements of Coetzee's style: On the one hand, there is the scrupulous, unadorned recording of events and mental states, which rewards the reader with a sense of impartiality. On the other hand, the channelling of events and meaning through one consciousness is just as much a feature of Coetzee's style. The particular socially and historically embedded consciousness is precisely what is supposed to be the cause of distortion, partiality, and moral blindness. Both these modes [...] carry their moral dangers' ('Truth and Love Together at Last: Style, Form, and Moral Vision in *Age of Iron*', in Anton Leist and Peter Singer (eds.), *J. M. Coetzee and Ethics: Philosophical Perspectives on Literature* (New York: Columbia University Press, 2010), p. 299).

96 Molly Hite, 'Tonal Cues and Uncertain Values: Affect and Ethics in *Mrs. Dalloway*', *Narrative*, 18:3 (October 2010), p. 250.
97 J. M. Coetzee, *Slow Man* (London: Secker & Warburg, 2005), p. 141. Hereafter *SM*.
98 Coetzee, 'Samuel Beckett and the Temptations of Style', p. 47.
99 Samuel Beckett, *Proust: And Three Dialogues with Georges Duthuit* (London: Calder, 1970), pp. 14–15.
100 Richard Begam suggests that Beckett constantly oscillates between scrutinising and redeeming his characters, objectifying and humanising them with equal measure. Begam notes that in *Murphy* Beckett 'attempts to negotiate between two conceptions of novelistic form', something that is evident in his 'peculiar procedure' of 'explicitly telling the reader that Murphy is not a puppet and then going on to suggest ways in which he is', a procedure that shows how Beckett is 'bound' to 'a set of narrative conventions that he can deconstruct but not transcend' (*Samuel Beckett and the End of Modernity* (Stanford, CA: Stanford University Press, 1996), p. 57).
101 S. E. Gortarski, 'Recovering Beckett's Bergsonism', in Linda Ben-Zvi and Angela Moorjani (eds.), *Beckett at 100: Revolving it All* (Oxford: Oxford University Press, 2008), p. 101.
102 Shameem Black, *Fiction Across Borders: Imagining the Lives of Others in Late Twentieth-Century Novels* (New York: Columbia University Press, 2010), p. 5.
103 Coetzee, 'Samuel Beckett and the Temptations of Style', p. 44.
104 Ibid., p. 44.
105 Zadie Smith, 'Revenge of the Real', *The Guardian, Review*, Saturday 21 November 2009, pp. 2, 3.
106 Coetzee, 'Samuel Beckett and the Temptations of Style', p. 49.
107 Ibid., p. 45.
108 Ibid., p. 47; J. M. Coetzee, *Disgrace* (London: Vintage, 2000), p. 72.
109 Coetzee, 'Samuel Beckett and the Temptations of Style', p. 49.
110 Coetzee, *Youth*, p. 155.
111 Coetzee, 'Popular Culture: Interview', in *Doubling the Point*, p. 105.
112 Coetzee, 'Beckett: Interview', p. 25.
113 William Carlos Williams, '*Parades End*' (1951), repr. in Richard A. Cassell (ed.), *Ford Madox Ford: Modern Judgements* (Basingstoke: Macmillan, 1972), pp. 135–6.

CHAPTER 4. THE DEAD HAND OF MODERNISM

1 Percy Lubbock, *The Craft of Fiction* (London: Jonathan Cape, 1921), p. 1.
2 Virginia Woolf, Letter to Harmon H. Goldstone, 16 August 1932, in *Letters of Virginia Woolf*, ed. Nigel Nicolson (London: Chatto and Windus, 1979), vol. V, p. 91.
3 In his 'Preface to the Fifth and Later Editions' from July 1892, Hardy observes that 'though the novel was intended to be neither didactic nor

aggressive, but in the scenic parts to be representative simply, and in the contemplative to be oftener charged with impressions than with convictions, there have been objectors both to the matter and to the rendering'. A paragraph later, he is more adamant still: 'Let me repeat that a novel is an impression, not an argument; and there the matter must rest' (*Tess of D'Urbervilles*, eds. Juliet Grindle and Simon Gatrell (Oxford: Oxford University Press, 2005), pp. 4, 5).

4 Ford Madox Ford, 'On Impressionism', *Poetry & Drama*, 2 (1914), p. 172.
5 Jesse Matz, *Literary Impressionism and Modernist Aesthetics* (Cambridge: Cambridge University Press, 2001), p. 1.
6 A term Zadie Smith cautiously assigns to herself, while critiquing it in Joseph O'Neill, in 'Two Directions for the Novel', in *Changing My Mind: Occasional Essays* (London: Hamish Hamilton, 2009), pp. 71–96.
7 Zadie Smith, Interview with Ian McEwan, *The Believer*, 26 (August 2005), p. 53.
8 Daniel Zalewski, 'The Background Hum: Ian McEwan's Art of Unease', *The New Yorker*, 23 February 2009. http://www.newyorker.com/reporting/2009/02/23/090223fa_fact_zelewski [Accessed Monday 7 December 2009].
9 Smith, Interview with Ian McEwan, p. 53.
10 Ibid., p. 53.
11 Jon Cook, Sebastian Groes, and Victor Sage, 'Journeys Without Maps: An Interview with Ian McEwan', in Sebastian Groes (ed.), *Ian McEwan: Contemporary Critical Perspectives* (London: Continuum, 2009), p. 124.
12 Rosa González, 'The Pleasure of Prose vs. Pornographic Violence: An Interview with Ian McEwan', *The European Messenger*, 1: 3 (Autumn 1992), p. 40; Reynolds and Noakes, 'Interview with Ian McEwan', p. 23.
13 Smith, Interview with Ian McEwan, p. 50; Zalewski, 'The Background Hum: Ian McEwan's Art of Unease'.
14 Reynolds and Noakes, 'Interview with Ian McEwan', p. 23.
15 Adam Begley, 'Ian McEwan: The Art of Fiction CLXXIII', *The Paris Review*, 162 (2002), p. 59.
16 Ibid., p. 36.
17 Laura Marcus, 'Ian McEwan's Modernist Time: *Atonement* and *Saturday*', in Groes (ed.), *Ian McEwan*, p. 85.
18 Gregory Jusdanis, 'Two Cheers for Aesthetic Autonomy', *Cultural Critique*, 61 (Fall 2005), p. 28.
19 Philip Roth, 'Rereading Saul Bellow' (2000), introduction to Saul Bellow, *Herzog* (London: Penguin, 2003), p. xvii (Roth's emphases).
20 Smith, Interview with Ian McEwan, p. 50.
21 Ian McEwan, *Atonement* (London: Jonathan Cape, 2001), p. 312. Hereafter *A*.
22 Behind the figure of Briony, McEwan tells us, 'was a sort of Elizabeth Bowen of *The Heat of the Day*, with a dash of Rosamond Lehmann of *Dusty Answer*, and, in her first attempts, a sprinkling of Virginia Woolf' (Begley, 'Ian McEwan: The Art of Fiction CLXXIII', p. 56).

23 Richard Robinson, 'The Modernism of Ian McEwan's *Atonement*', *Modern Fiction Studies*, 56:3 (Fall 2010), p. 475.
24 Cyril Connolly, *Enemies of Promise* (London: George Routledge & Sons, 1938), p. 57.
25 Smith, Interview with Ian McEwan, p. 50.
26 McEwan states that '[w]riting is a bottom-up process, to borrow a term from the cognitive world' (Zalewski, 'The Background Hum: Ian McEwan's Art of Unease').
27 Robinson, 'The Modernism of Ian McEwan's *Atonement*', p. 477.
28 Zalewski, 'The Background Hum: Ian McEwan's Art of Unease'.
29 I am thinking especially of Martin Amis, Jim Crace, Hanif Kureishi, Kazuo Ishiguro and Pat Barker, whose subtler experiments in expanding the remits of social realism I have discussed elsewhere, in 'Relocating Mimesis: New Horizons for the British Regional Novel', *Journal of Narrative Theory*, 36:3 (Fall 2006): pp. 424–49.
30 Woolf, 'The Method of Henry James' (1918), in *The Essays of Virginia Woolf*, vol. II, p. 346.
31 Cook, Groes, and Sage, 'Journeys Without Maps: An Interview with Ian McEwan', p. 124.
32 Ibid., p. 126. Very much in line with McEwan's sentiments about fiction as socially responsive *and* aesthetically adventurous, Gregory Jusdanis contends that it is possible 'to believe in the worth of literature without defending social privilege', such that 'we can defend art's social autonomy while rejecting the aestheticist version of autonomy' ('Two Cheers for the Aesthetic Autonomy', p. 28).
33 In light of McEwan's oblique satire of prize culture and artistic prestige in *Amsterdam* (1998), Dominic Head concludes that '[t]o the extent that postmodern art has been thought of as an intensification of modernist self-consciousness, this may be one way of articulating McEwan's contribution to it. His unsettling art upsets the equilibrium of knowledge and experience that modernism held out as a fleeing possibility' (*Ian McEwan* (Manchester: Manchester University Press, 2007), p. 287).
34 Martin Ryle, 'Anosognosia, or the Political Unconscious: Limits of Vision in Ian McEwan's *Saturday*', *Criticism*, 52:1 (Winter 2010), p. 36 (Ryle's emphases).
35 Ibid., p. 25.
36 Cook, Groes, and Sage, 'Journeys Without Maps: An Interview with Ian McEwan', p. 126.
37 McEwan, 'The State of Fiction', p. 51.
38 Ibid., p. 51.
39 Jo David Bellamy, Interview with John Barth, in Bellamy (ed.), *The New Fiction: Interviews with Innovative American Writers* (Urbana: University of Illinois Press, 1974), p. 15.
40 Woolf, 'The Narrow Bridge of Art' (1927), *Essays of Virginia Woolf*, vol. III, p. 429.

41 Jonathan Loeberg, *A Return to Aesthetics: Autonomy, Indifference, and Postmodernism* (Stanford: Stanford University Press, 2005), pp. 3–4.
42 Begley, 'Ian McEwan: The Art of Fiction CLXXIII', p. 49.
43 Theodor Adorno, *Aesthetic Theory*, ed. Gretel Adorno and Rolf Tiedemann, trans. Robert Hellot-Kenter (London: Continuum, 2002), p. 139.
44 Ibid., p. 140.
45 Ibid., p. 141.
46 Ibid., p. 144.
47 Ibid., p. 144.
48 Begley, 'Ian McEwan: The Art of Fiction CLXXIII', p. 59.
49 Adorno, *Aesthetic Theory*, p. 144.
50 Charles Altieri, 'Why Modernist Claims for Autonomy Matter', *Journal of Modern Literature*, 32: 3 (2009), pp. 1–21.
51 Adorno, *Aesthetic Theory*, p. 8.
52 Begley, 'Ian McEwan: The Art of Fiction CLXXIII', p. 59.
53 Reynolds and Noakes, 'Interview with Ian McEwan', p. 20.
54 Dorothy J. Hale, 'Aesthetics and the New Ethics: Theorizing the Novel in the Twenty-First Century', *PMLA*, 124:3 (May 2009), pp. 899, 900.
55 Ian McEwan, 'I Will Have to Make it Up', *The Guardian*, Review, 26 March 2011, p. 2.
56 Alistair Cormack, 'Postmodernism and the Ethics of Fiction in *Atonement*', in *Ian McEwan*, ed. Groes, pp. 73, 77.
57 Zalewski, 'The Background Hum: Ian McEwan's Art of Unease'.
58 Cormack, 'Postmodernism and the Ethics of Fiction in *Atonement*, p. 75. Kathleen D'Angelo makes a similar contention, when tracing the development of Woolfian methods in the novel, that '[t]hroughout *Atonement*, Briony transitions from a girl overpowered by her romantic imagination to a novelist who uses modernist technique to fulfil her elegiac impulse' ('"To Make a Novel": The Construction of Critical Readership in Ian McEwan's *Atonement*', *Studies in the Novel*, 41:1 (Spring 2009), pp. 89–90).
59 Zalewski, 'The Background Hum: Ian McEwan's Art of Unease'.
60 Toni Morrison, 'Roundtable on the Future of the Humanities in a Fragmented World', *PMLA*, 120:3 (2005), p. 717 (My emphases).
61 Smith, Interview with Ian McEwan, p. 56.
62 Jonah Siegel, 'Looking at the Limits of Autonomy: Response', *Victorian Studies*, 51:3 (Spring 2009), p. 497.
63 Head, *Ian McEwan*, p. 205.
64 Smith, Interview with Ian McEwan, p. 50.
65 Leo Charney, 'In a Moment: Film and the Philosophy of Modernity', in Leo Charney and Vanessa R. Schwartz (eds.), *Cinema and the Invention of Modern Life* (Berkeley: University of California Press, 1995), p. 283.
66 Virginia Woolf, 'The Moment: Summer's Night', in *The Moment and Other Essays* (New York: Harcourt, 1981), pp. 9–10.
67 Ibid., p. 12.

68 Ian McEwan, *The Child in Time* (London: Jonathan Cape, 1987), p. 14. Hereafter *CT*.
69 Barry Lewis, 'Postmodernism and Fiction', in Stuart Sim (ed.), *The Routledge Companion to Postmodernism*, 2nd ed. (London: Routledge, 2005), p. 114 (Lewis's emphases).
70 Mark Wollaeger, *Modernism, Media, and Propaganda: British Narrative from 1900 to 1945* (Princeton: Princeton University Press, 2006), p. 23.
71 Ibid., p. 23.
72 Adorno, *Aesthetic Theory*, p. 142.
73 Alex Zwerdling, *Virginia Woolf and the Real World* (Berkeley: University of California Press, 1986), p. 82.
74 Ibid., p. 55.
75 Famously unconvinced by *The Child in Time* as a 'determinedly feminism-friendly novel', Adam Mars-Jones sees that McEwan's 'nativity scene' at the end badly lets his critique of masculinism down. See *Venus Envy: On the Womb and the Bomb* (London: Chatto and Windus, 1990), pp. 19–33.
76 Jesse Matz has considered such contemporary appropriations of impressionism in terms of pastiche. Examining the works of Colm Tóibín and Michael Cunningham, Matz reminds us that 'Impressionism was never merely impressionistic. Conventional wisdom might equate it with surfaces as opposed to depths, appearances and not realities, hasty guesses rather than enduring truths, but no Impressionist was content with superficial, merely sensuous, appearances. James, Woolf and every other literary Impressionist worked with impressions that were all about undoing these very differences. James's impressions were not dim guesses, not vague presumptions or detached imaginings meant for subsequent disproof or enrichment; rather, they were part of a perceptual mode in which dim imaginings were a truer kind of truth, a form of higher intuition' ('Pseudo-Impressionism?', in David James (ed.), *The Legacies of Modernism: Historicising Postwar and Contemporary Fiction* (Cambridge: Cambridge University Press, 2011), p. 116).
77 Matz, *Literary Impressionism and Modernist Aesthetics*, p. 178.
78 Ibid., p. 178.
79 Nicholas Humphrey, *Soul Dust: The Magic of Consciousness* (Princeton: Princeton University Press, 2011), p. 40.
80 Ibid., pp. xi–xii.
81 Marco Roth, 'Rise of the Neuronovel', *n + 1*, 14 September 2009. http://nplusonemag.com/rise-neuronovel [Accessed 1 October 2010].
82 James Wood adopts the same kind of ominously diagnostic tone as Roth when observing that '[a] genre is hardening'. Realism has become 'hysterical' because '[t]he big contemporary novel is a perpetual motion machine that appears to have been embarrassed into velocity' ('Hysterical Realism', in *The Irresponsible Self: On Laughter and the Novel* (London: Jonathan Cape, 2004), p. 167).
83 Roth, 'Rise of the Neuronovel'.
84 John R. Searle, *The Rediscovery of the Mind* (Cambridge: MIT Press, 1992), p. 128.

85 Laura Doyle, 'Toward a Philosophy of Transnationalism', *Journal of Transnational American Studies*, 1:1 (2009), p. 2.
86 Woolf, 'Modern Fiction', *The Essays of Virginia Woolf*, vol. III. p. 33.
87 James, 'The Art of Fiction', p. 53.
88 Jonathan P. Eburne and Rita Felski, 'Introduction: What is an Avant-Garde', *New Literary History*, 41:4 (Autumn 2010), pp. v–xv.
89 Ibid., p. xi.
90 Ibid., p. xi.
91 Nellie McKay, 'An Interview with Toni Morrison' (1983), in Taylor-Guthrie (ed.), *Conversations with Toni Morrison*, p. 155.

CHAPTER 5. LICENSE TO STRUT

1 Virginia Woolf, 'Life and the Novelist' (1926), in *The Essays of Virginia Woolf, 1925–1928*, ed. Andrew McNeillie (London: Hogarth, 1986), vol. IV, p. 404.
2 Virginia Woolf, *Mrs Dalloway*, ed. David Bradshaw (Oxford: Oxford University Press, 2000), pp. 41, 32, 31, 32.
3 Ibid., p. 86.
4 Ibid., p. 84.
5 Chloe Ardellia Wofford [Toni Morrison], 'Virginia Woolf's and William Faulkner's Treatment of the Alienated', MA thesis, Cornell University (September 1955), p. 10.
6 Ibid., p. 10 (my emphasis).
7 Toni Morrison, *Song of Solomon* (New York: Vintage, 2004), p. 11.
8 McKay, 'An Interview with Toni Morrison' (1983), in Taylor-Guthrie (ed.), *Conversations with Toni Morrison*, p. 152 (Morrison's emphasis).
9 David Cowart, 'Faulkner and Joyce in Morrison's *Song of Solomon*', in David Middleton (ed.), *Toni Morrison's Fiction: Contemporary Criticism* (New York: Garland, 1997), p. 98. Barbara T. Christian replaces the notion of Woolf's influence on Morrison with an account of inspiring legacies as 'layered rhythms', while at the same time addressing Morrison herself directly, turning the conventional critical essay into thought-experiment of speaking one-to-one with the author, just as her textual analyses bring Woolf and Morrison into dialogue across time ('Layered Rhythms: Virginia Woolf and Toni Morrison', in Nancy J. Peterson (ed.), *Toni Morrison: Critical and Theoretical Approaches* (Baltimore: Johns Hopkins University Press, 1997), pp. 19–36).
10 Harold Bloom, 'Introduction', in Bloom (ed.), *Toni Morrison's Song of Solomon: Modern Critical Interpretations* (Philadelphia: Chelsea House, 1999), p. 2.
11 Timothy Caron observes that '[c]omparative readings of Faulkner and Morrison have increased with such frequency that this specific comparison might be said to comprise something of a subset of contemporary Faulkner criticism' ('"He Doth Betride the Narrow World Like a Colossus": Faulkner's Critical Reception', in Richard C. Moreland (ed.), *A Companion to William Faulkner* (Oxford: Blackwell, 2007), p. 495).
12 McGurl, *The Program Era*, p. 354.

13 As Morrison complained in 1981, anticipating critical theory's dominance over the course of the ensuing two decades: 'Whole schools of criticism have dispossessed the writer of any place whatever in the critical value of his work. Ideas, craft, vision, meaning – all of them are just so much baggage in these critical systems. The text itself is a mere point of departure for philology, philosophy, psychiatry, theology and other disciplines' ('For a Heroic Writers Movement' (1981), in Denard (ed.), *What Moves at the Margin*, p. 158.)

14 Michael E. Nowlin, 'Morrison and Faulkner', rev. of *What Else But Love?*, by Philip M. Weinstein, and *Unflinching Gaze*, ed. Carol A. Kolmerten, Stephen M. Ross, and Judith Bryant Wittenberg, *University of Toronto Quarterly*, 67:3 (Summer 1998), p. 734.

15 Toni Morrison, 'Faulkner and Women' (1985), in Denard (ed.), *Toni Morrison: Conversations*, p. 27.

16 Kathy Neustadt, 'The Visits of the Writers Toni Morrison and Eudora Welty' (1980), in Taylor-Guthrie (ed.), *Conversations with Toni Morrison*, p. 88.

17 Aaron Jaffe, *Modernism and the Culture of Celebrity* (Cambridge: Cambridge University Press, 2005), p. 7.

18 Nowlin, 'Morrison and Faulkner', p. 734.

19 Morrison, 'Rootedness', in Denard (ed.), *What Moves at the Margin*, p. 64.

20 Morrison has herself made a 'plea' of this kind 'for some pioneering work to be done in literary criticism', which is reflexive enough to overcome the way that 'grades are given on other people's scales' (McKay, 'An Interview with Toni Morrison', p. 152).

21 Toni Morrison, 'Foreword', *Song of Solomon* (New York: Vintage, 2004), p. xii (my emphasis).

22 Schappell, 'Toni Morrison: The Art of Fiction', in Denard (ed.), *Toni Morrison*, p. 81.

23 Ibid., p. 82.

24 Ibid., pp. 66–7 (Morrison's emphases).

25 Toni Morrison, *Love* (New York: Knopf, 2003), p. 3.

26 Susanna Rustin, 'A Life in Writing', interview with Toni Morrison, *The Guardian, Review*, Saturday, 1 November 2008, p. 12.

27 Toni Morrison, Foreword, *Jazz* (New York: Vintage, 2004), p. xix. Hereafter *J*.

28 Rustin, 'A Life in Writing', p. 12. Morrison repeats a phrase from an interview conducted fourteen years earlier, in which she recalls (in closer proximity to the year of winning the Nobel) that 'I felt I represented a whole world of women who either were silenced or who had never received the imprimatur of the established literary world.... But seeing me up there might encourage them to write one of those books I'm desperate to read. And *that* made me happy. It gave me license to strut' (Claudia Dreifus, 'Chloe Wofford Talks about Toni Morrison' (1994), repr. in Denard (ed.) *Toni Morrison: Conversations*, p. 99, Morrison's emphasis).

29 Toni Morrison, 'Roundtable on the Future of the Humanities in a Fragmented World', *PMLA*, 120:3 (2005), p. 717 (my emphases).

30 Ibid., p. 717.

Notes to pages 167–171

31 Robert Stepto, 'Intimate Things in Place: A Conversation with Toni Morrison' (1976), in Taylor-Guthrie (ed.), *Conversations with Toni Morrison*, p. 23.
32 Harold Bloom, *How to Read and Why* (London and New York: Fourth Estate, 2000), p. 269.
33 Sheldon Hackney, '"I Come from People Who Sang All the Time": A Conversation with Toni Morrison' (1996), in Denard (ed.), *Toni Morrison: Conversations*, p. 138.
34 Philip Weinstein, *What Else But Love? The Ordeal of Race in Faulkner and Morrison* (New York: Columbia University Press, 1996), p. 133.
35 Ruas, 'Toni Morrison', p. 108.
36 Weinstein, *What Else But Love?*, p. 149.
37 Toni Morrison, 'The Future of Time: Literature and Diminished Expectations' (1996), in Denard (ed.), *What Moves at the Margin*, p. 185.
38 McKay, 'An Interview with Toni Morrison', pp. 140, 142.
39 Faulkner, quoted by Malcolm Cowley, 26 October 1948 [notebook entry], in Cowley, *The Faulkner-Cowley File: Letters and Memories 1944–1962* (London: Chatto and Windus, 1966) p. 109.
40 Cecil Brown, 'Interview with Toni Morrison' (1995), in Denard (ed.), *Toni Morrison: Conversations*, p. 116.
41 McKay, 'An Interview with Toni Morrison', p. 152 (Morrison's emphases).
42 A notable exception is John Duvall's textually attentive account of Morrison's 'Faulknerian influence', and he launches his discussion by spotlighting Morrison's effort in McKay's 1983 interview to 'distinguis[h] herself from Faulkner, Hardy, and Joyce', while 'stress[ing]' in their place 'the particularity of African-American experience' ('Toni Morrison and the Anxiety of Faulknerian Influence', in Carol A. Kolmerten, Stephen M. Ross and Judith Bryant Wittenberg (eds.), *Unflinching Gaze: Morrison and Faulkner Re-Envisioned* (Jackson: University Press of Mississippi, 1997), p. 7).
43 Neustadt, 'The Visits of the Writers Toni Morrison and Eudora Welty' (1980), in Taylor-Guthrie (ed.), *Conversations with Toni Morrison*, p. 86.
44 Toni Morrison, 'Memory, Creation, Writing', *Thought*, 59 (1984), p. 389.
45 Jessica Harris, 'I Will Always Be a Writer' (1976), in Denard (ed.), *Toni Morrison: Conversations*, p. 8.
46 Michael Silverblatt, 'Michael Silverblatt Talks with Toni Morrison about *Love*' (2004), in Denard (ed.), *Toni Morrison: Conversations*, p. 218.
47 Ibid., p. 216.
48 Morrison, 'Rootedness', p. 59.
49 Zia Jaffrey, 'Toni Morrison' (1998), in Denard (ed.), *Toni Morrison: Conversations*, p. 142.
50 Hackney, '"I Come from People Who Sang All the Time": A Conversation with Toni Morrison', p. 127.
51 Silverblatt, 'Michael Silverblatt Talks with Toni Morrison about *Love*', p. 222.
52 Morrison, 'Memory, Creation, Writing', p. 389.
53 Jane Bakerman, 'The Seams Can't Show: An Interview with Toni Morrison' (1974), in Taylor-Guthrie (ed.), *Conversations with Toni Morrison*, p. 31.

54 Ibid., p. 31.
55 Bill Moyers, 'A Conversation with Toni Morrison' (1989), in Taylor-Guthrie (ed.), *Conversations with Toni Morrison*, p. 273.
56 Toni Morrison, Interview for *The Black List: Volume 1*, dir. Timothy Greenfield Sander, written by Elvis Mitchell (Perfect Day Films, 2008).
57 Nellie McKay, 'An Interview with Toni Morrison' (1983), in Taylor-Guthrie (ed.), *Conversations with Toni Morrison*, pp. 152–3.
58 Angela Carter, 'Notes from the Front Line', in *Shaking A Leg: Collected Journalism and Writings*, ed. Jenny Uglow (London: Chatto and Windus, 1997), p. 37.
59 Walkowitz, *Cosmopolitan Style*, p. 20.
60 See David James, 'Realism, Late Modernist Abstraction, and Sylvia Townsend Warner's Fictions of Impersonality', *Modernism/Modernity*, 12:1 (January 2005): pp. 111–31.
61 Eliot, 'Tradition and the Individual Talent', p. 45.
62 Stepto, 'Intimate Things in Place', p. 23.
63 Ibid., p. 23.
64 Ruas, 'Toni Morrison', p. 97.
65 Harris, 'I Will Always Be a Writer', p. 8.
66 Implying that *Jazz* exhibited a kind of formal autonomy not found elsewhere in her *oeuvre* (at least, at that point in her career, in the year she won the Nobel), Morrison noted that the novel reveals how the very 'artefact of the book' can become 'an active participant in the invention of the story of the book, as though the book were talking, writing itself, in a sense. It's an interesting and overwhelmingly technical idea to me' (Angels Carabi, 'Nobel Laureate Speaks about Her Novel *Jazz*' (1993), in Denard (ed.), *Toni Morrison: Conversations*, p. 95).
67 Schappell, 'Toni Morrison: The Art of Fiction', p. 81.
68 Ibid., p. 81.
69 Morrison, interviewed by *The World*, 'A Bench by the Road' (1988), in Denard (ed.), *Toni Morrison: Conversations*, p. 46.
70 Salman Rushdie, 'An Interview with Toni Morrison' (1992), in Denard (ed.), *Toni Morrison: Conversations*, p. 53.
71 Schappell, 'Toni Morrison: The Art of Fiction', p. 85.
72 The neglect of meter is apparent in an otherwise attentive discussion of *Jazz* by Eusebio L. Rodrigues, whose commentary on the way the novel's '[l]anguage is made to syncopate', as 'the printed words loosen up and begin to move', sounds compelling but remains tantalisingly impressionistic ('Experiencing *Jazz*', in Peterson (ed.), *Toni Morrison: Critical and Theoretical Approaches*, p. 247).
73 Schappell, 'Toni Morrison: The Art of Fiction', p. 81.
74 Morrison, Foreword, *Sula* (London: Vintage, 2005), p. xii.
75 Schappell, 'Toni Morrison: The Art of Fiction', p. 74 (Morrison's emphasis).
76 Silverblatt, 'Michael Silverblatt Talks with Toni Morrison about *Love*', p. 216
77 Ibid., p. 218.

78 Silverblatt, '"Things We Find in Language": A Conversation with Toni Morrison' (1998), in Denard (ed.), *Toni Morrison: Conversations*, p. 176. See also Morrison's introduction to Twain's *Adventures of Huckleberry Finn*, ed. Shelley Fisher Fishkin (New York: Oxford University Press, 1996), pp. xxxi–xli. There Morrison speaks of the 'seductive invitations' that arise in 'unarticulated eddies that encourage diving into the novel's undertow – the real space where writer captures reader' (p. xxxvi).
79 Roberta Rubenstein has argued that 'one of Morrison's ongoing concerns in *Paradise*, as in the two novels that precede it, is the naming of the *beloved imago* – the idealized, lost love object who is imaginatively constructed through nostalgic longing' (*Home Matters: Longing and Belonging, Nostalgia and Mourning in Women's Fiction* (New York: Palgrave, 2001), p. 148).
80 Toni Morrison, *Paradise* (New York: Knopf, 1998), pp. 6–7. Hereafter *P*.
81 Danielle Russell, *Between the Angle and the Curve: Mapping Gender, Race, Space, and Identity in Willa Cather and Toni Morrison* (London: Routledge, 2006), p. 55.
82 See Silverblatt's question from the interview, 'Michael Silverblatt Talks with Toni Morrison about *Love*', p. 218.
83 Angels Carabi, 'Nobel Laureate Toni Morrison Speaks about Her Novel *Jazz*' (1993), in Denard (ed.), *Toni Morrison: Conversations*, p. 95.
84 Ruas, 'Toni Morrison', p. 97.
85 Urmila Seshagiri, *Race and the Modernist Imagination* (Ithaca: Cornell University Press, 2010), p. 6.
86 Morrison, 'Rootedness', p. 59 (Morrison's emphases).
87 Claudia Tate, 'Toni Morrison' (1983), in Taylor-Guthrie (ed.), *Conversations with Toni Morrison*, p. 164.
88 Leonard Diepeveen, *The Difficulties of Modernism* (New York: Routledge, 2003), p. 244.
89 Ruas, 'Toni Morrison', p. 109.
90 Ibid., p. 109.
91 McKay, 'An Interview with Toni Morrison', p. 151.
92 Tate, 'Toni Morrison', p. 164.
93 Schappell, 'Toni Morrison: The Art of Fiction', p. 82.
94 Faulkner, Letter to Malcolm Cowley (November 1944), in Cowley, *The Faulkner-Cowley File*, p. 14.
95 Bakerman, 'The Seams Can't Show: An Interview with Toni Morrison', p. 35.
96 Ibid., p. 35 (Morrison's emphases).
97 Ruas, 'Toni Morrison', p. 108.
98 Emerson, 'History', in *Ralph Waldo Emerson: Essays and Lectures*, ed. Joel Porte (New York: Library of America, 1983), p. 239.
99 Carter, 'Notes from the Front Line', p. 37.
100 A. Alvarez, *The Writer's Voice* (New York: Norton, 2005), p. 18.

101 Thomas LeClair, 'The Language Must Not Sweat: A Conversation with Toni Morrison' (1981), in Taylor-Guthrie (ed.), *Conversations with Toni Morrison*, p. 128.
102 Maya Jaggi, 'An Interview with Toni Morrison', *Brick*, 76 (Winter 2005), p. 100.
103 Virginia Woolf, 'Creative Criticism' (1917), *The Essays of Virginia Woolf*, ed. Andrew McNeillie (London: Hogarth, 1986), vol. II, p. 124.
104 Morrison, 'Faulkner and Women', p. 27.
105 Ibid., p. 27.
106 Peter Osborne, 'Modernisms and Mediations', in Francis Halsall, Julia Jansen, and Tony O'Connor (eds.), *Rediscovering Aesthetics: Transdisciplinary Voices from Art History, Philosophy, and Art Practice* (Stanford: Stanford University Press, 2009), p. 167.
107 Zora Neale Hurston, 'Characteristics of Negro Expression' (1934), repr. in Bonnie Kime Scott (ed.), *The Gender of Modernism* (Bloomington: Indiana University Press, 1990), p. 181.
108 Ann Hostetler, 'Interview with Toni Morrison: "The Art of Teaching"', in Denard (ed.), *Toni Morrison: Conversations*, p. 198.
109 McKay, 'An Interview with Toni Morrison', p. 155.
110 Ibid., p. 155.

Index

Adorno, Theodor W., 143, 144, 153
Aestheticism, 107, 108
Alain-Bois, Yves, 67
Altieri, Charles, 17, 144
Alvarez, A., 185
Amis, Martin, 36
   on tradition and experimentation, 36
Apollinaire, Guillaume, 75, 77
Armstrong, Isobel, 15
Armstrong, Paul B., 34
Attridge, Derek, 4, 7, 25, 98, 101
Attwell, David, 109, 126

Barth, John, 16, 142
Beckett, Samuel, 22, 122–4, 129, 131, 133
   Lessness, 132
   Watt, 124, 128
Begam, Richard, 210n100
Bell, Kevin, 51, 52
Bellamy, Joe David, 30
Bellow, Saul, 59
   The Dean's December, 138
Bennett, Arnold, 207n56
Bennett, Jane, 70, 83
Berger, John, 69, 72, 78–80
Bernstein, J. M., 5–6
Bewes, Timothy, 97
Black, Shameem, 131
Bloom, Harold, 26, 27, 163, 167
Booth, Wayne C., 95
Borges, Jorge Luis, 44
Bowen, Elizabeth, 116, 139
Bowering, George, 81
Bradbury, Malcolm, 95
Braque, Georges, 68
Brennan, Timothy, 8
Brooker, Peter, 102
Byatt, A. S., 39

Caldwell, Gail, 81
Carey, Peter, 25, 27, 32

Caron, Timothy, 215n11
Carter, Angela, 172, 185
Caughie, Pamela, 41
Charney, Leo, 149
Christian, Barbara T., 215n9
Coetzee, J. M., 14, 22, 66, 96–134, 205n15, 206n18
   Disgrace, 132
   Dusklands, 100–1, 102–4, 123–7
   and ethical criticism, 25, 98
   'He and His Man', 27–9
   on influence and originality, 27–9, 100, 123, 133
   Life & Times of Michael K, 113–14, 117–20
   and postcolonial critique, 97–8, 101–2, 104
   on postmodernism, 99–100, 123, 127
   Slow Man, 128–32
   Summertime, 132
   Youth, 105, 108, 109, 122, 132
colonialism, 97, 98, 100, 125–6, 127
Connolly, Cyril, 139
Conrad, Joseph, 28, 47, 48, 52, 115
   and impressionism, 59
   The Shadow Line, 57–9
contemporary, the, 2, 3, 5, 6, 11
   generational distinctions within, 9, 11
   periodisations of, 11
Cooper, Douglas, 92
Cormack, Alistair, 145
Cowart, David, 163
creative writing, 21–4
   institutions of, 21, 22
   pedagogy and practice in, 22, 23
   in relation to the New Criticism, 21
Crowther, Paul, 90
Cubism, 24, 65–7, 69–70, 71–2, 75, 78–80, 83, 90, 93–5

D'Angelo, Kathleen, 213n58
Davidson, Ian, 86
defamiliarisation, 91–2, 127, 152
Defoe, Daniel, 27

DeLillo, Don, 38
  on artistic progression, 38
  on language, 38
Dickstein, Morris, 110
Diepeveen, Leonard, 182
Doherty, Thomas, 42
Doyle, Laura, 66, 158
Duvall, John, 217n42

Eburne, Jonathan P., 159
Eliot, George, 43
Eliot, T. S., 13, 43, 75, 173
Emerson, Ralph Waldo, 185
ethics, 7, 8, 47, 51, 66, 70, 71, 77, 86, 87, 92, 140, 148
  and artistic accountability, 77, 89, 106, 146
  of innovation, 13, 30, 83, 97, 101, 102, 121, 140, 157, 167, 184, 185
  of reading, 12, 15, 18, 25, 71, 98, 134, 144–6, 164, 165, 183

Faulkner, William, 13, 33, 168, 169, 176, 184
  on literary inheritance, 33
Felski, Rita, 159
Fiedler, Leslie, 10
Fitzgerald, F. Scott, 106
Flaubert, Gustave, 110
Ford, Ford Madox, 13, 22, 56, 59, 104–6, 107–8, 109–10, 114, 117, 121, 122, 133
  A Call, 115–16
  The Good Soldier, 62, 102, 105
  The Heart of the Country, 111, 112, 121
  'On Impressionism', 103, 135
  Parade's End, 112, 119, 120, 133
  and *progression d'effet*, 114
  Provence, 110
form, 2, 11–12, 13, 19, 35, 38, 41, 54, 61, 67, 69, 71, 72, 76, 79, 95, 101, 107, 143, 165, 169, 182
  and appropriation, 31–2, 33, 62, 84, 139
  critical reconceptualisations of, 5, 7, 14–15
  and experimentation, 5, 8, 13, 36, 37, 43, 47, 74, 80–1, 99, 108, 109, 142, 164, 166
  instrumentalism and, 98, 141, 143–4, 165, 183
  and involvement, 9, 15, 25, 42, 91–2, 126, 170, 179–81, 185
  the politics of, 3, 4, 7, 9, 18, 51, 52, 57, 96, 97, 113, 118, 133–4, 137, 162, 166, 167, 172, 173, 187
  as process, 15, 69, 73, 76–8, 86, 92, 170, 176–9
Forster, E. M., 34
Foucault, Michel, 7
Franzen, Jonathan, 8, 78

Friedman, Susan Stanford, 8, 72, 94, 205n4
Fry, Paul, 27
Fuentes, Carlos, 54

Gallagher, Susan VanZanten, 209n91
Gasiorek, Andrzej, 12, 19
Gee, Maggie, 11–12, 149
Gervais, David, 112
Gikandi, Simon, 97
Gleizes, Albert, 75, 76, 87, 95
Gortaski, S. E., 130
Green, Christopher, 92
Gunning, Tom, 25

Hack, Daniel, 196n152
Hale, Dorothy J., 145
Halio, Jay, 47
Hansen, Jim, 118
Hardy, Thomas, 39, 57, 116, 135, 157, 210n3
Head, Dominic, 148, 212n33
Heidegger, Martin, 67
Hemon, Aleksandar, 39
  on writing after postmodernism, 40
Henigan, Stephen, 81
Hoffman, Gerhard, 190n31
Hollinghurst, Alan, 38
homage, 109, 121, 134
Hudson, W. H., 115
Humphrey, Nicolas, 156
Hungerford, Amy, 5, 11, 23
Hurston, Zora Neale, 186
Hustvedt, Siri, 33
Hutcheon, Linda, 17, 18
Huyssen, Andreas, 16, 41

imperialism, 97, 101, 104, 119, 125, 127
impersonality, 57, 89, 90–1, 101, 115, 149, 162, 170, 173–5
impressionism (literary), 13, 38, 56, 57–60, 61, 71, 72, 116, 135–6, 139, 140–1, 146, 151, 155–60

Jablon, Madelyn, 191n48
Jaffe, Aaron, 165
James, Henry, 13, 21, 38, 107, 110, 115, 136
  The Ambassadors, 70
  'The Art of Fiction', 38, 48, 56, 57, 159
  'The Future of the Novel', 53
  on reading for form, 42
Jameson, Fredric, 19
  on aesthetics, 41
Jones, Grail, 87
Joyce, James, 96, 107
Jusdanis, Gregory, 138, 212n32

Kafka, Franz, 137
Kanaganayakam, Chelva, 89
Kundera, Milan, 8, 26, 31, 45–64
  The Art of the Novel, 45, 53, 56, 63
  The Book of Laughter and Forgetting, 60, 61, 62
  on influence, 26
  on modernism's institutionalisation, 53
  on narrative form, 54–5, 56, 57, 59, 60
  and the non-psychological novel, 57, 62
  on rehabilitating modernism, 45–6, 54
  parabasis in, 54, 55
  Slowness, 60
  The Unbearable Lightness of Being, 55–6, 62

Le Fauconnier, Henri, 75, 90
Lee, Hermione, 53, 197n36
Léger, Fernand, 65, 69, 72, 73, 77, 79–80, 83
Lehmann, Rosamond, 139
Leighton, Angela, 14
Levine, Caroline, 19
Levitt, Morton P., 198n52
Lewes, G. H., 107
Lewis, Barry, 150
Lewis, Pericles, 18
Lewis, Wyndham, 173
Lodge, David, 35
  on novelistic self-awareness, 37
  on realism, 36
Loesberg, Jonathan, 143
Lubbok, Percy, 135

Major, Clarence, 24
Manning, Olivia, 37
Mao, Douglas, 41
Marcus, Laura, 34, 138
Marinkova, Milena, 66, 70, 92
Matz, Jesse, 136, 155, 214n76
Mayers, Tim, 21
McCarthy, Tom, 39
  on the fate of modernism, 40
McEwan, Ian, 13, 17, 23, 38, 44, 84, 136–59
  and artistic autonomy, 141, 143–4, 147, 154
  Atonement, 28, 139–41, 144–6, 147, 158
  Black Dogs, 136
  The Child in Time, 150–3
  The Comfort of Strangers, 136
  on experimentalism, 142, 143
  and literary heritage, 136–8, 145, 210n22
  and neuroscience, 155–8
  Saturday, 28, 136, 147–9, 151, 154–5, 159
  and self-conscious fiction, 24, 138, 140, 144
  on style, 138, 139, 140, 148
McGurl, Mark, 3, 21–2, 57, 82, 164
McIlvanney, Liam, 4

Menand, Louis, 76
metafiction, 10, 15, 17, 18, 36, 101, 137, 172
Metzinger, Jean, 75, 78, 95
Miller, Tyrus, 20
minimalism (literary), 22, 66, 104–11, 112, 114–17, 118, 121, 122, 125–7, 166
Misurella, Fred, 55
modernism
  and contemporary culture, 5, 12, 23, 36, 39–40, 93, 151, 156–60, 164
  and difficulty, 171, 182–5
  the politics of, 3, 7, 8, 96, 100, 137, 144, 146, 172–3
  and postcoloniality, 13, 66–7, 97–9, 101, 104
  reperiodisation of, 16, 19–21, 24, 41, 79–81, 140, 186
  theorising the continuance of, 2–6, 7–11, 18, 26, 30, 46, 66, 95, 168–70
  and tradition, 43–5, 47, 53, 56, 59, 60, 62–4, 96, 110, 112–13, 133, 138, 154, 163, 172
modernity, 12, 13, 75, 95
Morrison, Toni, 1, 15, 17, 22, 66, 98, 106, 107, 122, 146, 162–87, 216n13, 216n20, 216n28, 218n66, 219n78
  on creativity, 23, 25, 28, 166, 168, 169, 170, 171, 172, 173, 175, 183
  Jazz, 166, 173–6, 181–2, 184–5
  on literary criticism, 169, 183, 186
  Love, 166, 176
  and musicality, 163, 169, 174, 175
  Paradise, 167, 176, 177–81
  on participatory reading, 171, 181, 182
  and the political, 165, 171, 172, 177
  and prestige, 164, 167
  on race and art, 169, 176, 181
  on risk and responsibility, 186
  Song of Solomon, 162–3
  Sula, 175
Mulhall, Stephen, 126

new modernist studies, the, 6
  methodological developments in, 41, 73
  reaffirming attention to novelistic craft in, 41–2
  and transnationalism, 41
Niedecker, Lorine, 80
Nixon, Rob, 35
Nowlin, Michael, 164, 165

Ondaatje, Michael, 13, 65–95
  Anil's Ghost, 76, 88–92
  on composition, 74, 75–6, 80, 82, 94
  and creative writing, 24
  and Cubist perspective, 71, 72, 74, 77, 78, 83, 87, 92, 95

Ondaatje, Michael (*cont.*)
  Divisadero, 76, 82
  The English Patient, 76, 83–7, 89, 93
  In the Skin of a Lion, 68–69, 93
  and interartistic affinities, 69, 72, 73, 76, 77, 93
  and literary tradition, 65, 66
  on narrative voice, 70, 76
  political critique in, 66, 70, 89
  Running in the Family, 75
Osborne, Peter, 186
Otter, Samuel, 6
Ozenfant, Amédée, 93

Parrinder, Patrick, 12
Pater, Walter, 107
Phillips, Caryl, 70
Píchavá, Hana, 59
postmodernism, 1, 5, 7, 19, 24, 36, 39, 99, 123, 146, 151
  periodising the wake of, 16
  political legacy of, 17, 19, 187
  and postwar writing, 10–11, 99, 142
Pound, Ezra, 80

Radway, Janice, 4
Ramazani, Jahan, 42, 205n5
realism, 36, 37, 76, 80, 139, 140
Richardson, Dorothy, 50
Roberts, Michèle, 44
Robinson, Richard, 139, 140
Rodrigues, Eusebio L., 218n72
Roskill, Mark, 91
Roth, Marco, 156–7
Roth, Michael, 29
Roth, Philip, 44–63, 138, 158
  American Pastoral, 47–8, 61
  and comedy, 47, 56
  Indignation, 61
  on innovation, 46, 61, 62, 63
  on Joseph Conrad, 52
  on the lessons of modernism, 46
  Nemesis, 48–52
  Portnoy's Complaint, 60
  on representing consciousness, 60, 61
Rubenstein, Roberta, 219n79
Rushdie, Salman, 174
Russell, Danielle, 178
Ryan, Ray, 4

Ryle, Martin, 141

Sanders, Julie, 31
Saunders, Max, 61, 194n110, 208n64
Scalan, Margaret, 89
Scruton, Roger, 203n90
Searle, John, 158
Seshagiri, Urmila, 2, 181
Shields, Carol, 44
Shostak, Debora, 198n35
Siegel, Jonah, 147
Silverblatt, Michael, 179
Smith, Zadie, 34, 132, 136, 147
Stein, Gertrude, 30, 71
  'Portraits and Repetition', 93
  Three Lives, 31
Steiner, Wendy, 81, 94, 200n5
Sturt, George, 111
  Change in the Village, 111–12

Taylor, D. J., 37
Tracy, David, 12

Vice, Samantha, 209n95

Walkowitz, Rebecca L., 7, 8, 13, 41, 172–3
Walsh, Robert, 32
Weinstein, Philip, 168
Widdowson, Henry, 27
Wilcox, Leonard, 13
Williams, Raymond, 2–4, 207n50
Williams, William Carlos, 133
Wilson, Angus, 101
Winterson, Jeanette, 36
  on tradition and literary innovation, 37
Wolfe, Thomas, 106
Wollaeger, Mark, 152
Wood, James, 157, 213n82
Wood, Michael, 33
Woolf, Virginia, 13, 57, 72, 135, 139, 140, 141, 142, 149, 155, 159, 161, 167, 178, 186
  Jacob's Room, 153
  Mrs. Dalloway, 150, 161–2

Young, Robert J. C., 77

Zuidervaart, Lambert, 189n8
Zwerdling, Alex, 153